Exploring the Roots of Flamenco

Traveling through Andalusia, Barcelona, and Madrid to learn about the culture of the Firedance

By Susan K Jones

Dedication

For Liz and Sarah, my travel companions

Contents

Introduction

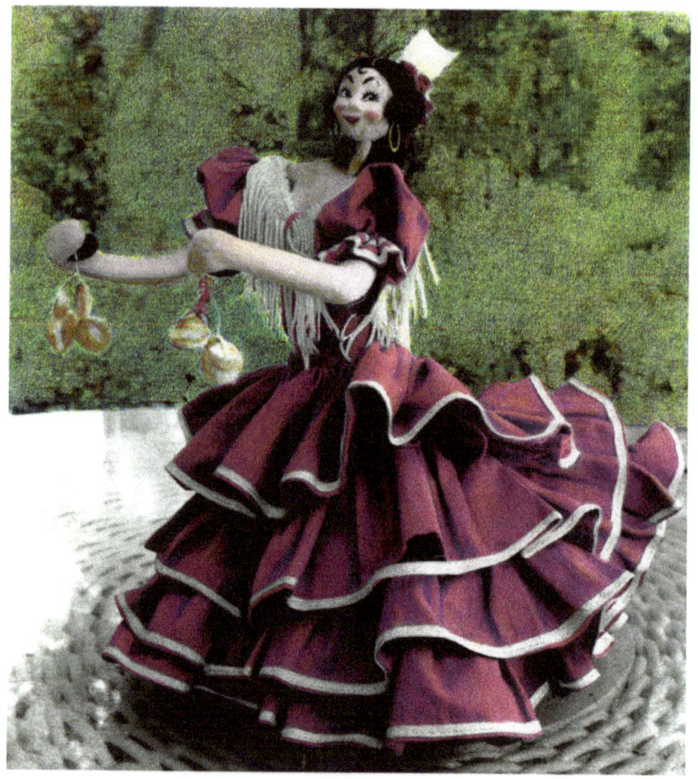

I have been enamored with gypsies since I was a young child, perhaps ignited by the flamenco doll my aunt brought me from Spain when I was six. As you can see, she is not very pretty but her dress is awesome and she can stand by herself. I envied the life she would have led; living in a caravan pulled by a horse, camping, and dancing around the campfire. Her life sounded wonderful, like the fairytales I read. I was too young to grasp the hardships gypsies faced.

Shortly after I finished graduate school, a flamenco teacher suggested that I work on a children's book about flamenco. I was captivated by the idea; it fit right in with my folklore studies so I began researching flamenco and the history of the gypsies of southern Spain. I searched for flamenco productions like those in ballet but quickly found that flamenco is a spontaneous medium that is never the same twice. Flamenco is built on raw emotion, sometimes light hearted or naughty but most times, dark and full of sorrow and anguish. It is a culture much like the American Blues; it fulfills the need of a people to express their travails, commiserate, and acknowledge a shared past.

The more I learned, the more I wanted to know. Flamenco did not lend itself to a children's book in my mind because it is a journey through darkness and passion to reach the performer's inner soul; it is a search for duende, best described by Federico Garcia Lorca as:

"the power that climbs up inside the performer from the soles of the feet, the spirit of the earth which scorches the artist and produces an inspired performance."

I spent the next two years reading everything I could find on flamenco, Spanish gypsies, and the folklore that permeates Andalusian culture. I read Don Pohren, Federico Garcia Lorca, Washington Irving, Ernest Hemingway and many more (I've included a list of sources at the end). These volumes paint a romantic picture of the life of aficionados and their discoveries of flamenco; a world of lush hillsides, tiny villages and colorful gypsies that sang and danced the nights away. Contemporary flamenco isn't as free and

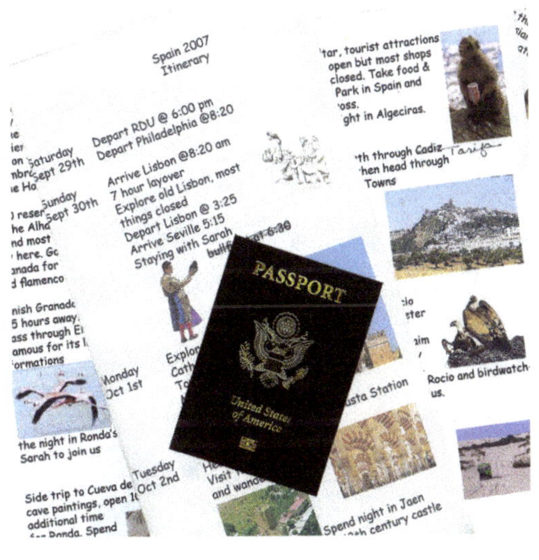

spontaneous; somehow, I ignored that fact. Today, Spain is becoming increasingly more modern but fortunately, the past is well preserved and authentic flamenco can still be found if you know where to look for it.

My research began to look more and more like a travel itinerary! In 2007, my best friend's daughter, Sarah, was in Seville studying flamenco. She and my daughter, Liz, grew up together; they were happy to join me on my adventure. Plans were made; in the fall of 2007, Liz and I traveled to Spain in search of the roots of flamenco.

On the surface, this is a journey to learn about the roots of flamenco and the culture of Andalusia. On a different level, it can be seen as a journey toward self-reliance and a transition from the traditional role of parent/child to that of friends. My daughter and I were partners in this adventure, jointly responsible for our safety and well-being, for not getting too lost, for ordering food and for having fun!

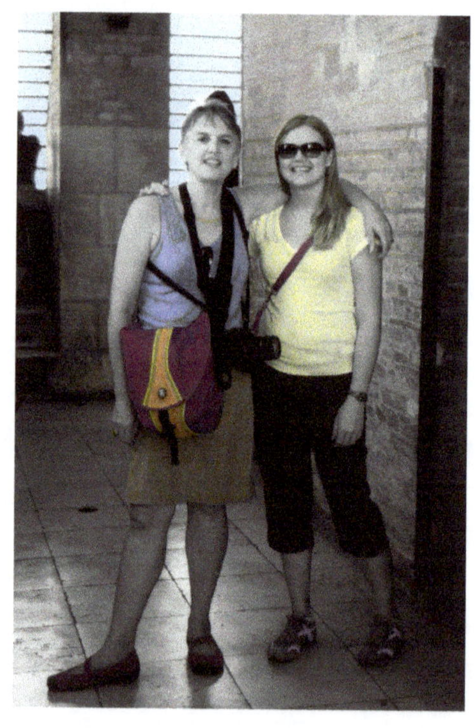

This is a combination of travel essay and history mixed together to portray a picture of the culture behind flamenco and provide a better understanding of the art that is flamenco. I hope that you will enjoy our journey and come away with the desire to learn more about flamenco and the wonderful people and places that bring it to life.

Lisbon

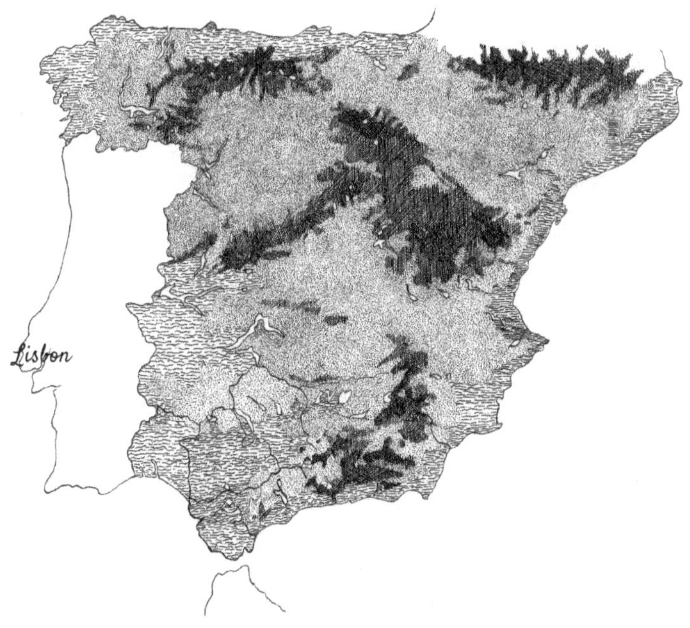

The Journey Begins…

Leaving felt strange; we hadn't taken a big trip without the whole family so this felt a bit liberating. The excitement of setting out on an adventure overshadowed any concerns or fears we might have had. Waiting in airports is so anticlimactic, especially in one as small as RDU. We were impatient to get started!

We had a long layover in Lisbon before we got to Seville so we wanted to get as much sleep as possible on the flight over. We opted to put our layover time in Philadelphia to good use and have dinner there, freeing up more time for sleep on the plane. Aided by modern sleep medicine, we arrived somewhat refreshed in Lisbon Sunday morning. I'm sure our excitement played a large part in our energy level!

Lisbon airport has a shuttle into town that is designed for passengers with layovers; it runs on a continuous loop so travelers can easily visit their lovely city. We were a little nervous about missing our flight but confronted with seven hours sitting in an airport vs. exploring Lisbon, we decided to take the risk.

There wasn't much of a crowd on this dreary, rainy, Sunday and very little looked open. The bus dropped us off in the city center. Our first mission was to find a café for coffee and lunch. This will become a recurring theme of our trip!

We got off the bus at Calçada Portuguesa, a large plaza paved with a wave mosaic made from black and white stones. The pattern is crisp and flows with the rhythm of the ocean across the plaza to a mosaic of Columbus's ship. Lunch was quick and tasty, and then we were on our way to explore.

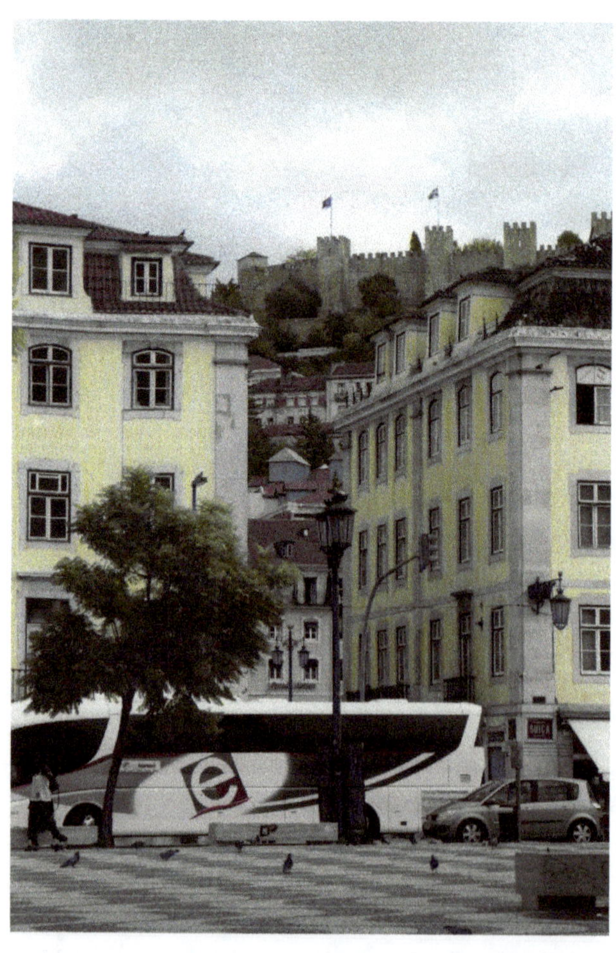

The first thing we noticed was that everything was uphill from this central location. Up steep hills! The central part of the city is a narrow valley that runs down to the water. According to the guidebooks, there is much to see along the waterfront so we decided that the smart thing to do was to save our energy and stay on flat ground. Unfortunately, there was major construction all along the boardwalk with massive barricades that prevented us from seeing the water. To see anything, we had to go up.

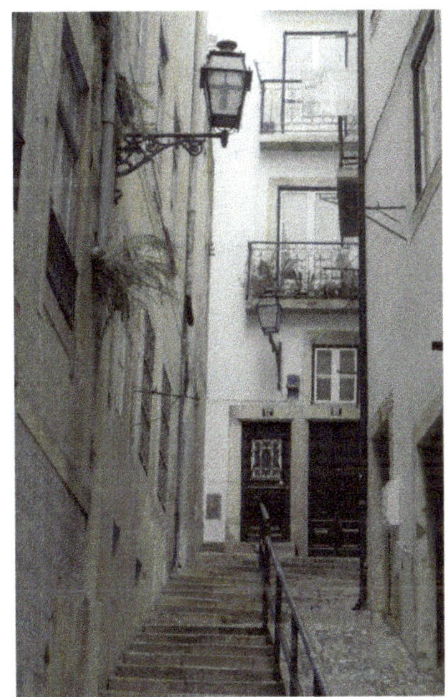

High above us was a castle. It became our destination as we started wandering up the narrow, steep, twisting lanes. The topography is very San Franciscan. I got shin splints from walking the streets of San Francisco, so I stopped as frequently as I could to take pictures!

Many of the buildings are old and in disrepair but everywhere you look, there is lovely tile work. Exterior walls of buildings are covered in tile, underneath balconies are decorated for pedestrians, small public spaces have walls and benches made from tile.

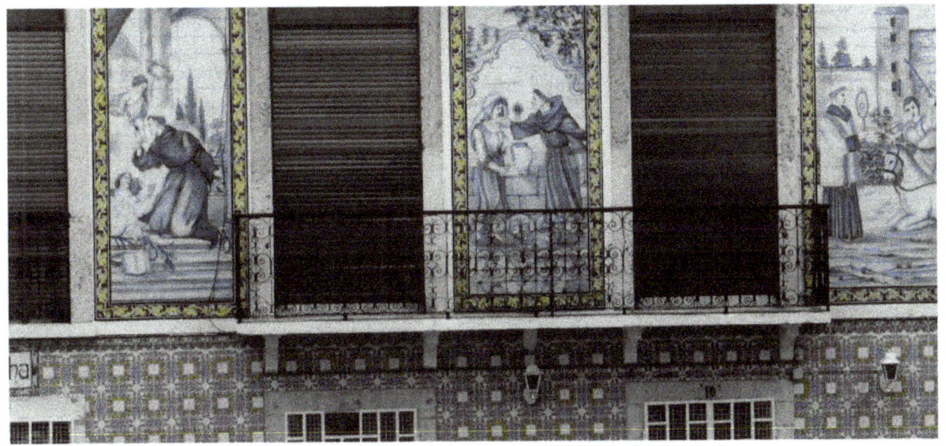

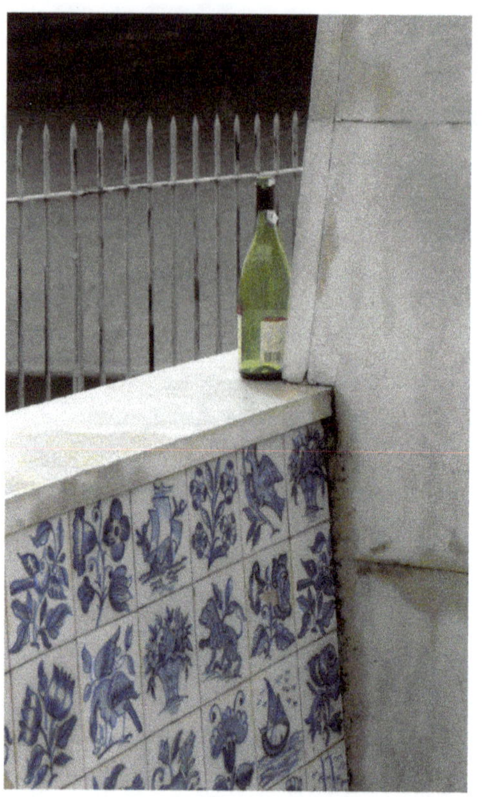

I associate this type of tile work with the Dutch so I was surprised to see it in Portugal. This type of tile, called azulejo, has been associated with Portugal for centuries. The tile originated with the Moors and is made up of simple geometric shapes in neutral tones dominated by blues and whites. Today azulejo tile is making a comeback, showing up in public venues where they are used to tell stories about history, religion, and culture. Spain also adopted the azulejo tile and it can be seen in many Moorish settings and prominent public venues.

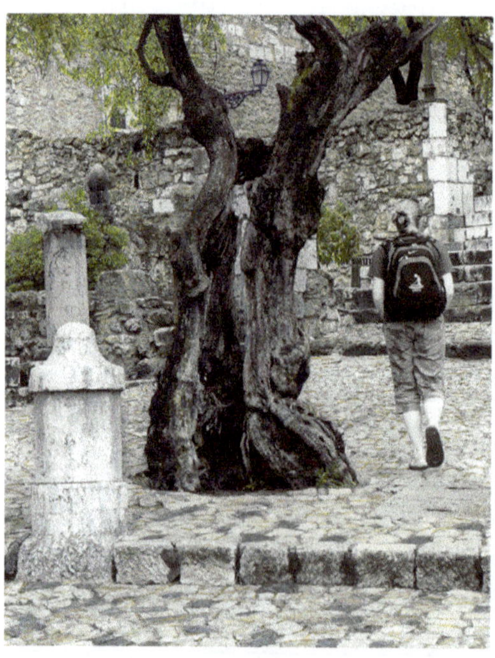

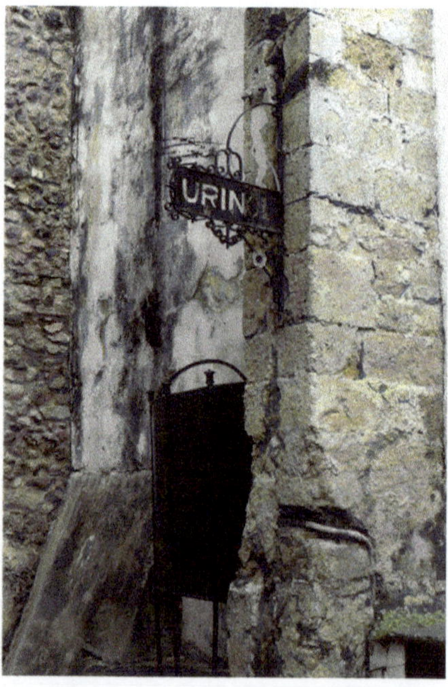

The castle of St George, Castelo de Sao Jorge, is situated on a high point, overlooking a sea of red tiled roofs, the Baixa district, before reaching the River Tagus, Rio Tejo.

The castle/fort was the seat of power for Portugal for over 400 years; it was heavily damaged by an earthquake in 1755 and basically rebuilt in the 1920s. Inside the fort, I was mesmerized by the gnarled old trees; they have so much character. We climbed up on the ramparts and enjoyed the views, then faced up to the trek back down. Shortly after we started our decent, we found a staircase; going down became quick and painless!

Getting a bus back to the airport was more of a challenge! The bus from the airport makes a large circle through the city with various stops. We decided to go back to where we got off the bus to re-board, figuring we'd take advantage of the scenic detour. The young men on the bus wouldn't let us on. According to protocol, we were supposed to cross the plaza and catch a bus there for the airport.

We followed directions and waited and waited; the bus finally came; it was the one we'd tried to board! They let us on this time.

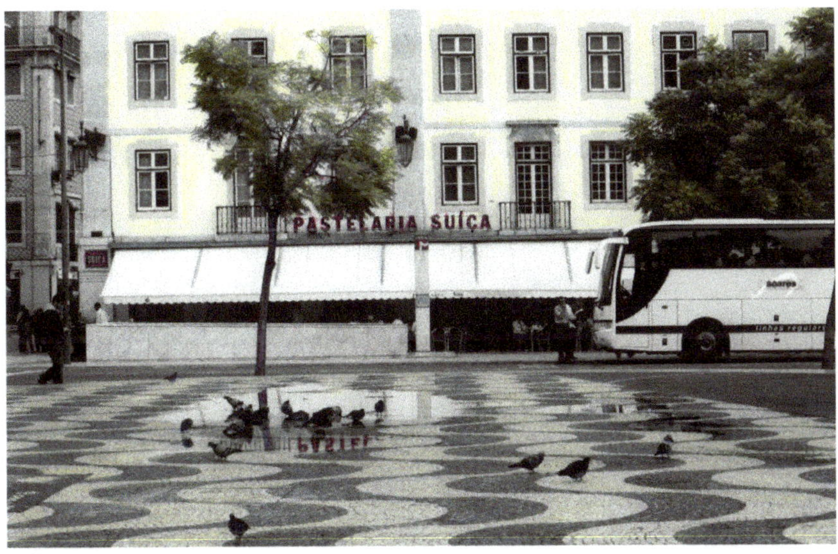

We made it back with a little time to spare, more amenable to getting on a plane again!

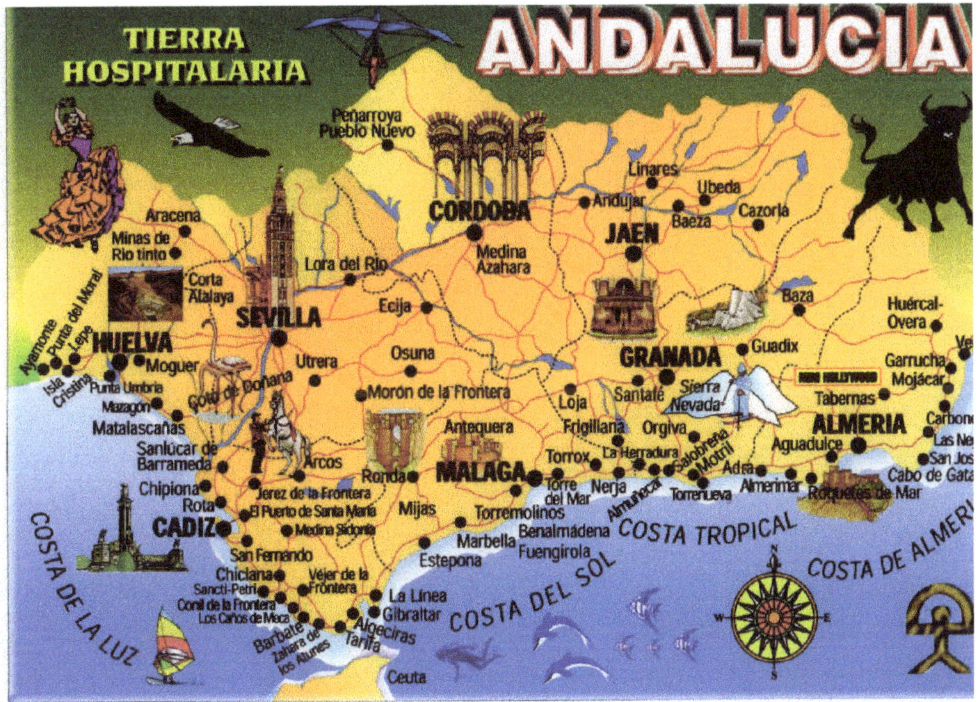

We arrived in Seville late in the afternoon, weary after a very long day. The airport in Seville was a bit bland and confusing. We'd gone through customs in Lisbon so we entered Spain through gates that were unprepared for English speaking visitors.

Baggage claim carousels were marked EU luggage with a downward pointing arrow. Being on a flight that originated in the European Union and with no other apparent choices, we were alarmed when all the baggage was claimed and our fellow passengers had departed leaving three Americans alone, luggage-less.

We noticed a sign over the last carousel: non EU luggage with an arrow pointing to a long, sturdy and impenetrable wall. Communicating with airport personnel was full of pantomime and charades. Pointing to the sign and a shrugging of shoulders was met with a blank stare; obviously they don't understand 'sign' language!

Dazed and a bit anxious, we fell in with the crowd in search of the airline's office. There, on the other side of the wall, forlornly, sat our luggage in front of an empty carousel beneath a sign: Non EU downward pointing arrow. The adrenaline rush of lost/found luggage revived us.

Our instructions were to call Sarah when we landed and she would meet us somewhere and take us to her apartment. Easier said than done! Each variation, with and without the country code, of her two phone numbers reached the same recording, "no such number". Not to be deterred, we dragged our luggage to the taxi queue with Sarah's address written out in Spanish. The driver had no clue where we were headed, but not to worry, he'd ask someone. The ride into Seville was fast on the highway and creeping through the maze they call calles (streets), more like alleyways. The driver was a very nice man, friendly and helpful, until he dumped us

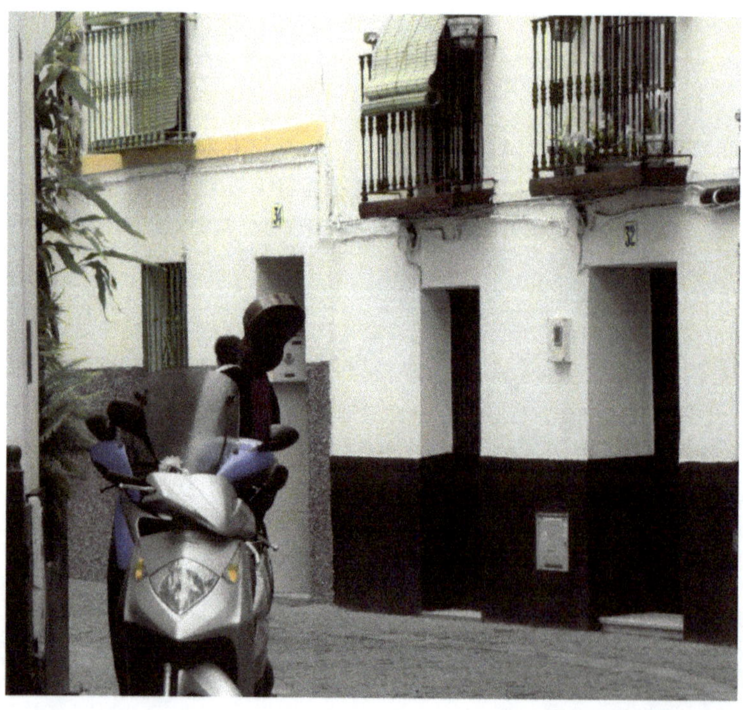

in a maze of streets that he could no longer navigate, saying "Number 38 is around here somewhere." Then he left.

Addresses in Spain are notorious for being next to useless. On this calle (street) the numbers were all odd and bore no relationship to the numbers across the narrow calle. The uneven, cobbled road was not meant for modern luggage wheels; my suitcase flopped from side to side but I was too tired to carry it. Finding Number 38 should be a piece of cake, after all, we were on the right calle but the numbers on both sides of the street were odd!

Frustration and fatigue bred boldness. I approached the first resident I saw, thrust the address into his hands and stood with pleading eyes. No, he didn't know where the even numbers were but thankfully he was up for the challenge. After a few meandering turns we were rewarded with Number 38. A push of the buzzer and our friend was at the entrance!

First order of business was cell phone lessons. There are extra buttons to push that the instruction booklet forgot to mention. The girls got their numbers programmed into each other's phones – that was the last I saw of our phone.

The second order of business was food.

The Spanish lifestyle is very different from Americans'. Everything shuts down from roughly 1:00 until 5:00, the hottest part of the day, for siesta. Business hours resume from 5:00 until 8:00; dinner is served late.

Sarah fixed us a traditional Spanish snack of delicious bread drizzled with olive oil. Liz and I had a chance to relax and revive. At eight o'clock sharp, we headed out. We arrived at the neighborhood bar before the crowd; the tables outside were full but there was plenty of room inside. Dinner is not served until 9:00 pm but many bars and pubs open up in the early afternoon for the social scene; they serve tapas with their beer and wine. Many restaurants in the larger cities have a menu in English. This was a small neighborhood bar and everything was in Spanish. Thus began our tapas tutorial.

Tapas

I like to think that the tapas tradition began with flamenco and the gypsies. Alcohol is the main ingredient for memorable flamenco and duende but gypsies didn't get drunk because they grazed steadily throughout the event.

Tapas are small portions of food that are served in bite sized pieces. There are a large variety of choices with Iberian ham, squid, varied seafood, and potatoes playing a large role. Liz and Sarah went through the menu and made us a key for restaurant emergencies. Our favorite safe, easy, and everywhere food became the tortilla Espanola, a potato omelet.

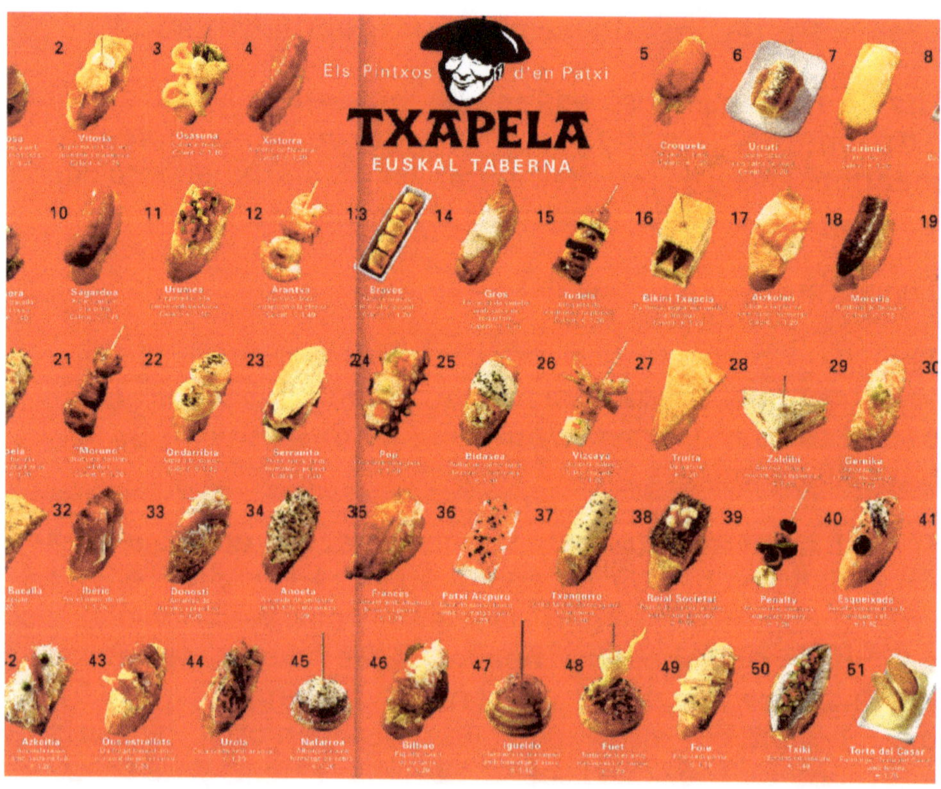

For our first tapas, we had chicken in almond paste, seafood croquettes, potatoes in a spicy tomato sauce, fresh tomatoes soaked in olive oil and spices, tiny quail eggs sunny side up, and some great goat cheese with plenty of tinto con limon (red wine and lemonade) to wash it down; an excellent introduction to the meals to come.

At this time, Liz and I were not food connoisseurs, we preferred quick and easy (and inexpensive) to spending our time and money on fancy meals. We had, however decided to forgo any temptation to eat American food; no McDonalds or Starbucks. Tapas, with their finger eating ease, were a good substitute.

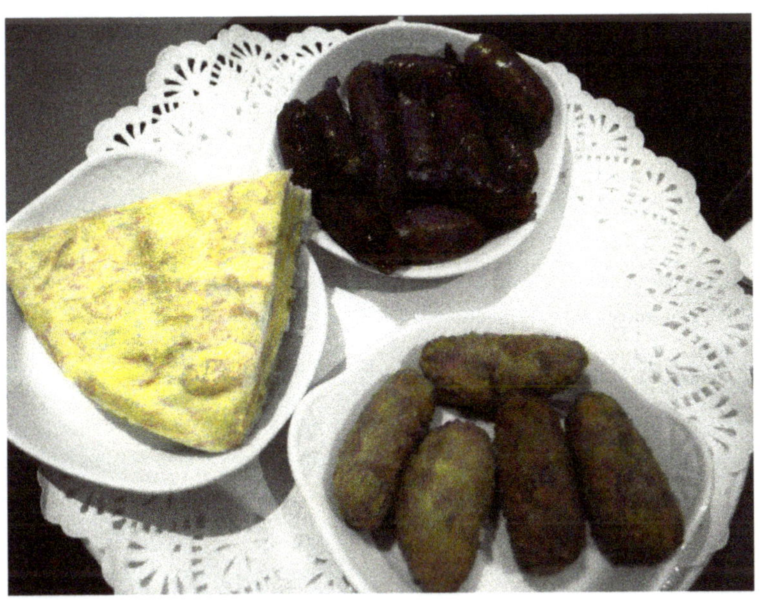

Tapas pros:

•   they are set out in glass covered dishes around the bar so you can order by pointing, minimal language barrier

•   there's no waiting

•   there's a large variety

- they're inexpensive which encourages braving new things, and

- they are easy to share/split

Tapas cons:

- that tasty looking croquette might be chicken or it might be bull's testicles so a little Spanish is useful

- most are breaded and deep fried (carbs & fat)

- vegetables are marinated in olive oil (at least it's healthy oil)

Religious Procession

Marching band music permeated the air when we emerged
from dinner. Parked cars lined both sides of the narrow,
one-way street; up the middle came a procession. The atmosphere was funeral like, quiet and respectful. Men dressed
in black suits were leading the procession, walking very slow
and somber.

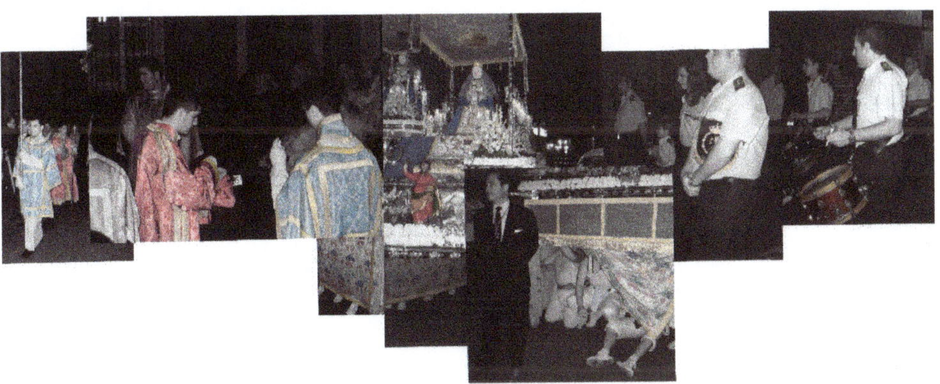

The men in processions are members of parish cofradia (a
confraternity) which is a brotherhood created to promote
charitable work. The men in the front of the procession were
the oldest of the group; they carried long gold staffs. Behind
them was a group of younger men carrying tall lit tapers.
These men wore white robes with a gold trimmed, blue tunic
over them; very festive and colorful in contrast to the first
group. In their midst was a man in a red robe, swinging a pot
of burning incense, billowing smoke. Directly behind them
was a candle laden float bearing the Virgin and baby Jesus.
A small percussion band sporting a military style uniform
brought up the rear. Military presence is an important part
of the procession; it asserts the military's job of defending
the church; very different from the American separation of
church and state.

As we approached the street, the procession halted. The atmosphere immediately lightened as the men broke formation and began quietly talking among themselves. The taper-bearers encircled their leader as he began to stir the incense. In ritualistic manner, he fanned the smoke toward each taper-bearer. The candle light, the scent, and the smoke lent a mystical air to the proceedings. Bystanders began to mill around among the participants, taking pictures and examining the Virgin up close. In the center front of this float was a flamenco dancer implying that this particular Virgin watches over the dancers and protects them from harm. Many Virgins are dedicated to protecting bullfighters.

Underneath the float were rows of white shoes. When the procession stopped, the float was lowered and the curtains around the base were raised to reveal a group of large, muscular men dressed in white (stevedores). I was very surprised to see them; when the procession is moving, the Virgin seems to float magically by. The source of magic is seldom revealed. Witnessing the stevedores brought everything back to reality. Stevedores are not members of the cofradia; they are hired to carry the float. During lengthy celebrations, they may carry floats for a different cofradia every night.

The floats are generally 20'x9'x15' tall and weigh as much as 1/2 ton; it can take the procession up to 12 hours to cover their route. Small, narrow streets make carrying a float even more of a challenge. To prevent accidents a man walks directly in front of the float and guides the stevedores with taps on the float's frame. Using a simple code, they can maneuver very tight spaces without a single bump.

Spain is a Catholic country; the Virgin plays a large role in the people's lives. I felt very fortunate to stumble upon a religious procession and to be able to get up close to the float. Religious processions are common occurrences throughout the year in celebration of a parish's or a city/village's Saint's Day but there isn't a calendar, you just get lucky (or disappointed when everything is closed).

While the gypsies proclaimed Christianity to avoid religious persecution, they pride themselves for their nonconformity to religion. Yet Semana Santa, with its religious processions, is very important to them; why? Quite possibly, it is because theirs is a religion more in tune with the Virgin. Mothers play an important role in gypsy society and through hardships, many grieve for their sons just like the Virgin. Or possibly, like Christ, they are the outcasts of society and easily identify with his suffering.

During larger celebrations, an observer may sing a saeta to the Virgin or Christ. Saetas are old song forms that were incorporated into flamenco in the early 1900s. In the larger cities, cantaors may strategically place themselves on balconies to serenade the passing procession (many are actually paid performers). This doesn't preclude spontaneous song from the crowd but you are more likely to find spontaneity in the smaller villages. This procession was a lovely taste of Spanish life. We were very lucky to be in just the right place at the right time.

> Under the canopy goes
> The brightest star;
> Its eyes look like fountains,
> Weeping for its solitude.
>
> My mother of hope,
> Tell your son Jesus
> That there isn't in the world over
> A virgin as beautiful as you.
>
> Response:
> The Virgin embroidered her cloak
> And she embroidered it so beautifully
> That she wore it for the first time on Good Friday,
> At Christ's burial.

Seville

We awoke to the sun streaming in. With very little sleep in the last 24 hours, we were surprisingly energized.

Housing in Spain is not unlike housing in most large cities; cramped quarters and very expensive. Sarah had gotten lucky; she was house sitting for a couple of flamenco friends that were in the states. Their belongings were stored in the spare room so the 'living area' was little more than an efficiency. But all the creature comforts were there: a clothes washer, a TV, an iPod, internet, and a big comfy sofa. The shower was incredibly small, every time I bent my elbow, the door popped open! No desire to linger there! The smallness made the apartment easy to personalize and thus feel like home.

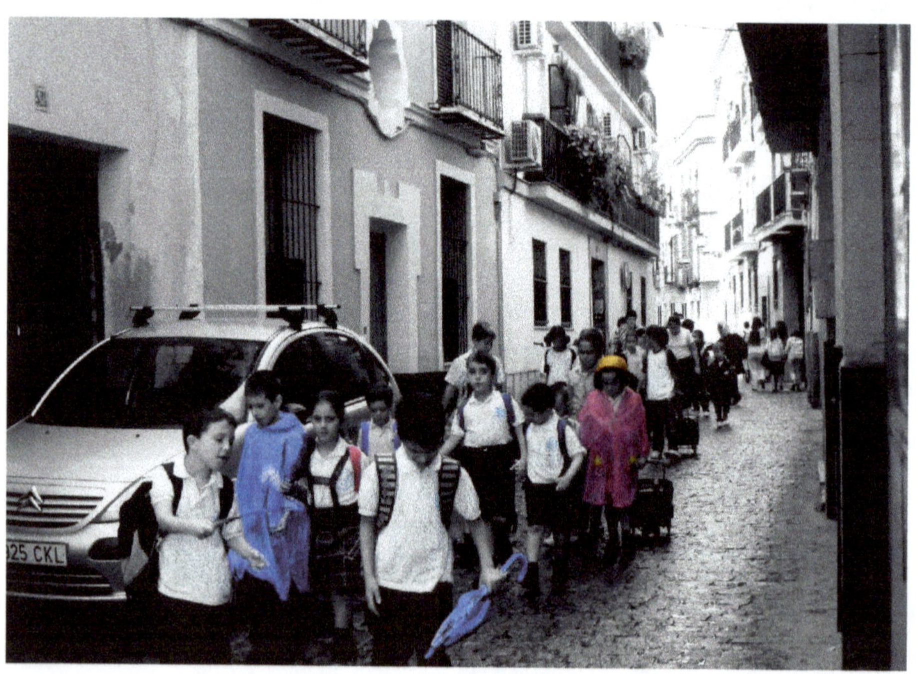

The meandering calles of the neighborhoods are not on the local tourist maps so we had a good incentive to rise early so Sarah could lead us to the Plaza Nueva on her way to Spanish class. The marathon trek reminded us of our lack of sleep; café con leche became our highest priority!

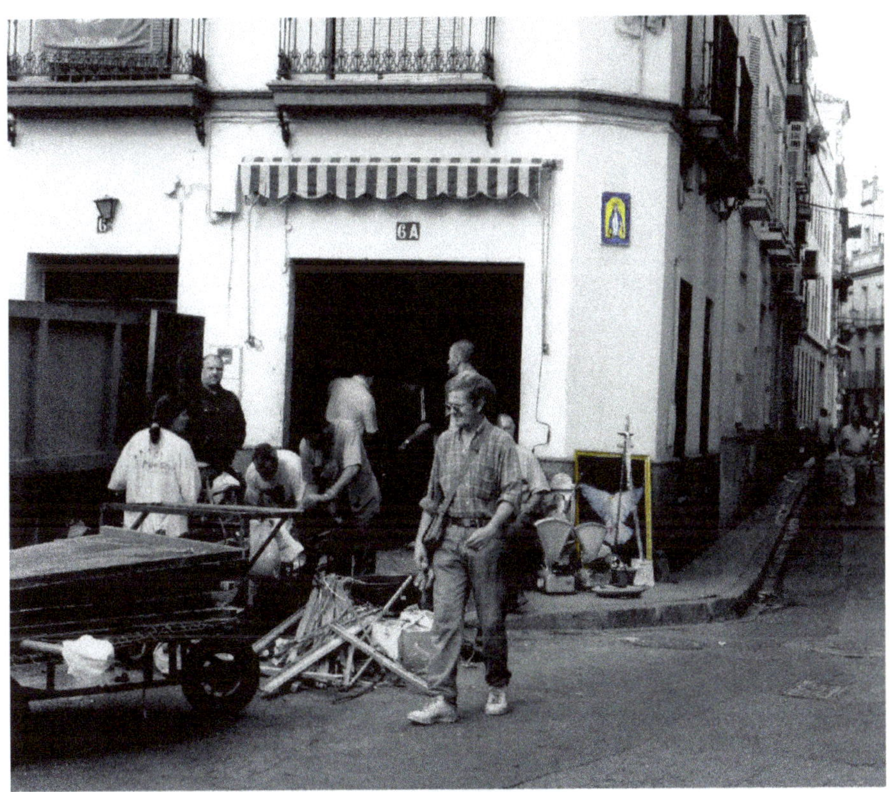

Museo del Baile Flamenco

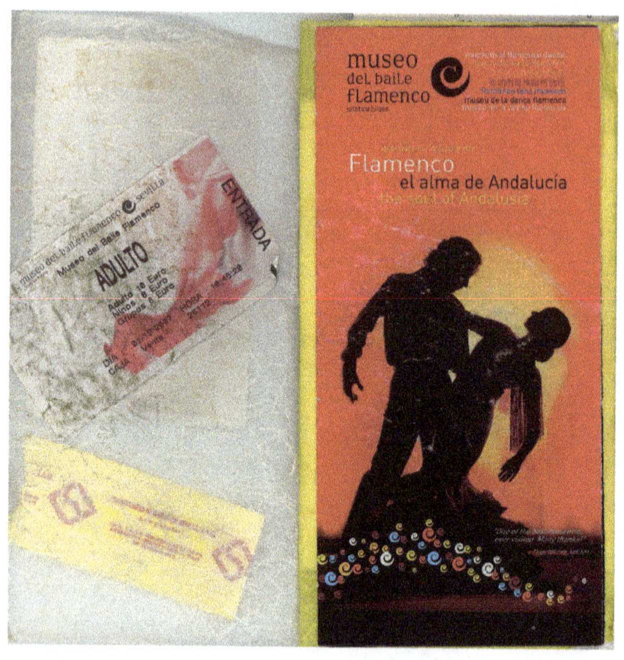

Our goal for Seville was a total immersion into flamenco. Over coffee, we studied our map. The old section of Seville is surprisingly compact. We found ourselves very close to the Museo del Baile Flamenco.

The Museo del Baile Flamenco was the first flamenco museum in the world. Cristina Hoyos, a dancer, opened the museum in 2006 with the mission of explaining the mystery of the dance.

The museum is housed in an 18th century palace built on an ancient Roman foundation made from stones cut by Tartars. The walls of the museum are built on top of an urn containing the Bible, Koran, Talmud, and Hindu scriptures; a symbol of peace and understanding.

Despite the rain, light from a skylight streamed down three floors and flooded the lobby of the museum, creating an energetic environment. Large polka-dot flamenco shoes added a bit of whimsy.

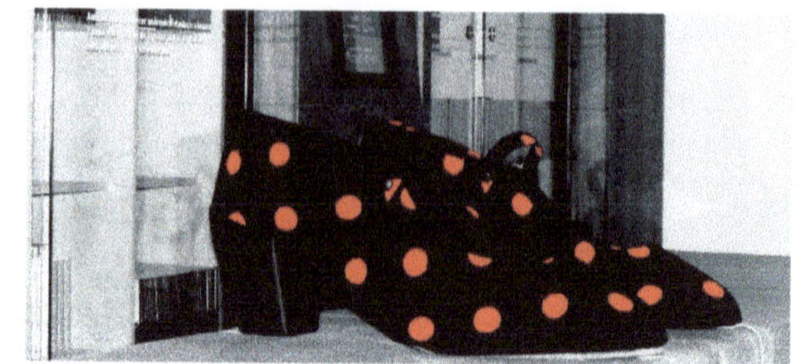

The official tour begins on the third floor. The elevator opens to a mezzanine surrounding a shaft of light. The perimeter walls are hung with black and white portraits of flamenco's famous and most respected stars. The portraits portray the hardships of the gypsy race, enhancing the penetrating eyes and somber expressions. The only one familiar to me was Carmen, but I had the wrong Carmen. I was thinking of the famous story, *Carmen*, written in 1845 by a Frenchman, Prosper Merimee, a tragic romance of love and betrayal.

The skylight shaft is filled with the high-backed Andalucian chairs that are used by flamenco guitarist. Suspended with the chairs are two lemon trees which are symbols of Andalucia and the art of flamenco.

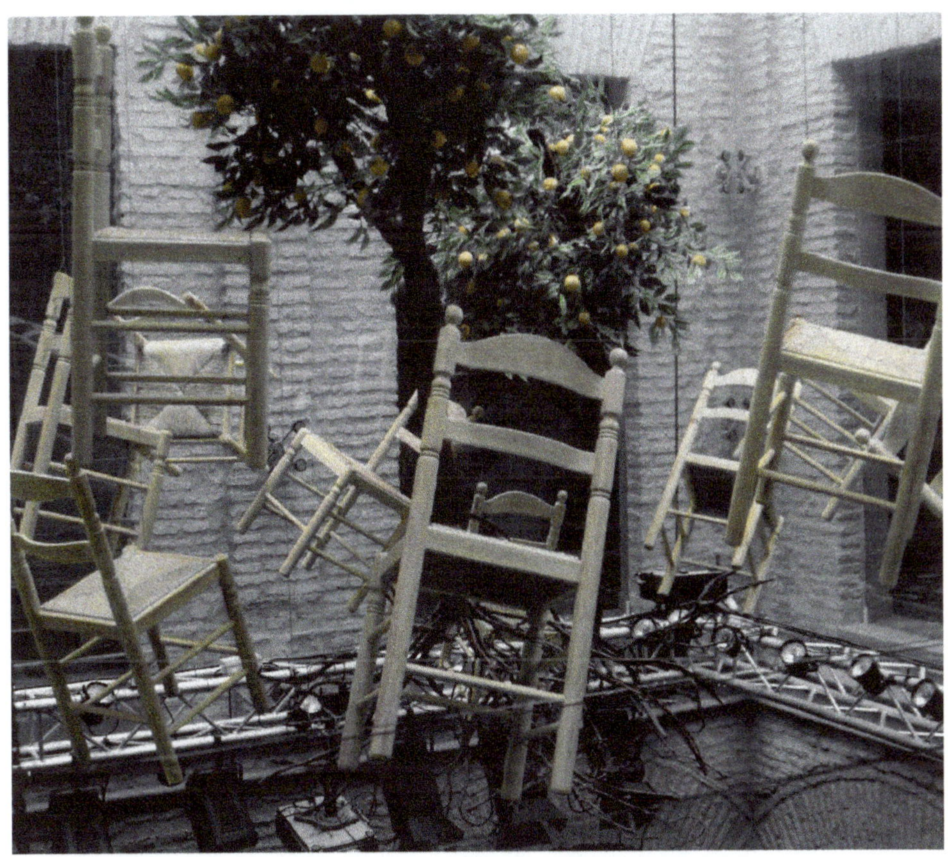

Moving into the exhibit area, the mood becomes bright and festive as you enter the most colorful part of the museum, the display of costumes. The colorful costumes bring the dance to life. The wide variety is astonishing. The traditional polka-dot with the long train is there of course; I have always associated flamenco with polka-dots. I was surprised to see the variety of combinations and the limited use of polka dots. As I reflect back, I wonder at the cheerfulness for a genre based on poverty and oppression. The gypsy race thrives on its laissez faire, nomadic lifestyle; perhaps the bright colors reflect the gaiety they possess despite their hardships.

The lighting in the next exhibit is dim and hazy, reminiscent of smoke filled café cantantes. This audio visual section of

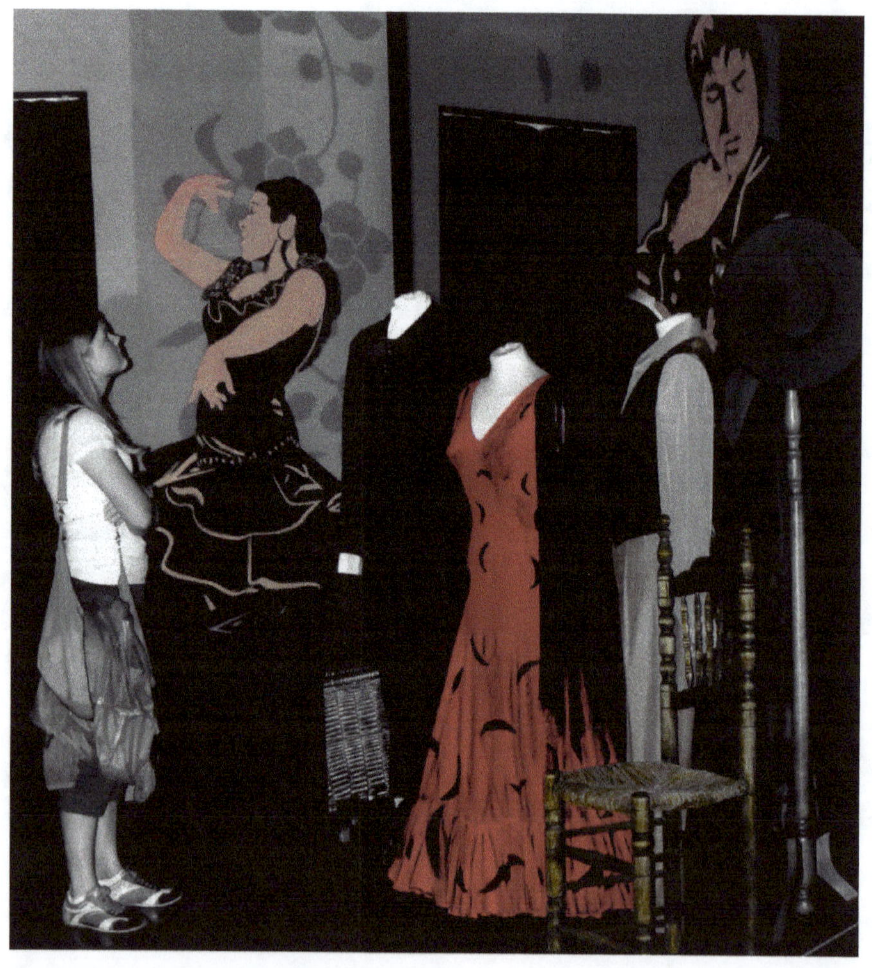

the museum gives a sense of what a performance was like. When you walk in, you are immediately a spectator. Life size performers fill the wall to your right. The music is lively and the dancing, energetic. Video screens are setup with cantaors, guitarists and English interviews with performers, blending together for a better understanding of the meaning of flamenco. The vintage black and white footage may be the best flamenco you'll see in Spain. Many purists think that the flamenco performed for tourists isn't flamenco at all; tour books tend to agree.

In the mid-19th century, wealthy young men seeking exciting evenings and willing to pay, led flamenco from the gypsy communities to café cantantes. These young men were revolting against the refinement and sophistication of the aristocracy by adopting the dress, mannerisms, and speech of the gypsy community and by providing the money to launch flamenco as a commercial entertainment.

Once café cantantes became established, flamenco began to flourish outside of Andalusia in cities like Barcelona and Madrid. Flamenco changed venues again in the 1950s and became the showy and gaudy tourist attractions of today.

Per standard museum practice, you exit through the gift shop. I was enamored with the available literature since books on flamenco are in short supply in the US. Unfortunately for me, they haven't printed English translations. All that history just beyond my reach!

The dresses and practice skirts on display are beautiful; the ruffles add an amazing weight. The shoes, while a standard style, come in numerous colors and designs. Serious dancers have their shoes custom made for a perfect ft. The mantillas (shawls) are radiant; they are hand embroidered with vibrant colored thread on a heavy weight silk. The fringe is hand knotted. This accessory is heavy too, it's a wonder that the bailora can move. My single purchase was a pair of castanets. Castanets are not a part of pure flamenco; the purist relies on their hands (clapping, snapping fingers, beating chair or table) and feet (stomping) for accompaniment.

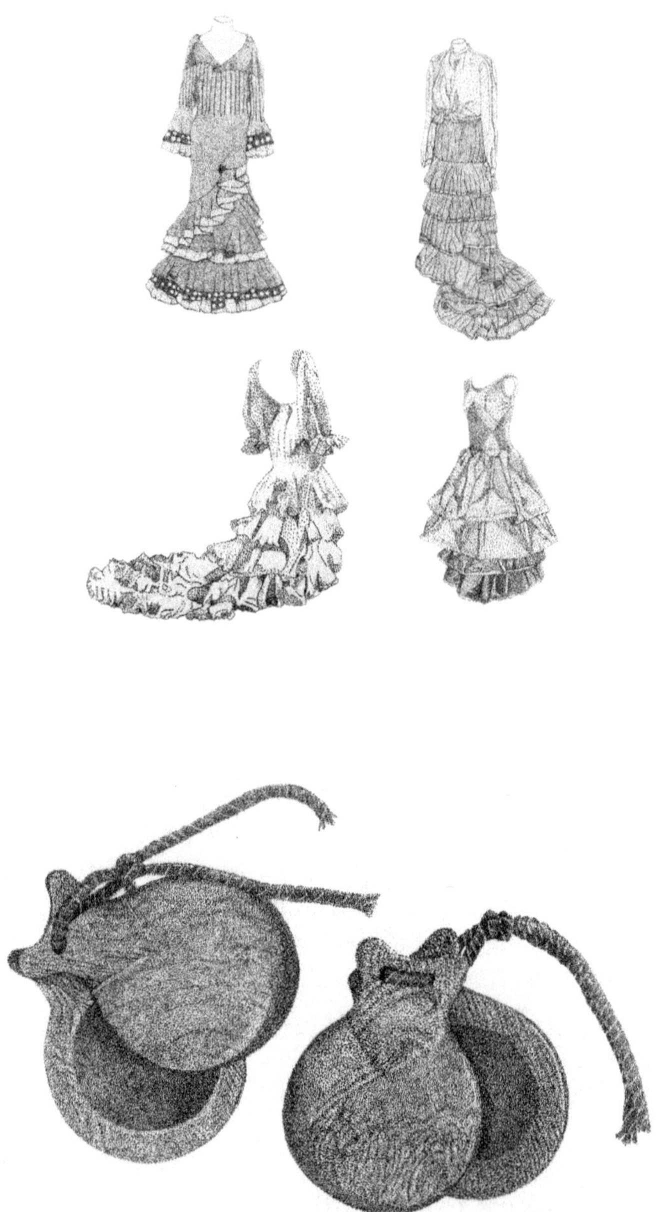

History of Flamenco

The history of flamenco has many parallels to American Blues. It encompasses a way of life that began in the rough, lower classes and was born of a race that was unsettled, emotional, and unpredictable yet appreciated by the educated and moneyed. At its best, it is an impromptu communal activity.

Flamenco song is "a resonant tear on the river of the voice"…"Anguish is made flesh"

Frederico Garcia Lorca

Flamenco music is not for the untrained ear. It sounds like an angry chant and takes some getting used to. Song was the first and is still the most important element of flamenco. It contains elements of Jewish, Byzantine Christian, and regional folk styles blended together with a strong Indian and Arab presence. The gypsies transformed these gentle, lyrical ballads into coplas (three or four line songs) in a manner more expressive of their feelings of rejection and hostility.

The early cantaor's song resounds with his sense of hurt as well as that of his audience, drawing them emotionally into the performance. Flamenco songs gain their meaning from how the cantaor shapes them through improvisation, hence there is no set music. The guitarist's accompaniment must follow where the singer leads.

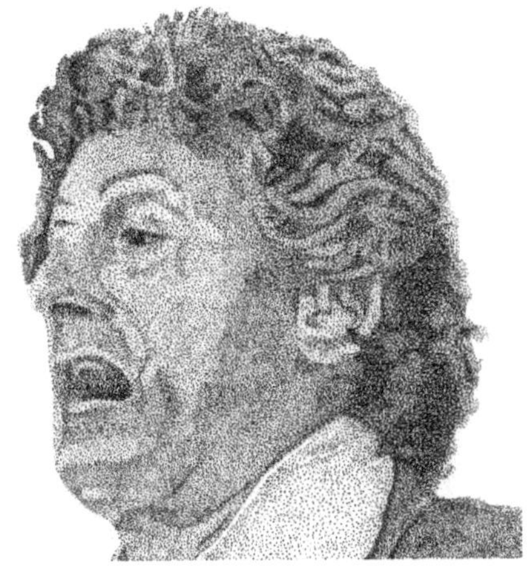

The modern flamenco guitar has been around since the 1870s. Its origin was a four string instrument, a blend of an Egyptian string instrument, a kithara asiria, and the Moors' guitarra morisca. A fifth string was added in the ninth century and the sixth string in the 1790s.

The dance, my favorite part, was the last element to become a part of flamenco. It also has strong roots in Indian and Arabic tradition. Early dance embraced the footwork and hand work of India's Katsk, Kathakali, and Bharata Naryam while observing the early Islamic teachings forbidding women to call attention to their legs.

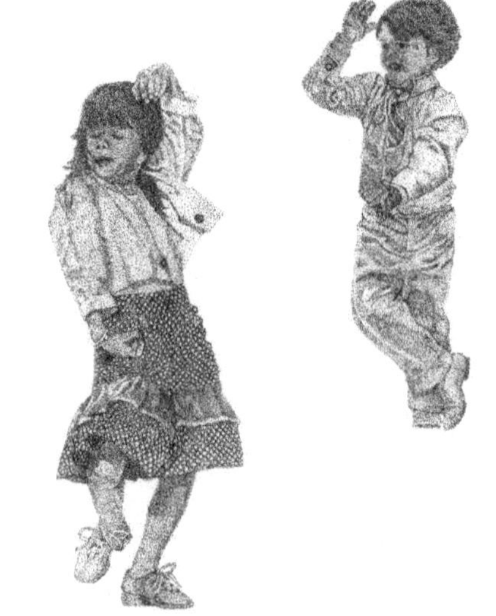

Bailaora (a female dancer) moved little from one spot. With arched back and serious expression, she moved her hips gracefully while her arms formed beautiful, circular movements. The dance is an expression of inner emotion that is based on experience and emotion, not athleticism, so it is often performed by older people. For me, the dance will always be the epitome of flamenco and, along with the matador, the symbol of all things Spanish.

Carmen Amaya was born in Barcelona in 1913 into a gypsy family; her father was a flamenco guitarist. She began dancing at age four and performing at age seven.

Her innovative, dynamic, unfeminine dancing and wild lifestyle made her a legend. Prior to Carmen, bailora used only the upper body and facial expression to convey the drama and meaning of the dance; feet and legs were demurely covered. Carmen pushed the boundaries.

Often wearing the traditional male costume, she introduced fast and exciting leg work ("sounded like the rattle of machine guns" – Walter Terry) into the female role while preserving the traditional female elements, paving the way for today's bailora.

Carmen formed her own company, predominately members of her extended gypsy family. She traveled extensively and became synonymous with flamenco and the fiery women of Spain of the 20th century.

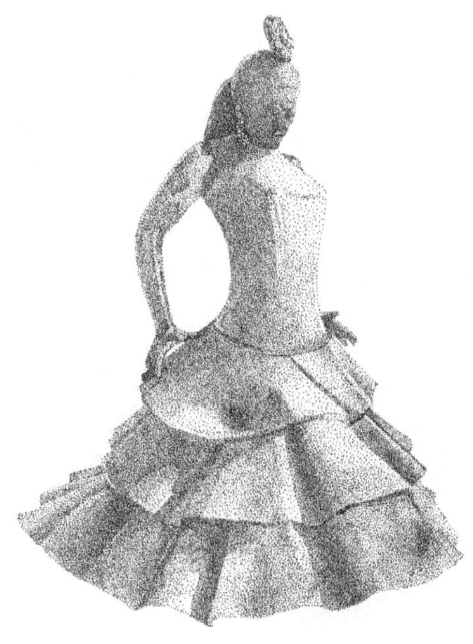

Seville City Center

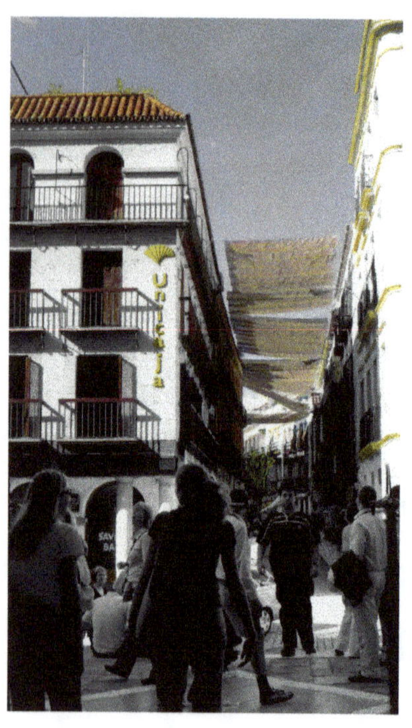

The city center encompasses Seville's most famous shopping district, the Calle Sierpes. The streets are a narrow, pedestrian only maze filled with small boutiques; generally a single room with only a single ware. Every block seems to have a shop devoted to one facet of flamenco; a dress store, shoe store or mantilla store. The shops are filled with exquisite displays of color in the windows and, alas, very high price tags. I was officially on a quest now to find a deal on a black mantilla with 'all-over' embroidery in bright reds, greens, and purples, at a price I could afford.

Siesta time was approaching and it was time to meet Sarah. The girls wanted to shop before lunch. The larger chains stay open during siesta so the girls planned to settle me in at a café, gulped a café con leche, then dash off to explore. I chose to linger over my coffee and catch up my journal.

When we arrived at the café, all the outdoor tables were full. An elderly woman motioned that we should join her. I was uncomfortable with the notion of forced small talk through pantomime but felt it inhospitable to decline the offer.

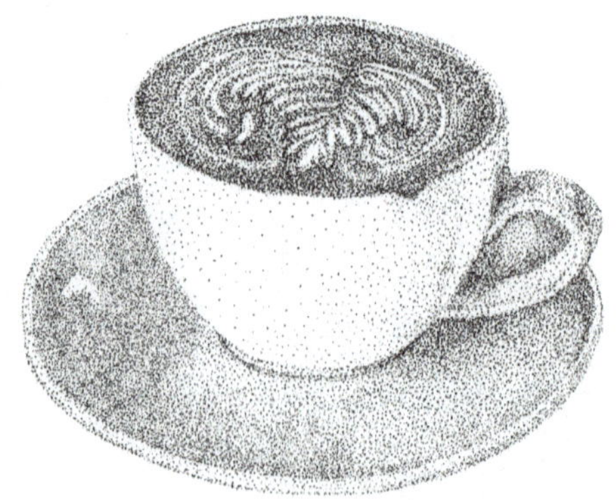

Much to our surprise and relief, the only acknowledgment was a warm smile. She continued to enjoy her repast as though we weren't there. The girls hurried through their coffee and left me to handle the tab. I was soon left alone with my journal and iPod.

Out of the corner of my eye, I noticed a small group of English speakers looking for a table. Enjoying the kindness of the older woman, I offered them seats at my table. The table was messy with the remnants of the girls' coffee so I asked a waiter to clear the debris, totally unprepared for the ensuing uproar. My waiter, who had been invisible, came roaring out the door waving his hands in the air shouting what I could only imagine were obscenities. The general idea seemed to involve my leaving without paying the check. I had made no move to gather my stuff and depart however and my attempts to ask for la quinta didn't seem to penetrate his despair. A young man traveling with my new companions, came out of the café, quickly assessed the situation, and hurried to intervene. The waiter calmed enough to take my money but he was still miffed. I was grateful when every-

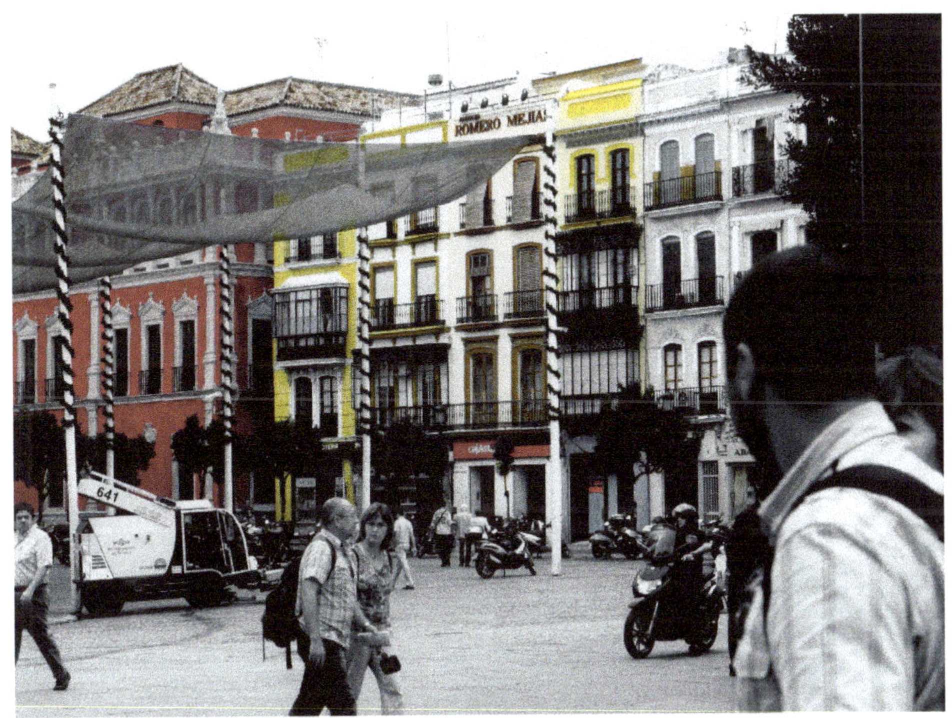

one's focus returned to their own conversation and I was allowed to return to my journal.

I now know the fastest way to summon the check: prepare to leave!

The girls returned empty handed. We had a few hours before Sarah's flamenco classes so we grabbed a quick lunch and visited the Cathedral. The café served cute little miniature sub sandwiches. There were twenty or more choices on the menu and they were inexpensive enough to try a variety.

You order your food by checking off what you want on a piece of paper; luckily they had an English version which takes away some of the guess work but you still have to know what the translation is referring to. When your order is ready, they call your name and you pick it up at the pick-up window. Turns out, our names didn't sound very familiar in Spanish, we had to listen carefully. I tried a variety of things; my favorite was the chocolate! We made note of the name of the chain in hopes of finding another.

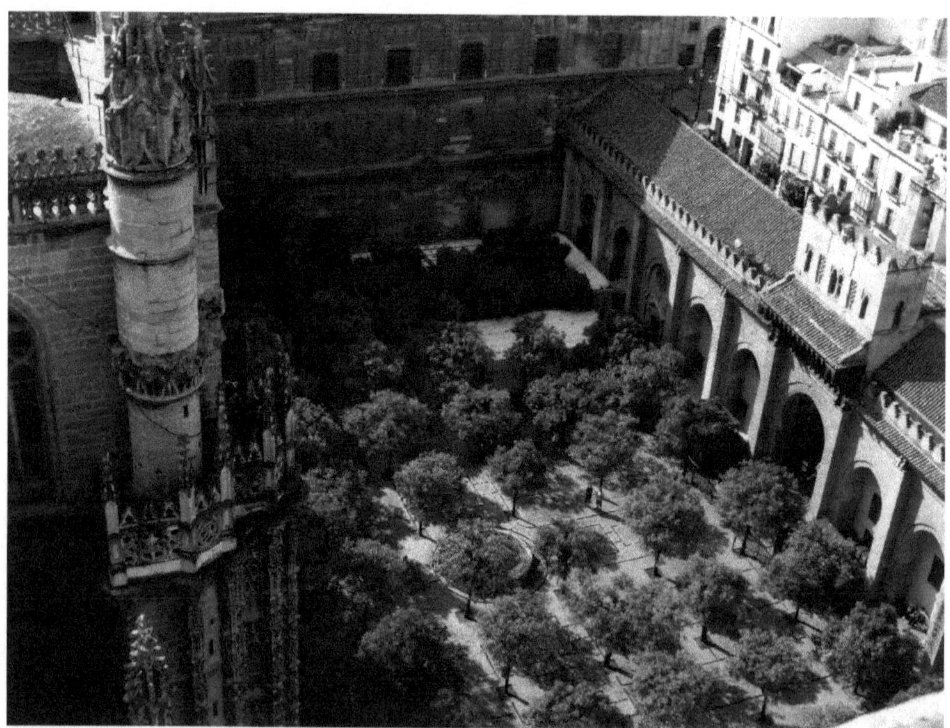

We spent a wonderful siesta exploring the Cathedral and Giralda. The Cathedral is in the Guinness Book of Records for the largest interior of a cathedral in the world; it is the third largest cathedral overall, after St. Peter's in the Vatican and St. Paul's in London.

The Cathedral was built between 1401 and 1507 on the sight of a Moorish mosque. All that remains of the mosque are the Patio de Los Naranjos (orange trees) and the Giralda, the bell tower. Inside, the Cathedral is pretty much like the inside of most European cathedrals. The sides are lined with private chapels which house wonderful art work. Most of the chapels are inaccessible which makes it hard to see the paintings.

What interested me the most was the tomb of Christopher Columbus. His tomb is carried by four men representing the four kingdoms that made up the Spanish crown at the time of his voyage – Castile, Navarre, Aragon and Leon.

I had never thought about Columbus' significance to Spain, after all, we are the land he discovered. Christopher Columbus' discovery, how-

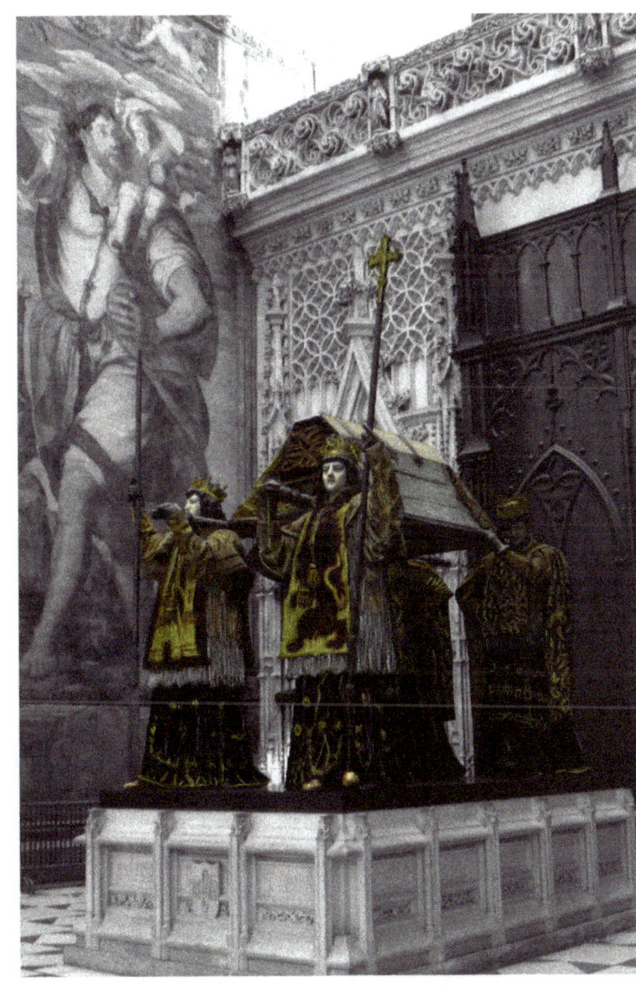

ever, played a large role in Spain's prosperity through trade with the New World.

Historic sites throughout Andalusia explain the Andalusian's role in Columbus' history. The crew of the initial voyage was mainly from Andalusia, thus most the first colonists of the American islands were Andalusian. Monuments and statues throughout Spain are dedicated to him and October 12th is Columbus Day in Spain, a national holiday. Columbus died in 1503, convinced he had found a new route to Asia, never knowing that he had discovered a new world.

The guide books make climbing the Giralda Tower sound like a challenge. The tower is 330 feet high. No building can,

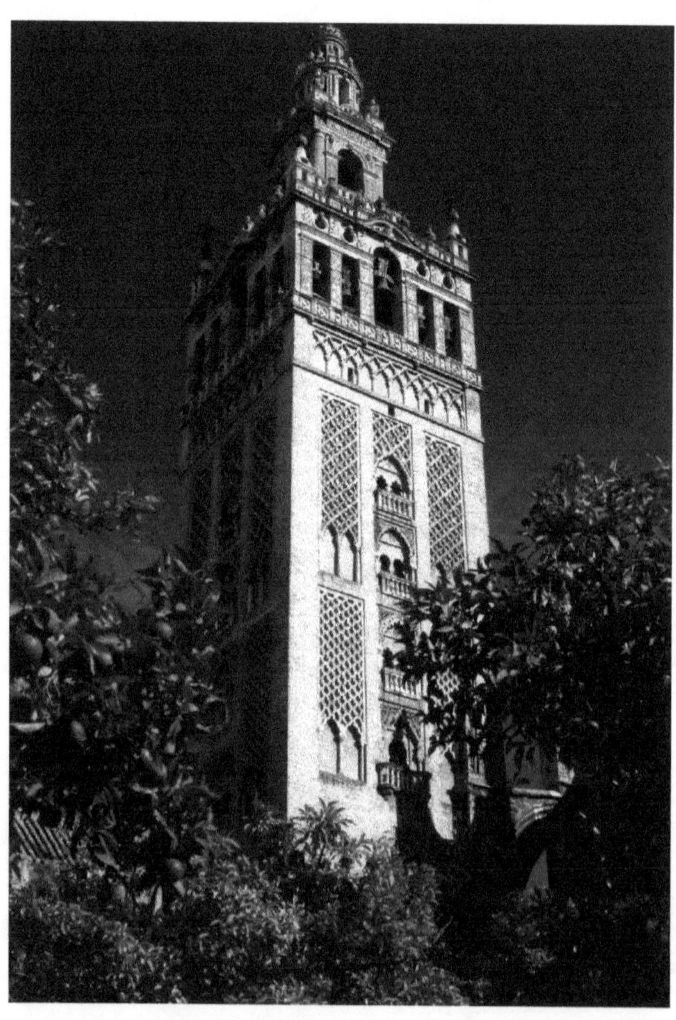

by law, be taller than the statue atop the tower. It is a leisurely walk up a long incline of 35 ramps. Steps would have worn me out but the spiraled incline was very comfortable; no rush and interesting vistas from the tower windows. The ramp is wide enough for two men on horseback so there is plenty of space for tourists to walk at their own pace without getting in anyone's way. Men on horseback climbed the tower to ring the bells five times a day to call the Muslims to prayer.

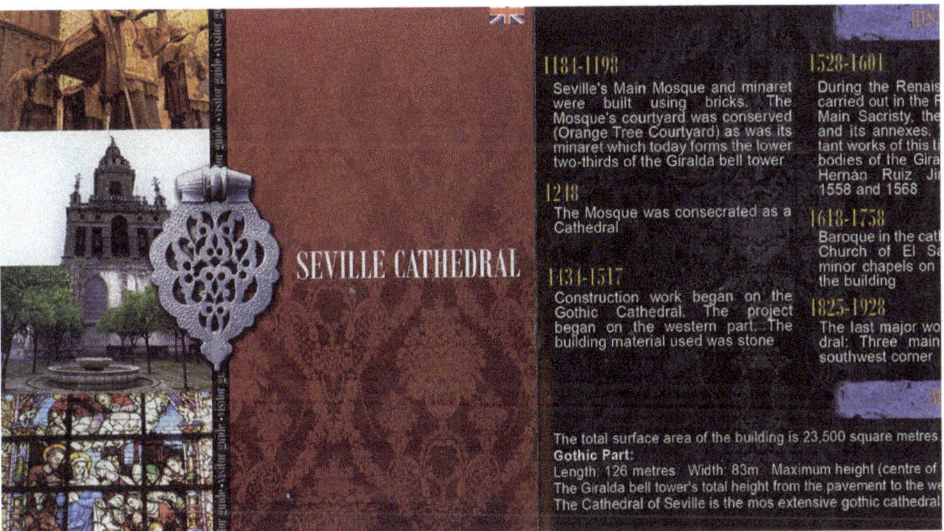

When we emerged from the Cathedral, siesta was over. Liz and I tried to find the shop that had flamenco clothing on sale to show Sarah but everything looked the same and we couldn't figure out which way we'd come!

Flamenco Estudio de Arte

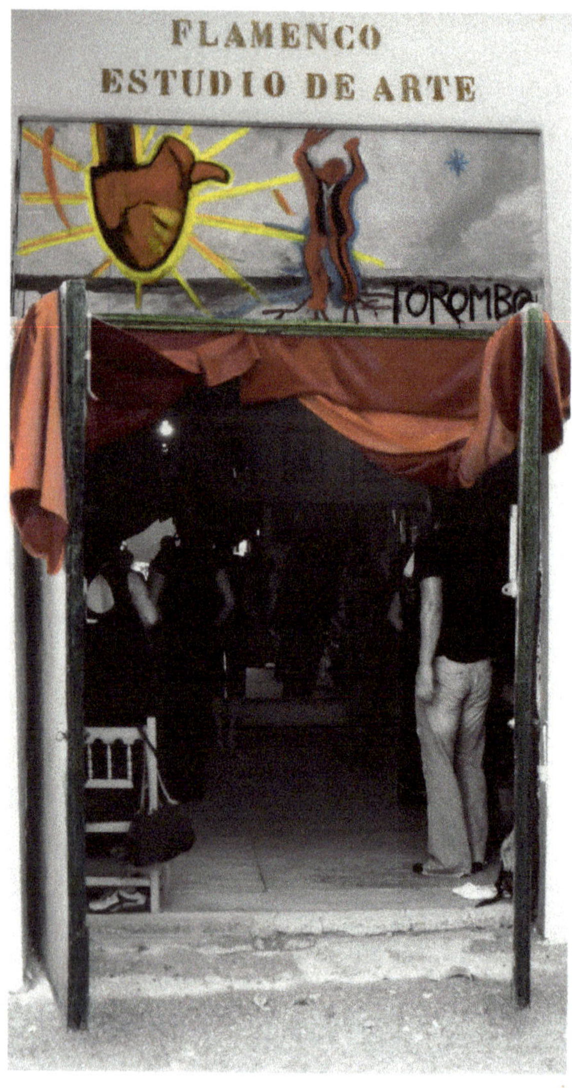

Time for flamenco, part two. Sarah changed quickly into her rehearsal clothes, long black pants under a long black practice skirt in very hot Seville. She quickly explained that the long pants were to absorb the sweat, delightful.

The evening was devoted to live flamenco, beginning with a visit to dance class at 6:00. Students arrive at the local bar with liters of water and depart en masse for class. There were many languages and nationalities among the students; flamenco has a broad international appeal. We walked from the bar into what used to be an area of stables. The individual stalls are fairly large and have been converted into a business park similar to an industrial park in the States.

The large wooden doors swing open to a dimly lit room with a mirror running across the far wall. The studio is a small room (a rather large stall) that is dimly lit with no A/C or even fans. I was surprised at the rusticness of the studio. I was expecting a well-lit, air-conditioned space. The floor is well worn plywood and the walls are white washed but have long since lost their luster; the walls are adorned with flamenco portraits.

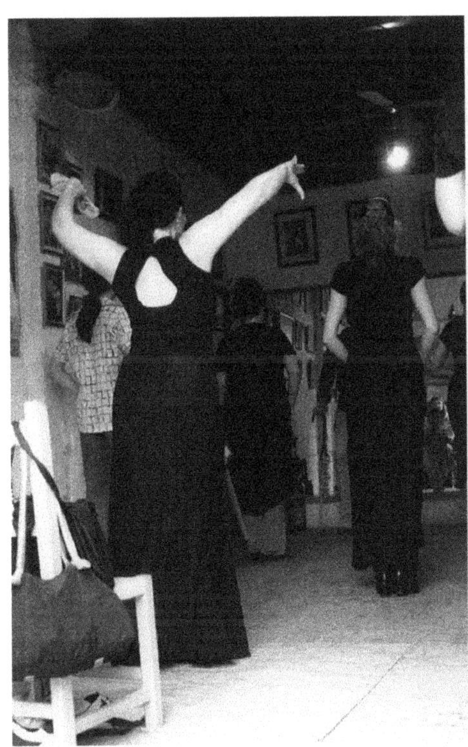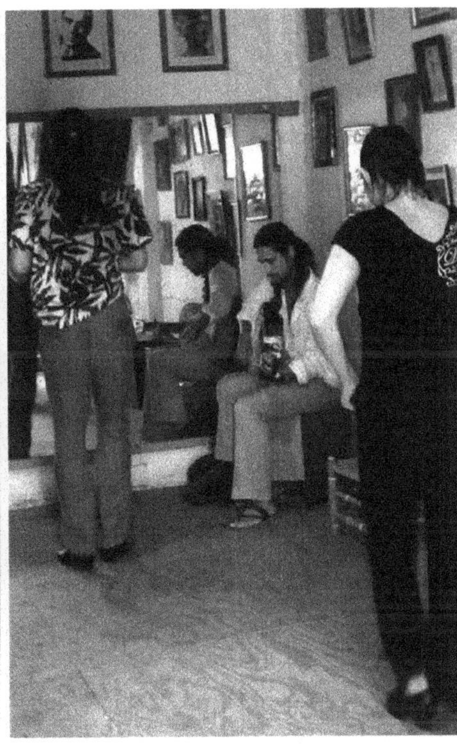

To the right is a staircase leading to a hayloft which doesn't appear to serve any purpose other than a nice place to display flamenco guitars. In the front of the studio is a single chair for the guitarist and there are a few chairs along the back wall to hold the students paraphernalia and, tonight, Liz and myself. It is a very cozy, intimate space. My hope was to be inconspicuous and as out of the way as possible while photographing. In that small of a space, not possible.

The teacher is a renowned performer of only 19. He stood in the front of the room and directed class with his cane, reminiscent of my ballet teacher many years ago. A tap of the cane and feet were flying, the noise deafening and the sweat pouring; upper bodies didn't move.

Flamenco sounds like American tap. Rather than heavy metal plates on the bottom of the shoes, flamenco shoes have
many small tacks covering the heel and toe areas. The students stand straight and tall with hands clasped behind their
back. I tried to mimic the footwork in slow motion, no way.
The instructor moved among the dancers and studied their
footwork, demonstrating and instructing, leaning in close to
be heard.

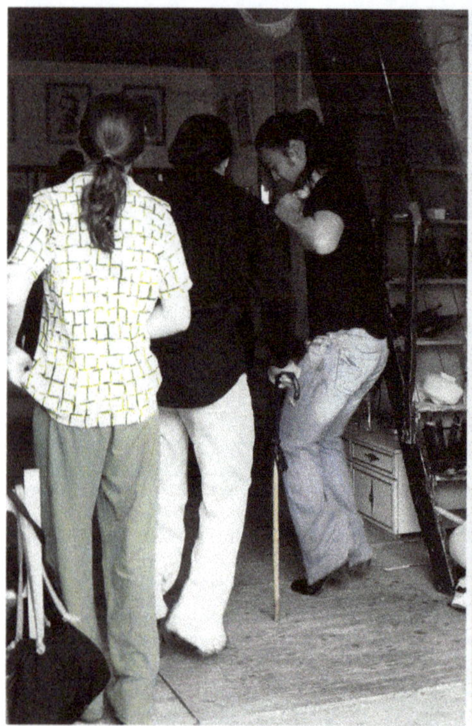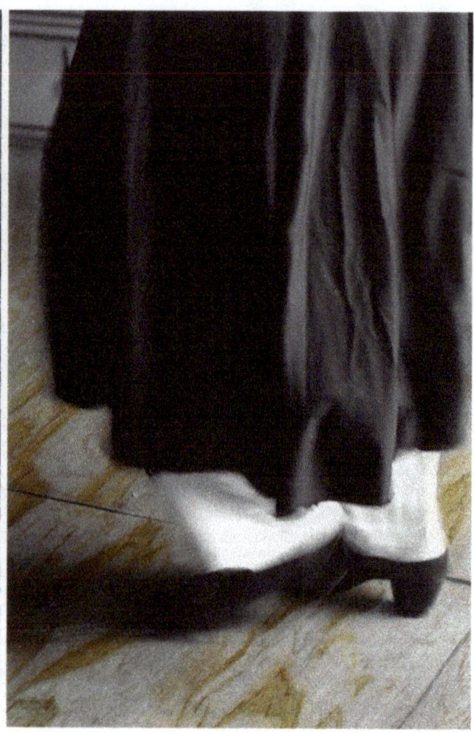

Warm ups are intense but not a single complaint was ut-
tered; they danced furiously until the cane rapped, took
a water break, and started again. What dedication! These
young people had traveled far; visas are for a limited time
period so no time is wasted in social chatter.

Plaza de Espana

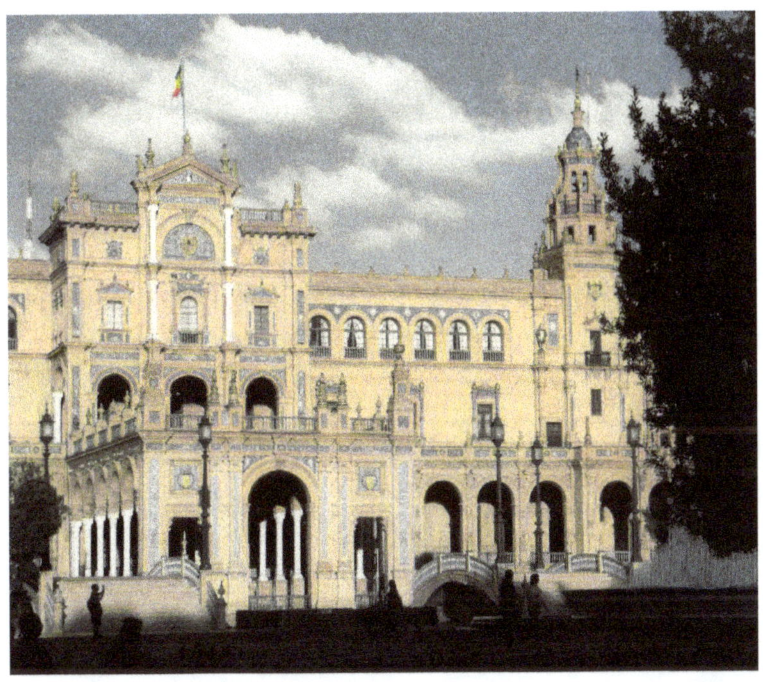

Time is short for us too so we head out before classes are over to visit the Plaza de Espana and the famous Tobacco Factory in Triana. The Plaza de Espana was the Spanish Pavilion at the Ibero-American Exposition of 1929. The plaza is undergoing renovation, repairing the tile work that makes the plaza a 'must see' in Seville.

The Ibero-American Exposition was a world's fair for countries with an historical tie to Spain through either colonization or political union. Twenty-three countries took part in the event which covered 170 acres around Parque Maria Luisa. The buildings that housed exhibits took 19 years to build. The US building was to be used later as the consulate but is now home to an art foundation. America displayed a menagerie of electrical appliances, a movie theatre and government exhibits.

The largest building surrounds the Plaza de Espana on three sides. It housed an exhibit related to the discovery of the American continent. At one time it was occupied by government offices and by the general office of the regional army. Currently the building appears to be empty; in all my guidebooks, nothing is mentioned about its current use. The building has a large tower at each end. Sunlight hit the façade of the central section, glistening off the tiles, giving it the glow of a fairytale castle. The architecture of the building is a mix of styles including Gothic and Renaissance; known today as Sevillian (or Andalusian) Regionalism. The choice of exposed red brick for the building materials is unique for this area.

As we came around the side of the building, I was enchanted by the railings. The balusters are painted pastel shades of blue, green, yellow, and orange; they remind me of carousels. The hand railing is covered with azulejos tile and there is a row of the tile running beneath the balusters.

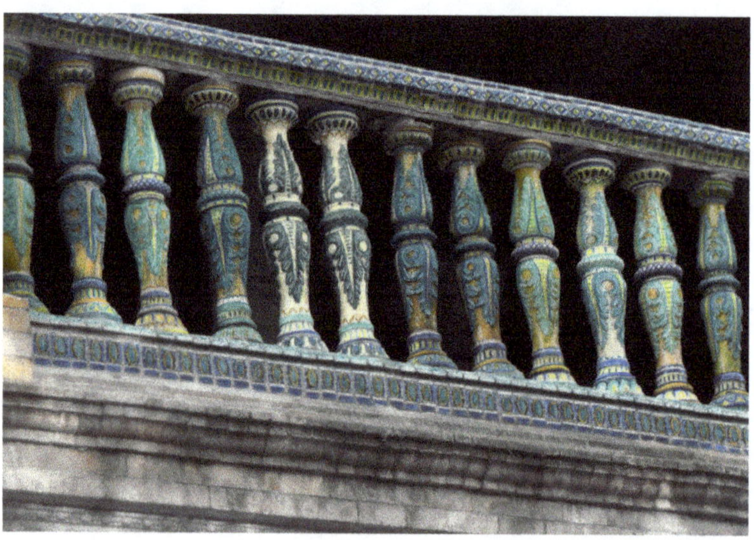

Azulejo tile is a painted, tin-glazed, ceramic tile that was introduced to Spain by the early Muslims. The tiles generally have interlocking curvilinear, geometric, or floral motifs. The Muslim tradition was to cover everything with tile to avoid 'horror vacui' (a fear of empty spaces). At one time, Seville was the major center of the tile industry. The use of tile spread throughout Spain and Portugal; it covers walls, the underside of balconies, and creates murals in unexpected places.

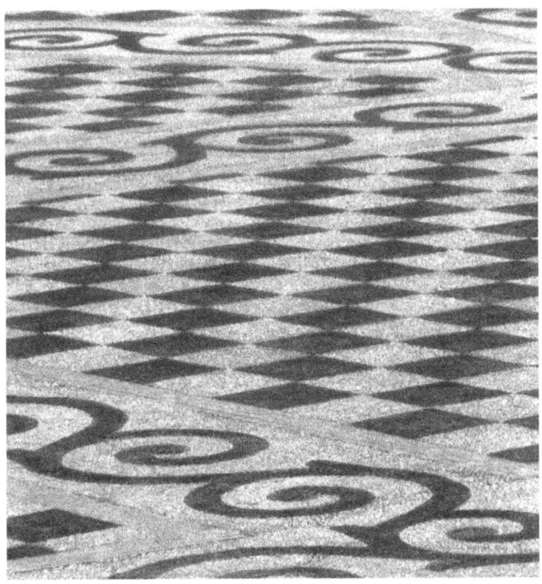

Inside the grounds of the Plaza, you are in for a visual treat. Large black and white pebbled mosaics of Moorish design surround a large fountain in the plaza. The designs are flawlessly executed and very mesmerizing. Encircling the perimeter of the plaza is a moat; it had been drained for the restoration so the full effect was lost. There are four bridges across the moat representing the four kingdoms that came together over 500 years ago to form Spain. Fabulous tile work adorns everything!

The tile on the railings here are a blue and white pattern that reminded me of delft tile, but only in the coloring; the swirling, intricate patterns are of a traditional azulejo design. Across the moat, at the base of the building, are tile murals depicting historic scenes from every province in Spain. The portico is framed by a series of arches. Between the arches are medallions with the bust of Spain's famous; kings, explorers, writers, and artists. The sheer size and bright colors are astounding.

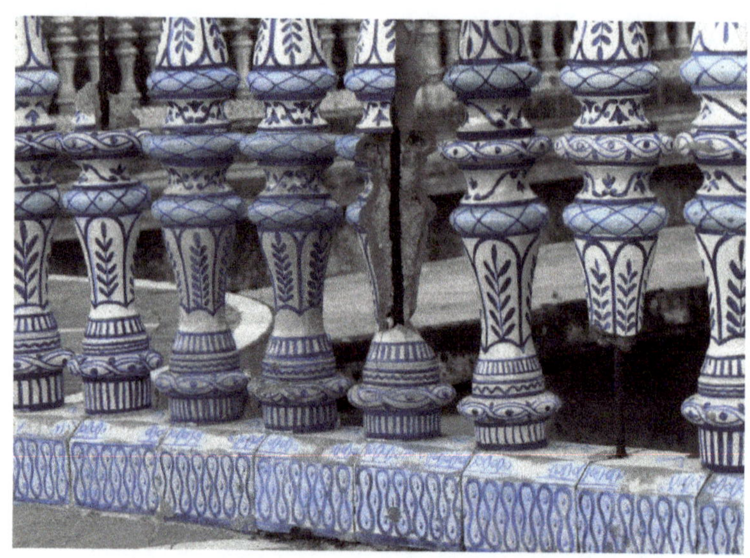

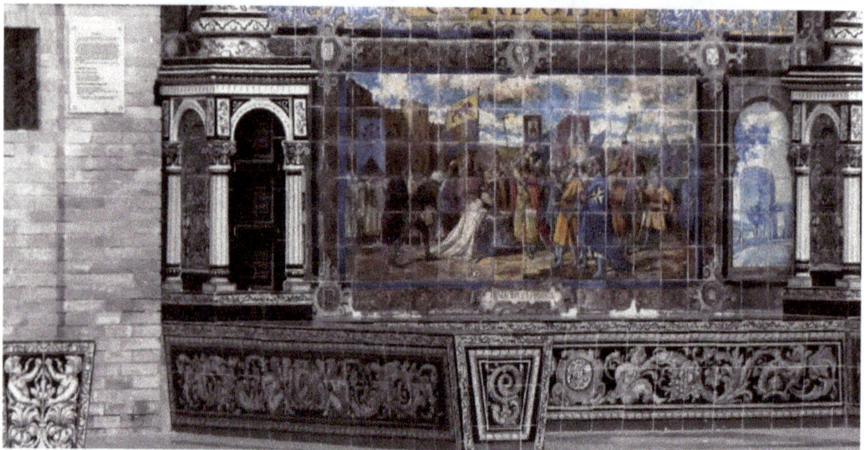

Time marches on…

Leaving the Plaza de Espana, we walked through parts of
the University of Seville to the bridge over the Guadalquivir
River into Triana. The tobacco factory is along the river. It
plays an important role in the famous story, *Carmen*, written in 1845 by a Frenchman, Prosper Merimee. It is a tragic
romance of love and betrayal. Carmen, the main character,
is given the attributes of the classic Andalusian woman:
defiant yet demure, feminine yet independent, a temptress
capable of turning men mad with desire. The story highlights
the spirit of camaraderie and self-confidence that the cigar-

reras (tobacco factory workers) gained from working in the tobacco factory in Seville. Tobacco factory jobs were the first time these women had had the opportunity to gain financial independence. Sharing childcare among them; these women worked in teams that became extended family.

Adaptations of the story to theatre and cinema incorporate flamenco thus coming to represent Spanish gypsies and flamenco to many. Today the tobacco factory building is occupied by the University of Seville. There is a high fence with formidable looking guards at every entrance. Our lack of Spanish made us timid so we walked along the fence, catching glimpses of the famous building, then back over the river to catch a bus back to the apartment.

We had counted the stops on the bus route map at the bus stop so we'd know when to get off the bus because only a few of the stops have names on them. What we weren't aware of is that the bus stops many times for each dot on the map! Needless to say, we got off too early! We didn't know where we were so we followed the bus route home! It was a relief to see the old Roman wall; the apartment was near!

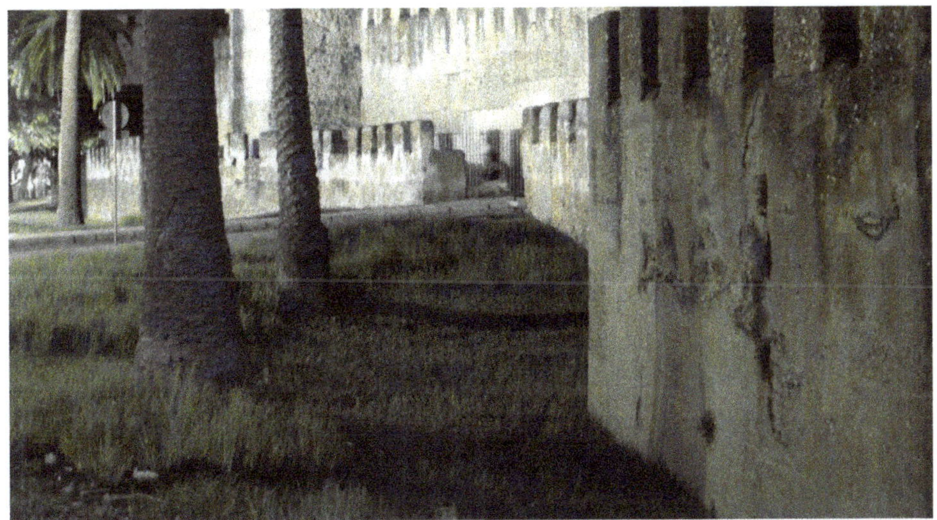

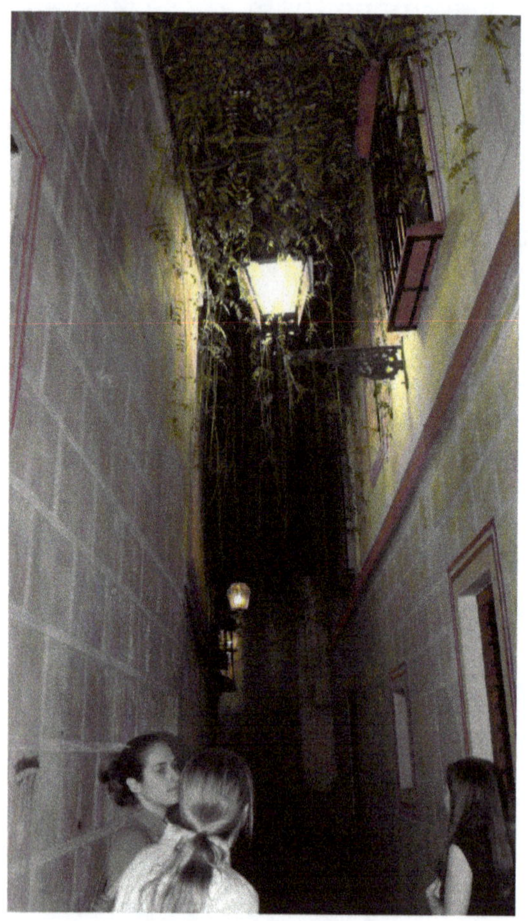

A quick change and we were headed out to dinner and live flamenco. It was a typical Spanish evening; dinner at 10:00 pm. Spain has many flamenco venues; most are very expensive and geared to the tourist industry. Not one of my guidebooks recommended a single show. Sarah provided us with an authentic experience; a café cantante where some of her friends perform.

Walking through the maze of streets disoriented me. We were in a very different neighborhood, not many people about. The bar is in a tight alley with unadorned walls on either side. We reached an unmarked entrance, a large industrial door. Clearly you had to be invited, otherwise you'd never know it existed. Admission was free. I thought of speakeasies and prohibition; very secretive.

It felt like we were walking into one of the mid-19th century cafes with the bars that served tapas and alcohol, the tables and chairs for the aficionados, and the small, low stage, with Andalusian scenes for a backdrop, for the performers. The room was already filling up when we got there, patrons were three deep at the bar and the only seats left were in the very back. We found a bench along the back wall where we could stand to see and not block anyone else's view. We ordered different tapas this time, and of course, tinto con limon! As 11:00 neared, the crowd doubled and the air became hazy with the smoke.

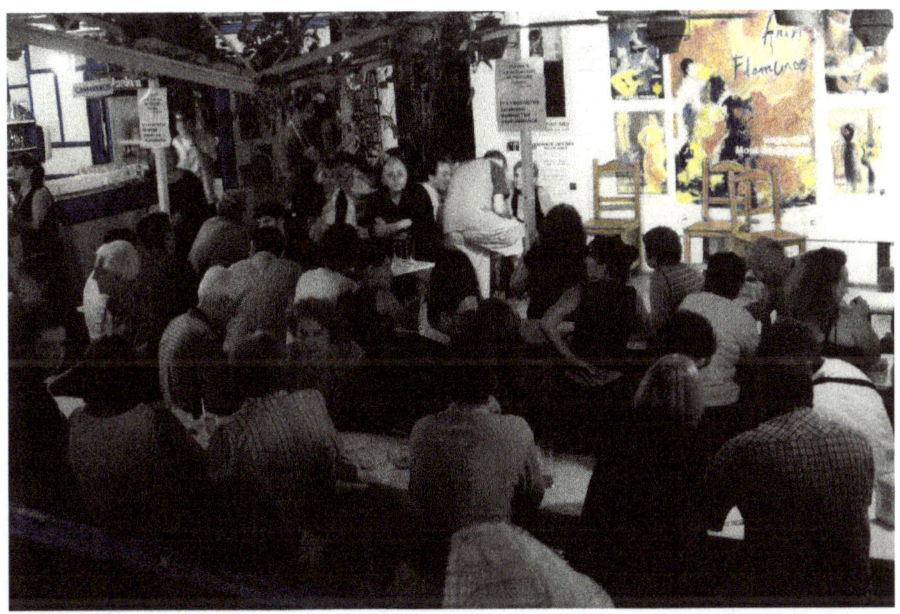

At 11:00 a trio walked onto the stage; a cantaor, a guitarist, and a bailora. They were dressed in casual, contemporary clothes. The stage was very small. There were three chairs for them.

The audience quieted. The performance began with a soft, rhythmic beat made by clapping their cupped hands. The cantaor, eyes closed and arms outstretched, joined in singing a song of anguish. I couldn't understand a single word but the meaning was clear. The bailora and the guitarist continued to beat the rhythm with palmas and pitos. The guitarist began to play, following the cantaor's lead. Listening to this man sing, I came to appreciate the importance of his role. In this small, informal environment it was easy to feel his emotion and gain a better understanding of flamenco.

The bailora was graceful and regal. She arose, shushed the audience and began to dance. In the first set, her movements were concentrated within the upper torso. She made very little eye contact with the audience; she was meditative, feeling the dance within. Her gracefulness was surprising. Flamenco is an art form that is not reserved for the young and athletic. The raspy voice of the old and the grace of the matron are most respected.

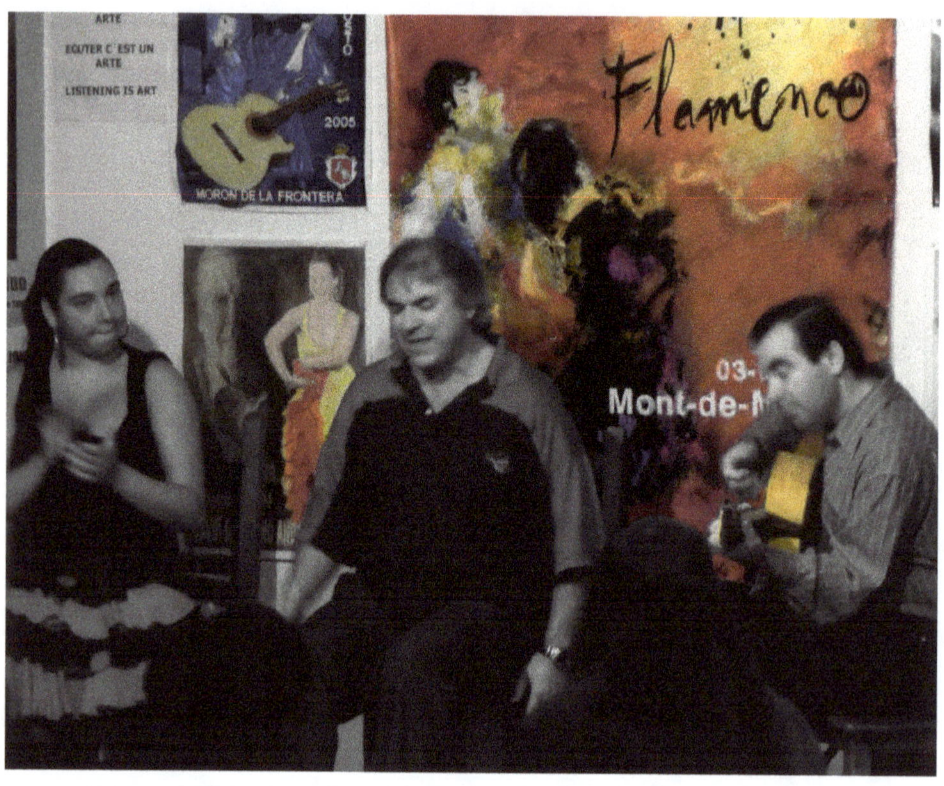

Whenever the crowd got too noisy, the bailora would raise her finger to her mouth and shush the audience. Clearly the group expected the audience to be respectful and participate. We weren't just here to be entertained with background music.

The second set was livelier. The joyousness and fun was apparent from the first note; more alcohol had been consumed and the crowd was a bit more boisterous. The bailora sternly shushed the crowd when the whispering got too loud. Her dance this time had the fast footwork of the post-Carmen Amaya era.

During this set, the cantaor invited a friend of his from the audience to honor us with his voice, a real treat. He was the epitome of gypsy; swarthy with a carefree, mostly toothless, grin. He had a sparkle in his eyes and was very animated; gesturing to include the audience and the other cantaor in his song. He thoroughly enjoyed being the center of attention.

When the bailora began to dance, he flirtatiously joined in and they danced a sevillana, a courting dance in which the man woos the woman in a display reminiscent of mating flamingos. They circle and become unbearably close but never touch until the end when he is allowed to put his arm around her waist. Sevillanas are not flamenco, they are the dance of the people.

The bailora's distaste for him was apparent in both her expression and her movements. Undaunted, he pursued her in such a lively manner, he won her over.

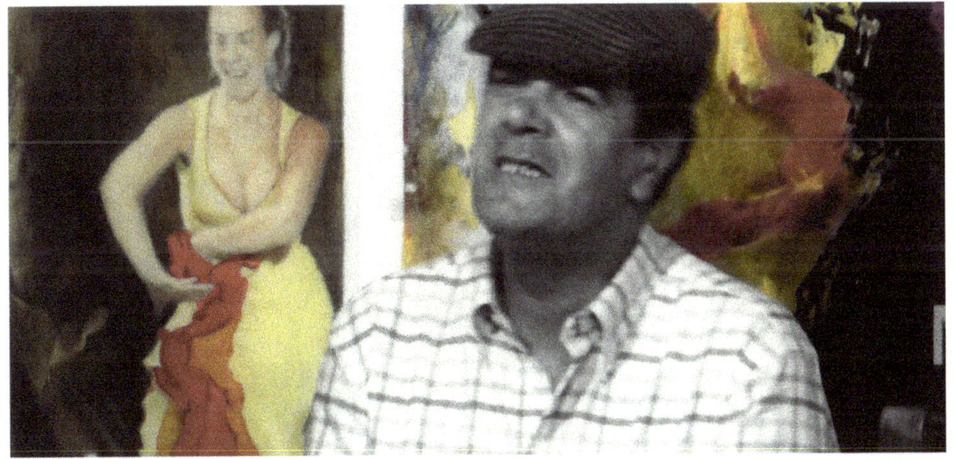

An Adventure

After the show, we carried our sangria out to the patio to enjoy the cool evening air. Sangria is a fruity wine drink that is very popular in Spain. This pitcher, however, had a strong medicinal taste and really packed a punch! It is apparent why flamenco becomes more emotional as the juega goes into the night. The crowd began to filter out around 1:00 am. We left in good spirits, planning to walk home.

We left the bar, blissful and carefree. After a few blocks, the seclusion became eerie so we decided to hail a taxi, unaware of the adventure yet to come.

As we were nearing our destination, we began to argue about who was going to pay the cab fare. Sarah had a wallet full of change and was trying to get it out quickly when she dumped her handbag. Change rolled everywhere! This was funny until the cab pulled away and Sarah realized that she didn't have her house keys! T'was a very sobering moment! Good humor prevailed as we searched the curbside for the keys. No luck.

We stopped by the apartment building but no lights were on in neighboring apartments and the outside door was securely locked. We had nowhere to go but the neighborhood bar. The patrons were all older men, drinking coffee, their taxis lining the street.

Since we felt certain that the keys had fallen out in the taxi, we were excited to see so many of them in one place. Our feeling of relief was short lived when we realized that all the taxis were white like ours and all were from different companies! With no other choice, we began collecting phone numbers and hit the pay phone. Every dispatch told us the same thing, "call back in the morning".

We walked back to the apartment, just in case someone had magically arrived home late and could let us into the building. We reasoned that if we found someone to let us into the building, we should be able to get them to loan us their key to the laundry drying space on the roof. We could then climb the fence between the laundry patio and Sarah's patio and go in through the window. Nobody was up.

Finding a place to sleep in a city full of hotels should be simple but for one major obstacle, our passports were safely locked in the apartment! In Europe, you can't get a hotel room without a passport. We decided to try to get a room at the hotel where we had reservations for our last night in Spain; not sure what we thought that connection would do for us. Upon reaching the hotel, I felt our luck changing when the night clerk turned out to be a young man, perhaps eager to help three damsels in distress.

Sarah's Spanish was helpful but there was a language barrier nonetheless. After about twenty minutes of pleading, we found a loophole! Sarah knew her passport number which was good enough for him! The hotel's computers were doing their nightly backup; what's thirty more minutes? At 3:00 am we finally piled into the bed, there were a few more giggles and then we zonked; it was a very long day.

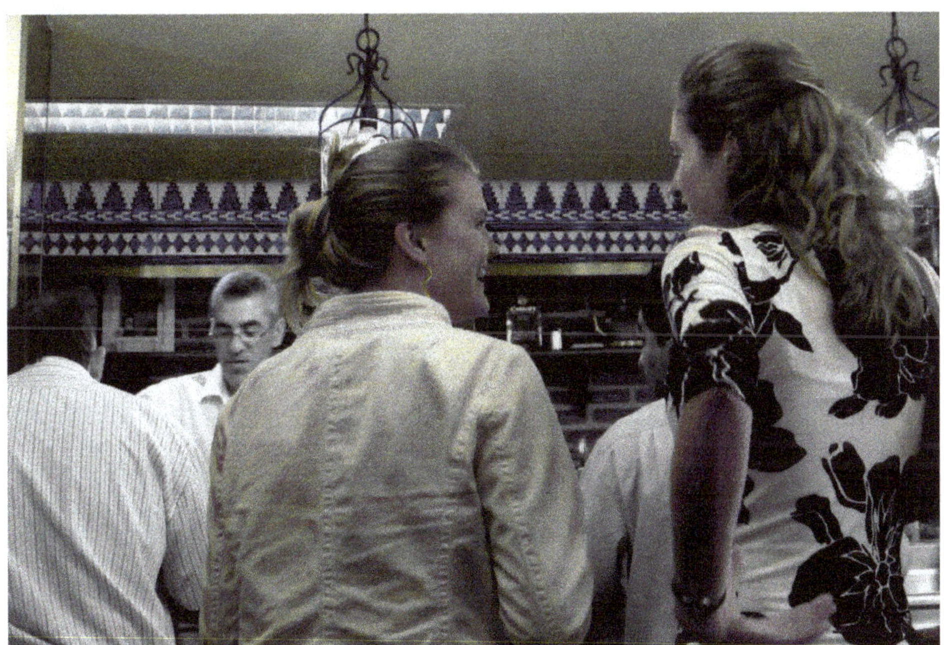

The morning began with more phone calls to cab companies. No one was around when we passed by the apartment building and rang all the doorbells. We were too late again! There were no keys; on to Plan B. Breakfast and café con leche. We dined on toast while we discussed our options. It was looking like we needed a locksmith. An older flamenco friend agreed that we had no choice. Sarah had a local Spanish 'mother' whose job was to help foreign flamenco students find classes and deal with emergencies. Sarah went to her for advice and a phone. Sarah returned, no phone call had been made. It seems that the Sevillians don't like locksmiths, they charge too much, better to just wait until someone comes home. We disagreed and sent Sarah straight back.

A flamenco friend, that we'd seen at breakfast, happened by with her husband as we waited on the stoop; he listened to our tale of woe and came up with a brilliant plan. Construction was going on all around us, surely there was a gallant knight up for a rescue. With the girls in tow, the quest was on.

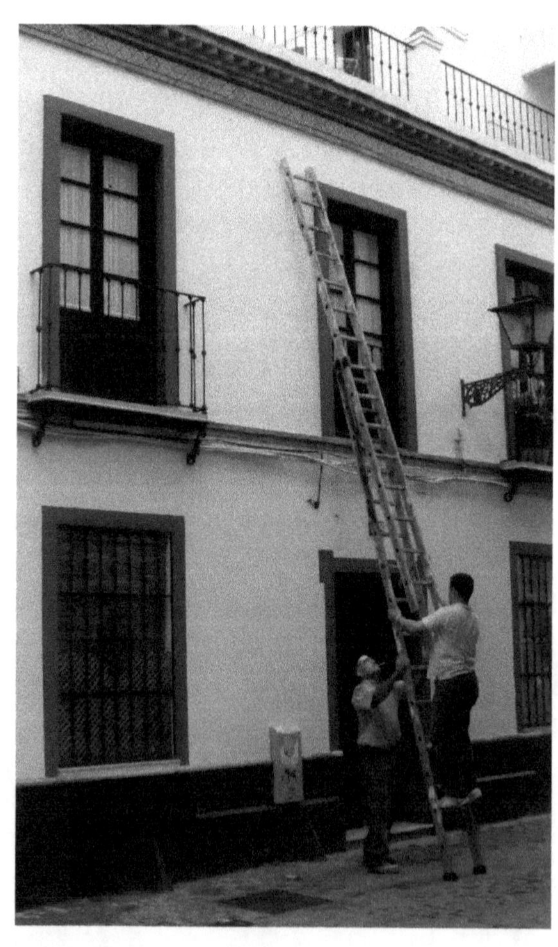

They returned in short order with two men and a ladder. Almost as quickly, the ladder was in place and our knight disappeared over the balcony. The locksmith arrived just as our knight appeared at the front door with keys in hand! We'd left them in the back of the door!

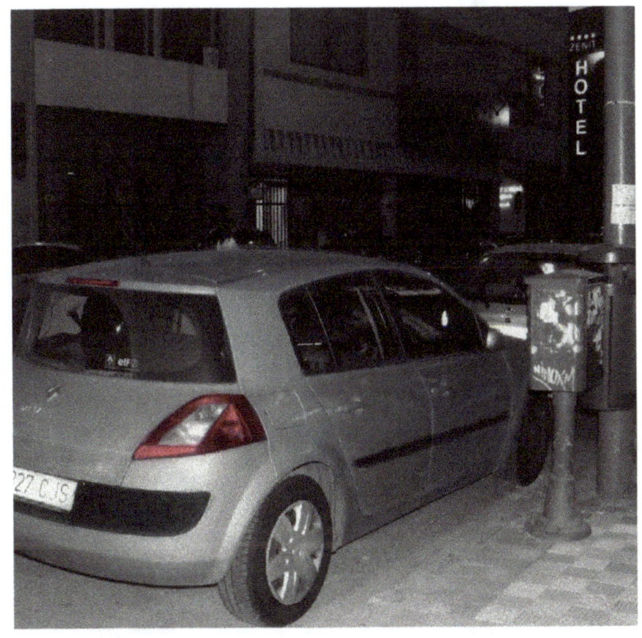

By the time we had showered and packed up, we were running four hours late picking up our rental car. The rental car company was not happy with us but what could we say? They didn't speak much English and we spoke no Spanish so we just grinned at them and they found us a car.

Their only joy came when they got to tell us that our Mini Cooper had been rented to someone else since we were late. This turned out to be a blessing, there's no way we'd have fit everything in the trunk when Sarah was with us!

We waved goodbye to Sarah and were on our way!

Jaen

Our evening destination was Jaen. We had reservations in
the government Parador of Jaen, a 13th century Arab fortress
perched high on a hilltop overlooking the city. Loosely translated, Jaen means caravan route. It was at the crossroads
of an important trade route. The ruins of the fort are further uphill behind the parador. From this vantage point, the
Moors were able to see approaching parties; the cliffs made
an attack difficult.

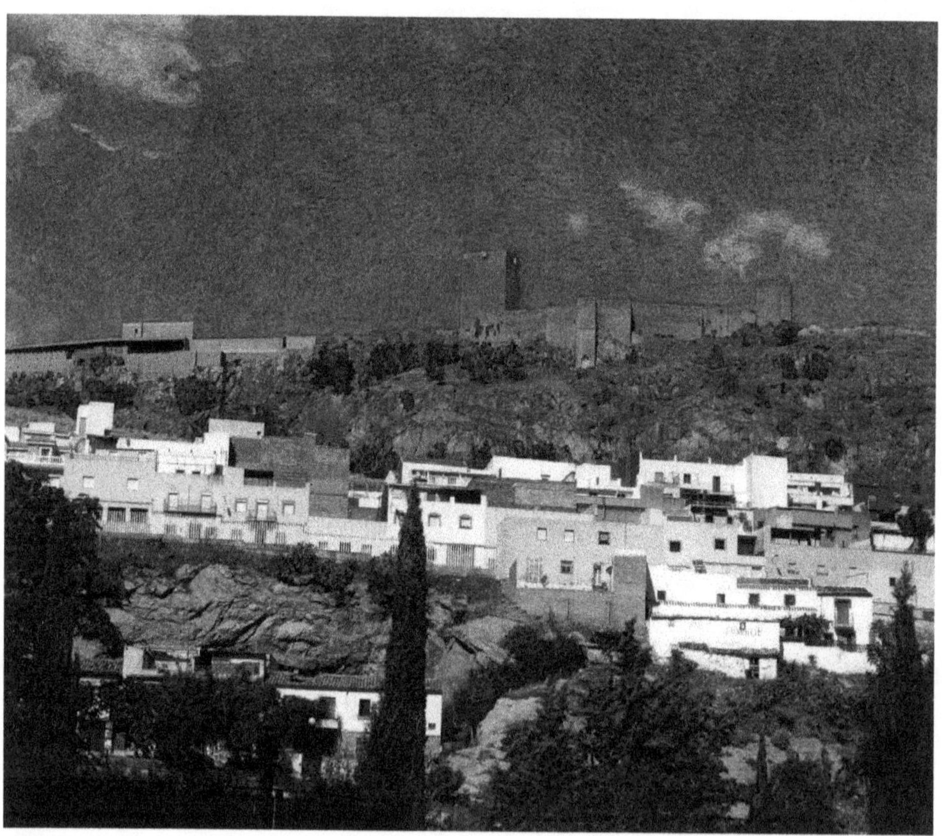

It was very dark en route to Jaen; it was getting late and
a storm was brewing. I was comfortable driving 90 km/hr,
any faster and I out ran my headlights! Liz and I arrived at
the Parador at 10:30 having had nothing to eat. Luckily the
dining room didn't close until 11:00. We don't usually eat at

fancy restaurants so this was a real treat. We had salad, fruit and nothing fried! They serve sherry with your bread basket and you have to ask for water. We felt very pampered as we headed to bed.

I had chosen to stay at this Parador because it was once a medieval castle. It was restored in 1968, maintaining the tall arches and large metal chandeliers. Our room had a beautiful carved wooden door to a small balcony with a splendid view.

We managed to sleep through breakfast! But before we went into to town in search of nourishment and caffeine, we wandered around the fortress.

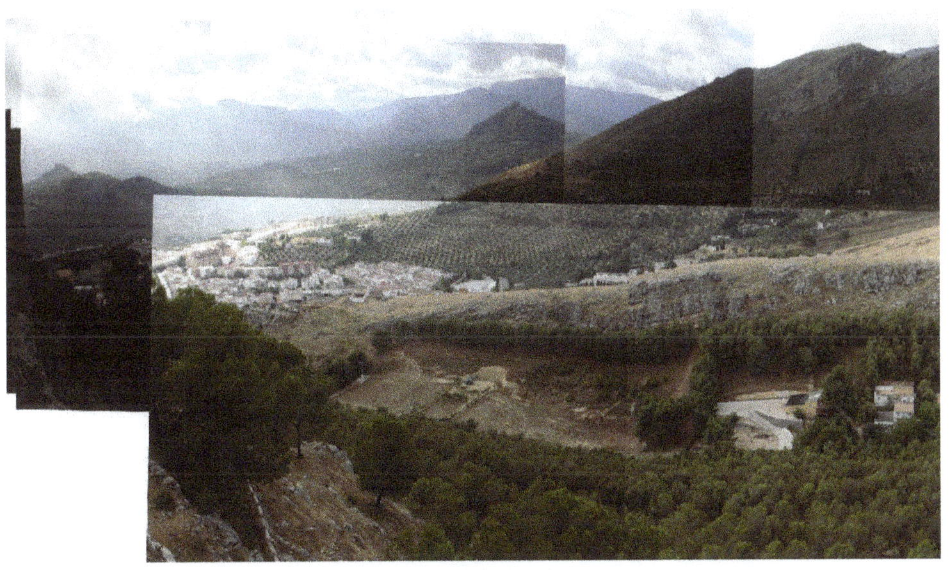

It has an amazing 360 degree view of the town below, from the valley of the Guadalquivir to the ridges of the Sierra Morena. Jaen is the World Capital of Olive Oil; as you look out, you see field after field of olive trees. The official entrance to the old fort is guarded by a knight in armor who began to speak and move as we walked by, startling us.

Rain began falling as we reached town. The guide book said that parking was great next to the bullring. It took us an hour to circle the center city twice, through all the pedestrians and heavy traffic, before we noticed the bullring. I'd been looking for an old Spanish structure; it looks like a modern sports arena! By the time we parked, the rain had stopped and we'd seen most of the city, not bad for being lost.

Alas, we arrived just in time for siesta. The pedestrians had disappeared, nothing was open. We wandered around the outside of the cathedral (touted to be one of the most important Renaissance-style cathedrals) and admired the architecture, found a small café for a quick lunch, then headed for the caves of Guadix.

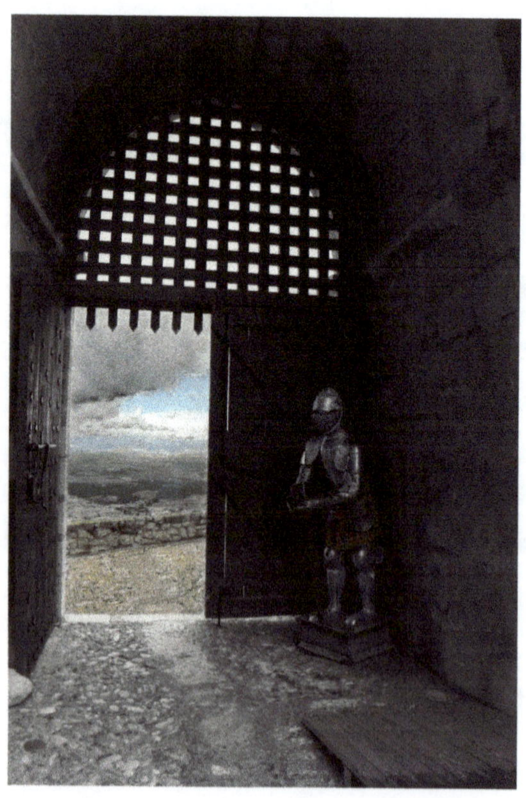

Guadix

Guadix, loosely translated means 'River of Life', rivaled Granada with its poetry and bards in earlier days. We came to see the cave dwellings.

Ten thousand people, roughly half the population of Guadix, live in caves and take advantage of the constant 20 C temperature. Some of the caves have been fixed up as second homes for city dwellers and some are mere hovels with a curtain for a front door. Churches, bars, and shopping are all found in caves in the harsh eroded hillside. It was still siesta when we arrived, not many people were about but the Guadix Cueva Museo de Costumbres Populares (cave museum) was open.

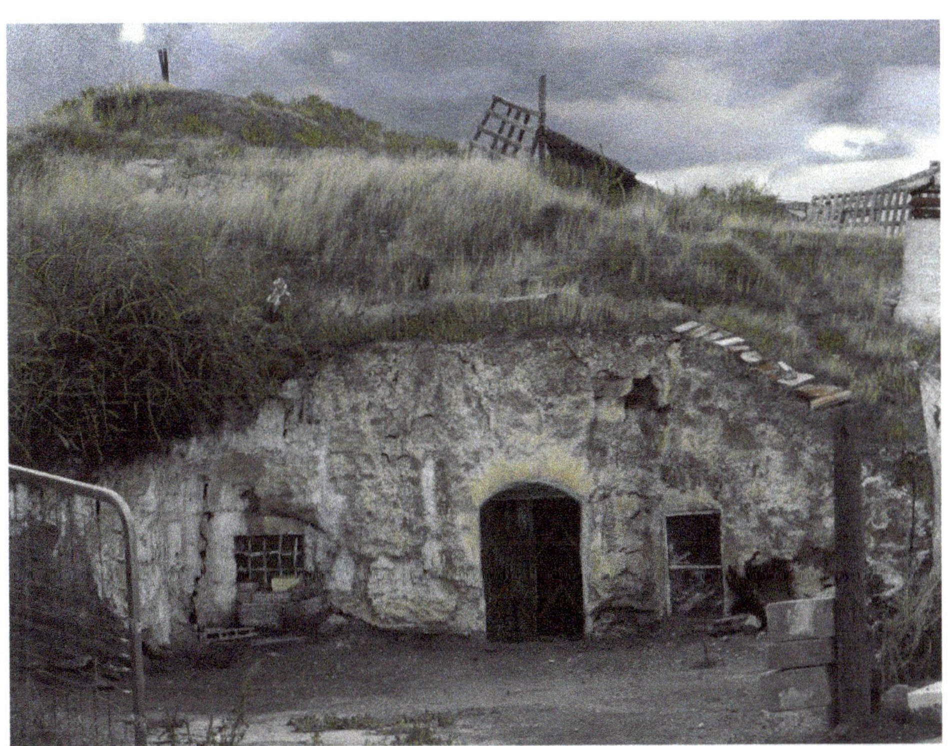

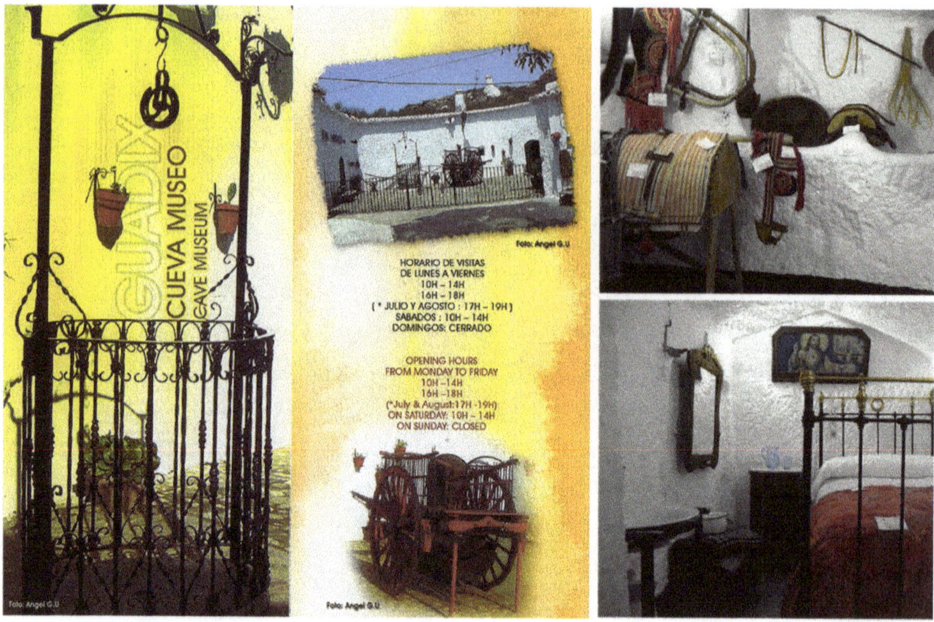

The museum is a cave dwelling decorated in the fashion of a typical home. The rooms are small, mere alcoves with bright, white washed walls.

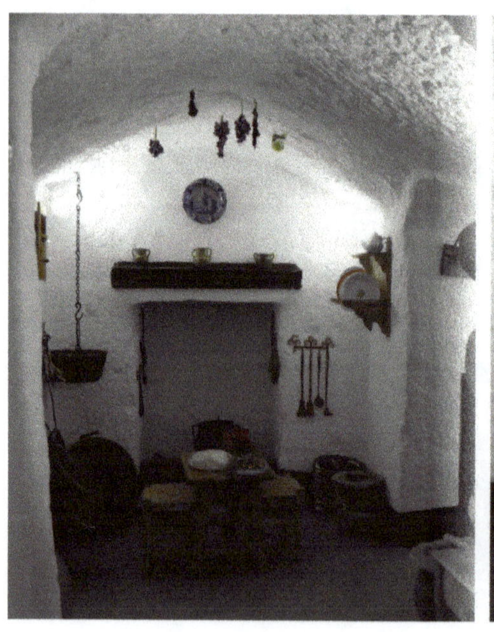

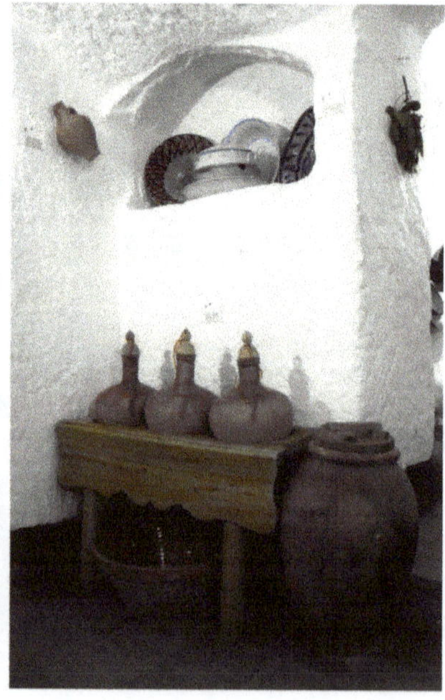

The first thing I noticed was the musty damp smell; when inhabited, the smell would have been more like a barnyard because the livestock lived in the rear of the dwelling.

Guadix and the surrounding valley are located on an elevated plateau in the northern foothills of the Sierra Nevada. The

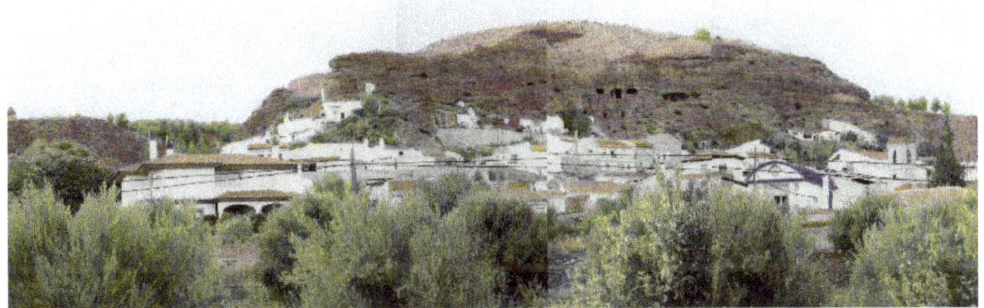

mountains were formed up to 65 million years ago when the African and Eurasian continental plates collided, closing off the Tethys Sea, leaving behind ochre colored mountains and a small body of water, the Mediterranean Sea.

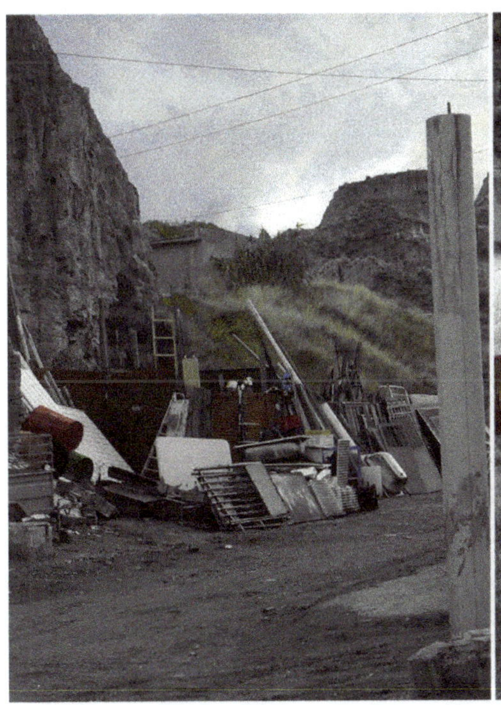

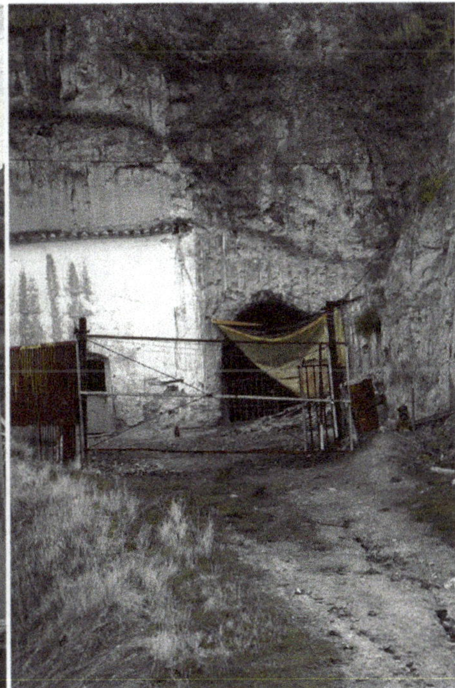

This area has the largest concentration of cave dwellings in Europe. Caves have been used as homes in Spain since prehistoric times and are referred to as Troglodyte habitats.

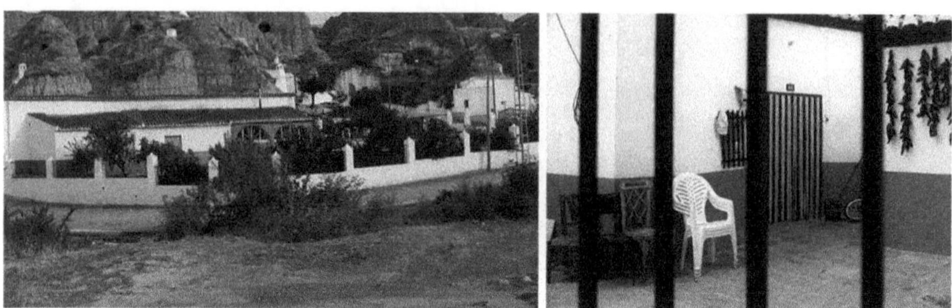

During the Muslim period, people began excavating the caves for dwellings. During the Roman period, Julius Caesar built a town here to mine silver. Later the Moors raised mulberry trees to feed silk worms for their thriving silk industry.

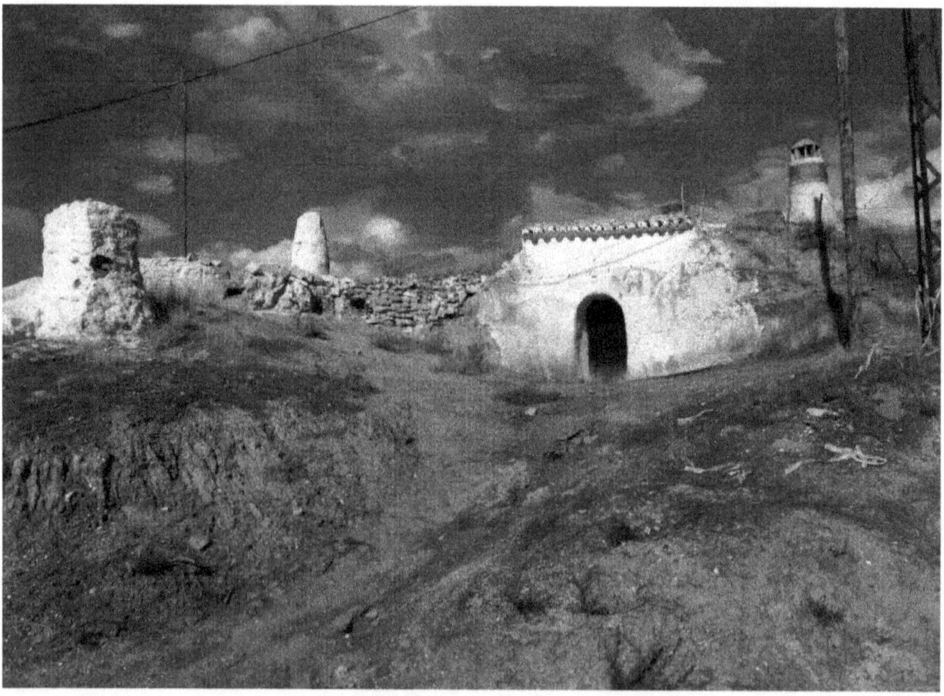

Today Guadix is still agricultural. Esparto rush, a grass used to make rope, rope soled sandals (espadrilles), baskets, and to reinforce plaster is the main crop; sheep are still herded on the mountain slopes.

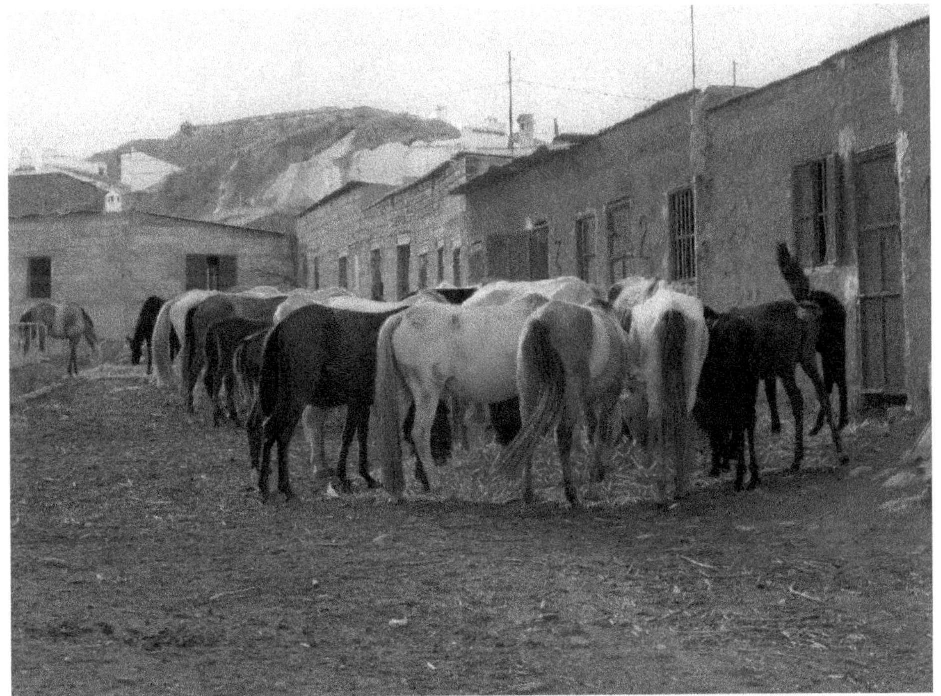

We wandered the streets of the community; I felt like a voyeur, invading a private world. White washed chimneys sprout out of the surrounding hillsides. The chimney and front door provide the only ventilation. Some of the grander caves have a house-like façade with windows; otherwise, there are no windows. Patios or small courtyards in front of the cave provide space for family gatherings. Most caves have modern conveniences; aerial antennas stick out of the hillside and overhead wires bring electricity and phone service.

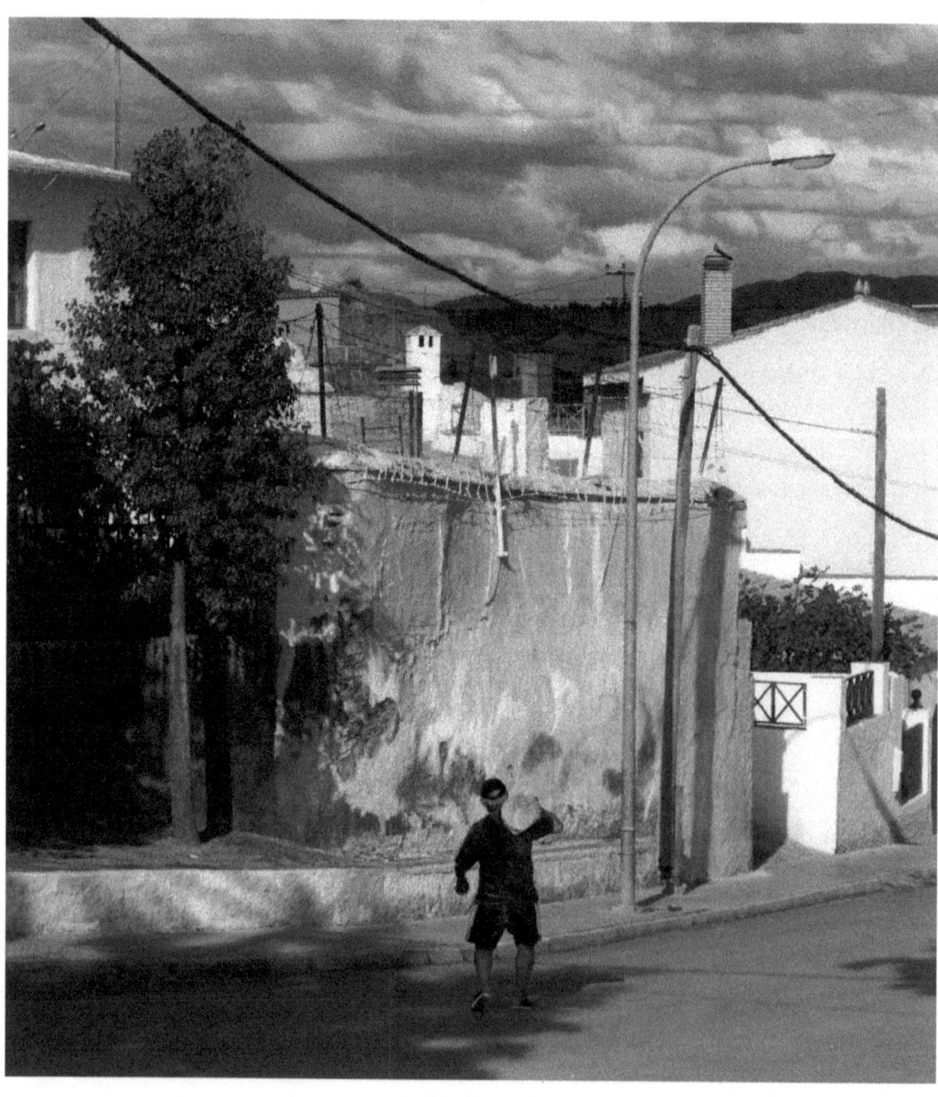

En Route to Granada; Home of Fredico Garcia Lorca and the Alhambra

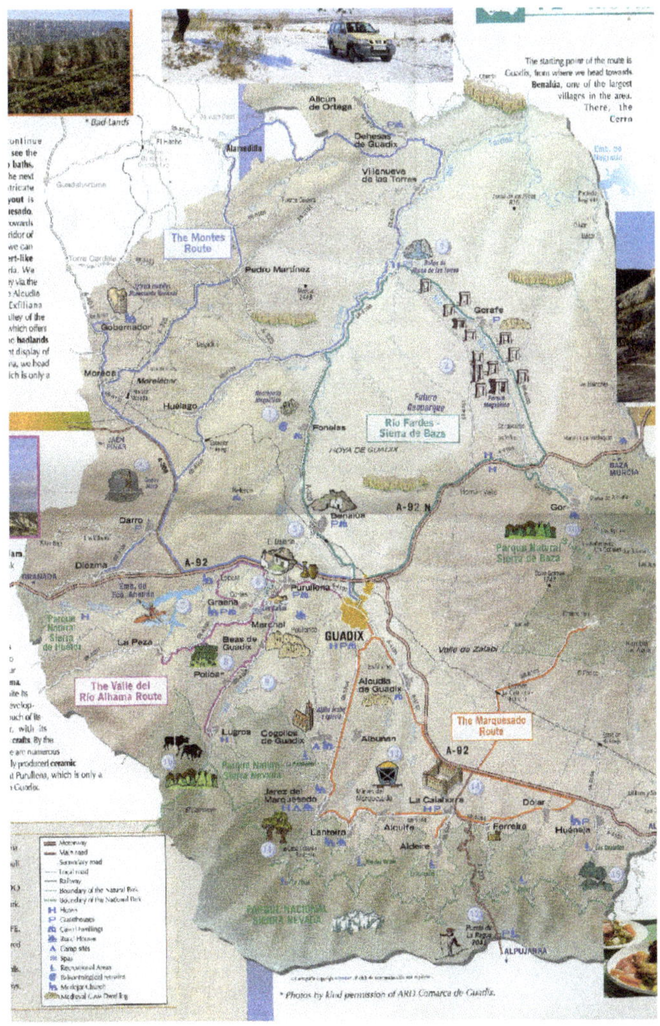

There are several scenic routes around Guadix through megalithic dolmans, caves with paintings, and medieval caves, castles, and forts. We headed west taking the Valle del Rio Alhama Route through vineyards, bull pastures, and medieval and modern caves on our way to Granada.

We stumbled across a shepherd with his flock but did not see any of the famous bulls grazing. Night was falling; we traversed much of the scenic route in the dark, missing the vega of Granada and outlying countryside.

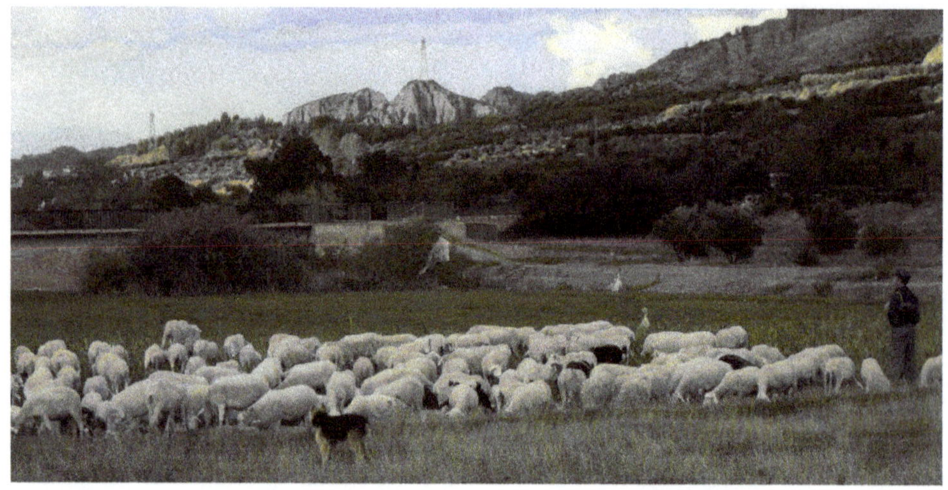

Frederico Garcia Lorca, the poet of the people, was born in the vega of Granada in 1898. Lorca was fascinated with gypsy culture. His love of the Andalusian way of life, its aesthetic values, musical dance styles and mystique pervades much of his work. His collection of poems, *Gypsy Ballads*, was the bestselling book of Spanish poetry in the 20th century. His most famous play, *Blood Wedding*, attained international acclaim. The play effectively tied bullfighting and flamenco to the Spanish way of life.

Lorca became a spokesman for the movement to keep flamenco pure; giving lectures and organizing the Cante Jondo festival,

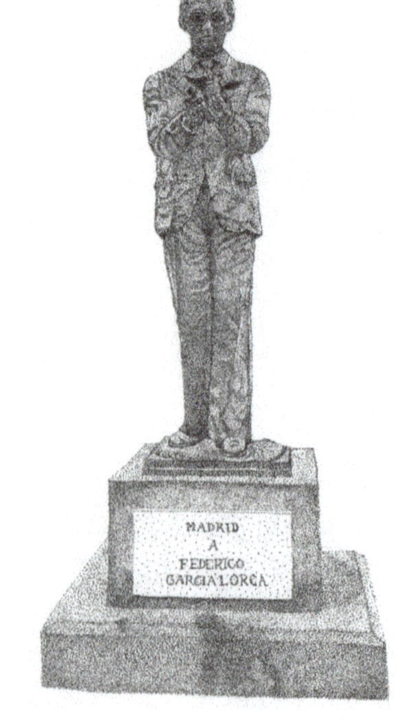

along with flamenco composer Manuel de Falla. The festival was first held in Granada in 1922. Lorca defined flamenco song as a "resonant tear on the river of the voice." He saw cante jondo, not as the folklore of Spain, but living proof of Granada's universality.

Much of Lorca's work was inspired by Granadian duende. He saw duende as a red-skeleton that targets tormented and suffering artists by making them confront the Present and Death. In a lecture he gave in 1933, *Play and Theory of Duende*, he proposed 3 distinct spiritual entities that inspire creativity: muses, angels, and duende. According to him, duende only accounted for 1% of the art produced; to have great art, the artist must confront his death. He describes duende elegantly in this paper:

"one must draw close to the earth and acknowledge one's own death and the mortality of all things, and the limitation of reason and intelligence."

"Duende unexpectedly comes and without warning goes."

"power climbs up inside the performer from the soles of the feet, the spirit of the earth which scorches the artist and produces an inspired performance"

Lorca's paper on duende spread to NYC after WWII (1945) and became a major topic of discussion within the artist community. His theories permeated the first generation of Abstract Expressionists.

Lorca was executed by Franco's firing squad in the early days of the Spanish Civil War; he was accused of being a Russian spy.

Granada and the Alhambra

Granada was the last Muslim stronghold in Spain. It took 2 1/2 centuries for Christian armies to muster the final push to rid Spain of the Moors. Fortunately, they didn't rid Spain of all that the Moors endowed them with!

It was dark for the bulk of the trip to Granada. Getting into the Alhambra was a little tricky but we only had to circle once before we discovered a gate with a guard and do not enter sign.

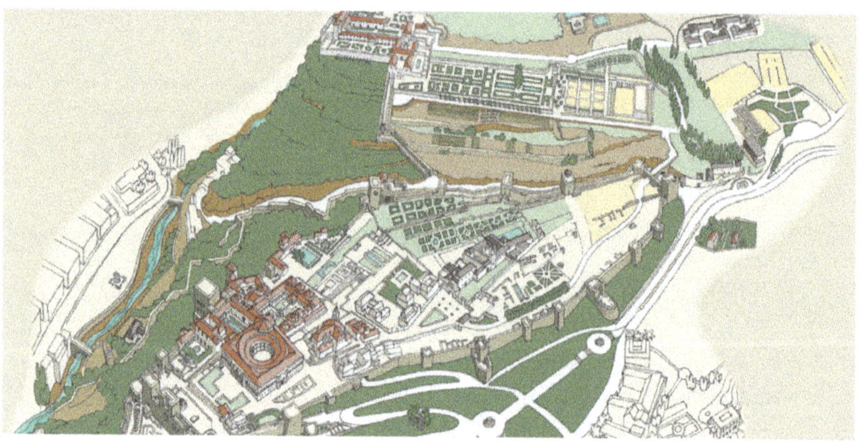

At night the Alhambra grounds are empty; we dropped our luggage off at the inn then headed to find the car park. The hotelier suggested we pick up our tickets for the Alhambra so we didn't have to go out so early tomorrow to get them. Sounded like a grand idea! There weren't many people there but we ended up waiting in line a very long time; one person was taking for ever. When they finally finished, the crowd gave them a round of applause! I wasn't the only impatient one. The line then moved much quicker, but when it was our turn we found out we couldn't pick the tickets up more than an hour before our entry time… we had another 11:00 dinner of sandwiches and tinto com limon.

Our hotel in Granada, Hotel America, is a small inn on the grounds of the Alhambra. Our room wasn't much larger than the bed but what an awesome setting. Waterfalls and fountains soothed our weary minds on our walk back to the inn.

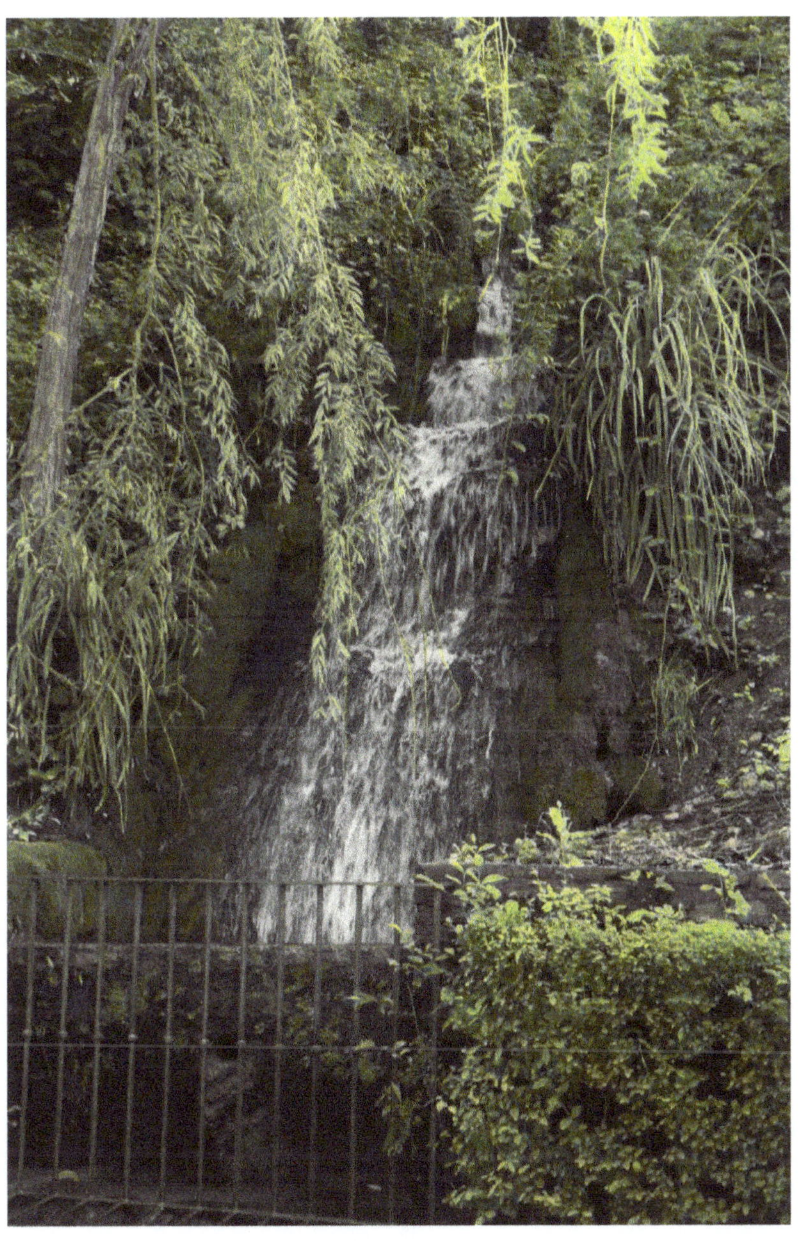

We awoke to a cold, overcast morning. A throng of people were gathered for our timed entrance but once inside the palace people disbursed and, at times, you could view a space without inhabitants.

Every inch of the palace is covered with intricate designs and filigree work; carved into rich, wooden panels, laid out in beautiful tile, carved in white marble and alabaster pillars, with lavish plasterwork, arches, and walls. It's amazing that the delicate peristyles and fragile fretwork have survived over so many centuries and much neglect.

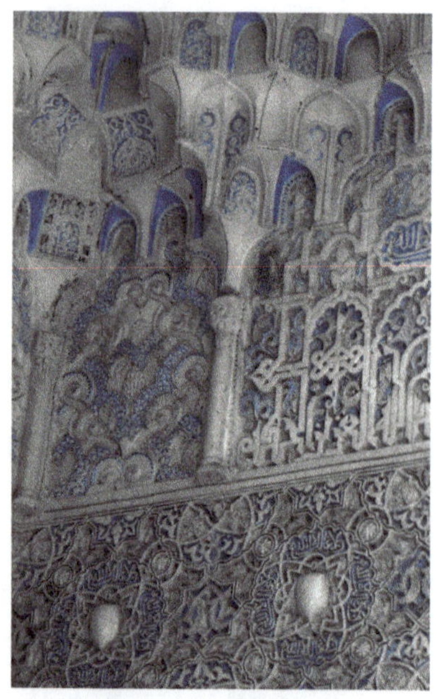

Fountains and pools are everywhere; you're never far away from the soothing sound of trickling water. One of the Moors' most significant engineering feats was the

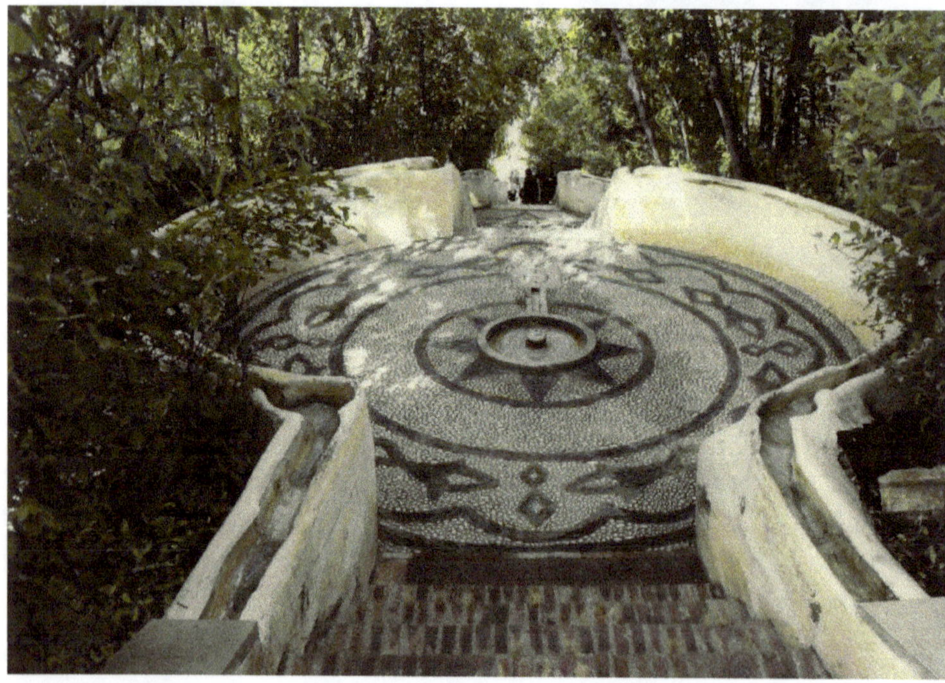

diversion of the Darro River, originating in the high Sierras, to supply the Alhambra with plentiful water.

This fountain, Escalera de agua, is known as the water stairs and dates from the 16th century. It is a long staircase set amongst bushes and trees. It has water splashing down inside the hollow hand rail and is a unique and eye-catching sight.

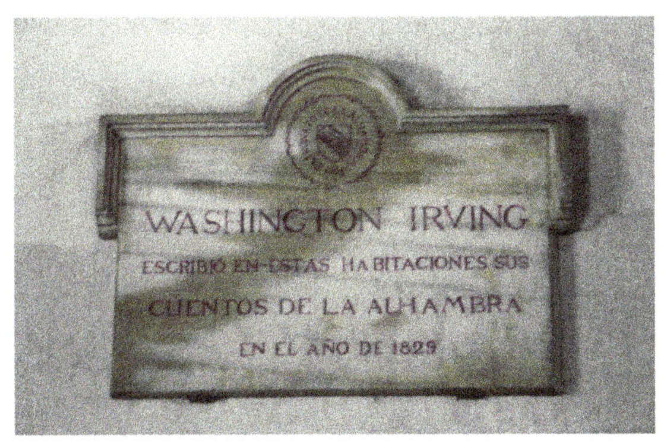

The American writer, Washington Irving, visited Granada and lived in an apartment in the Alhambra for several months in 1829 while he was serving as Ambassador to Spain. His book, *Tales of the Alhambra*, paints a romantic picture of life in the Alhambra during this period of decay. The inhabitants in the early 1800s were many of Granada's poor; gypsies, beggars, and thieves. The royal palace was looked after by Dona Antonia Molina and her family.

Irving writes delightful descriptions of each part of the Alhambra, recounts the colorful lives of its current inhabitants, and educates with tales from the past. Irving tells of his evenings at Dona Molina's tertulias, filled with the sound of castanets and song. He recorded the folklore and myth that had passed down through the generations in the oral tradition; tales of forbidden love and buried treasure, of romance and magic. It is easy to picture gypsies gathered in the 'patios' around the fountains, bathed in moonlight, dancing the night away, enjoying life.

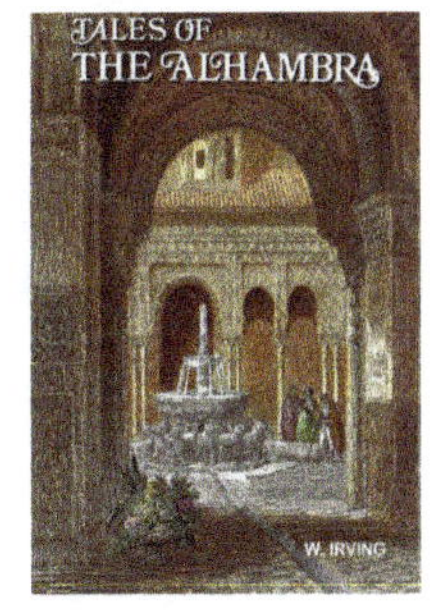

Throughout *Tales of the Alhambra*, Irving throws out snippets of history from the 11th century until his visit in 1829. In 1238, Al-Ahmar, founder of the Nasrid Dynasty, moved into the Alcazaba and began reconstruction of the building that made up his court at the Alhambra palace. Construction was completed in 14th century by Yusuf I and Muhammed V.

In 1492 the Moors were vanquished by the Christians and Ferdinand and Isabella moved their court to the Alhambra. It was within the walls of the Alhambra that Columbus was called back by Queen Isabella and the treaty was signed that led to the discovery of the New World. King Charles V decided to build a royal palace in the Alhambra in 1526, not to move his court there but to make a statement on the superiority of Christianity over Islam.

The palace, built in Italian Renaissance style, was under construction for ninety years and uninhabitable until 1923 when construction was resumed. Today, the Palace houses the Museum of the Alhambra where we visited the Court of the Lions' lost and forlorn lions. Examples of furniture and the accoutrement of daily life are also on display.

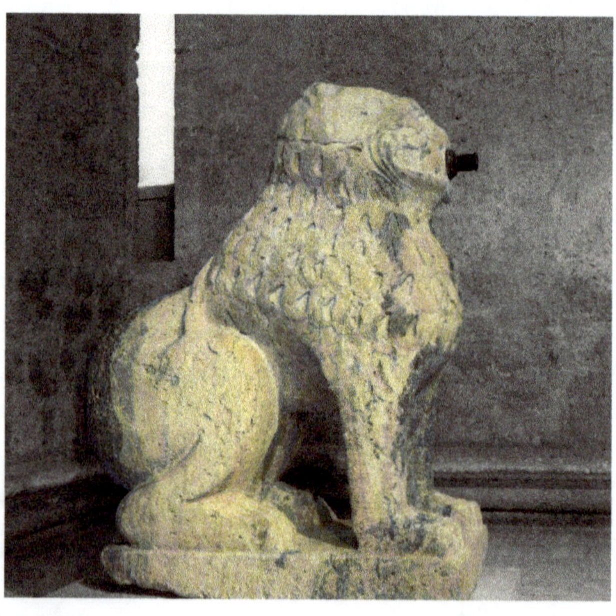

The morning was warming up as we headed to the Generalife, "garden of paradise," which is on a plateau above the palace. The gardens are magical; it's easy to imagine the young princesses playing in the gardens or gazing out over the village and vega far below.

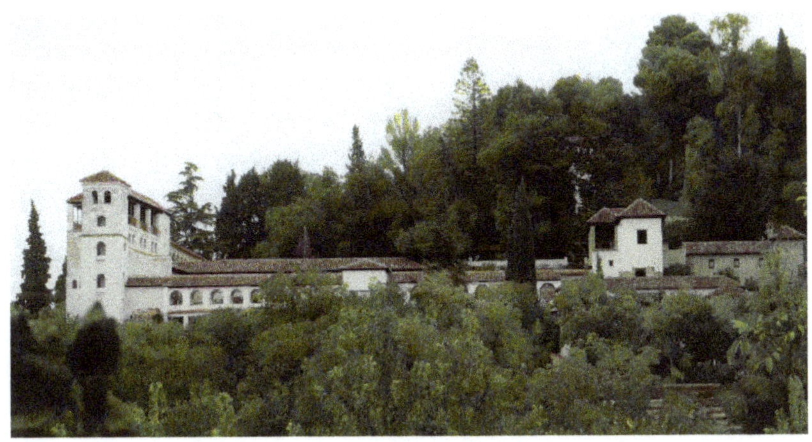

Walking up the path to the Generalife is like taking a walk in the country as you traverse the orchards and fields.

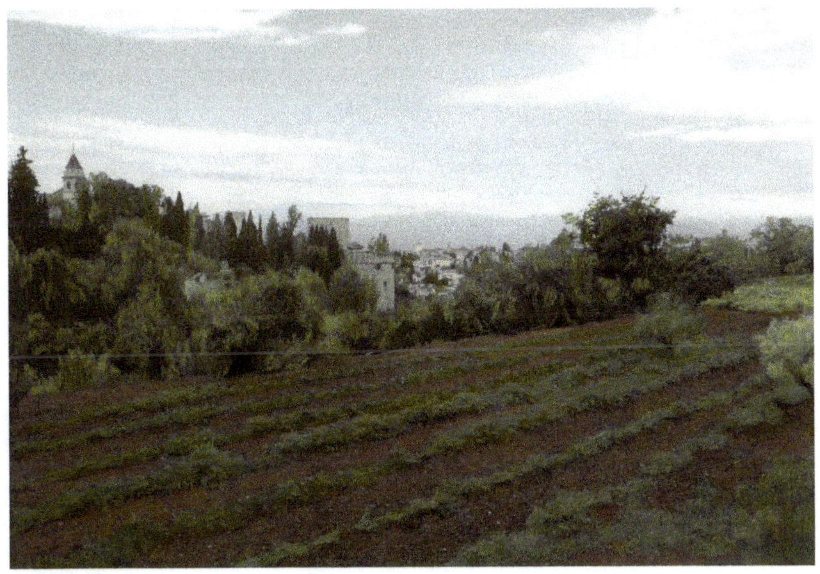

Entering the garden is entering another world. I am fascinated with the hedges which are tall, with densely packed foliage, trimmed into precise geometric shapes marking the

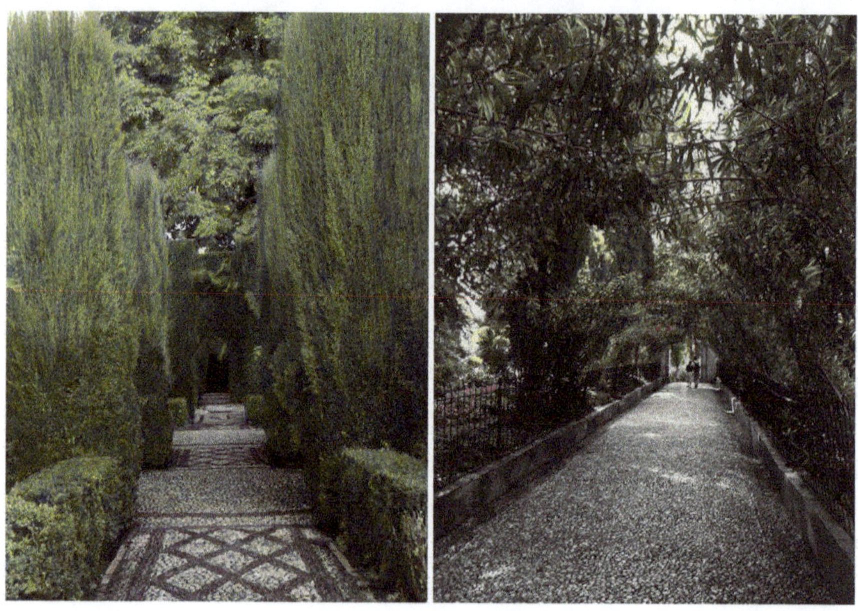

boundary of garden rooms and enclosing paths with an abhor shape, creating intimate spaces.

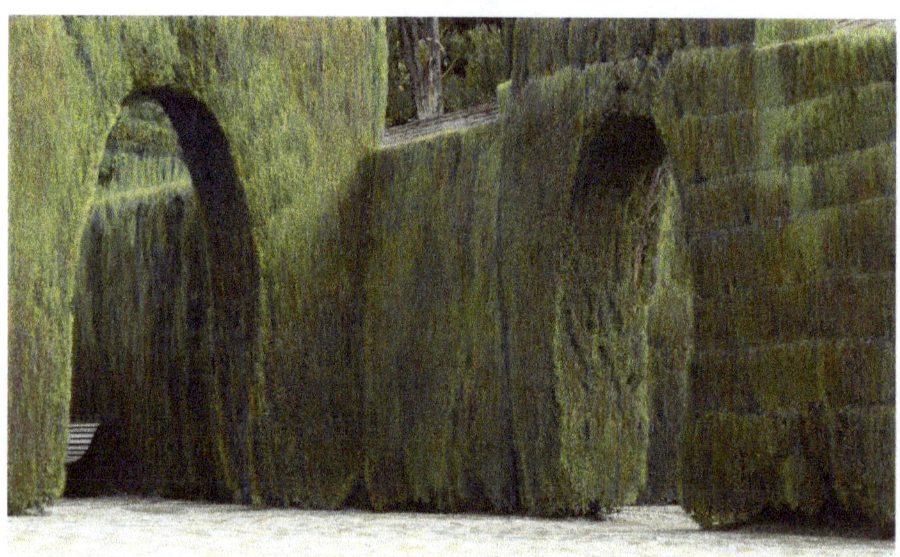

Canals run through two larger courtyards nearer to the residence, the Court of the Main Canal which brings in water from the Royal Canal to the Generalife, and the Soultana's Court, originally the site of the Palace Bath.

On the west side of the Court of the Main Canal is a central observation point decorated with the lavish plasterwork from the early 1300s. Arched openings are low to the ground so that privileged visitors could recline on the floor with their arm on the sill and contemplate their surroundings, much of which remains unchanged today.

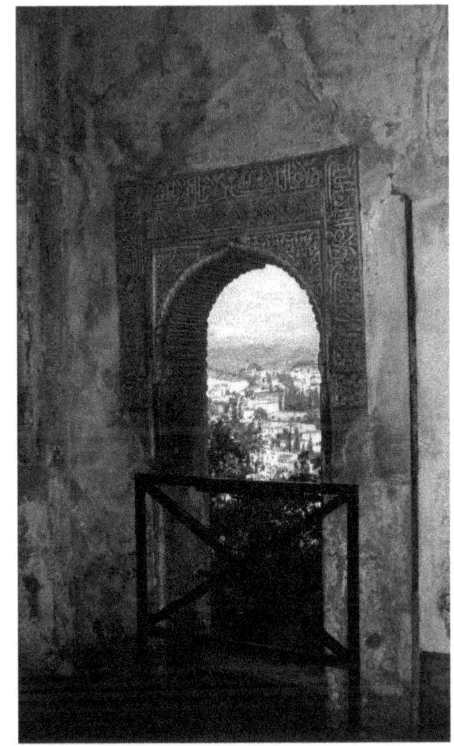

Exiting from the High Gardens, we followed the Promenade of the Cypress Trees back to the entrance of the Alhambra grounds and headed to the Alcazaba or fortress on the opposite side of the Palace.

The fortress dates back to at least the 11th century when the Zirid Dynasty settled their court here. Arab texts from the 9th century mention new construction within the Alhambra suggesting that some form of construction was built during the Roman period or earlier. Over the centuries, earthquakes and battles have reduced the fortress to ruins.

The clouds reconvened and the skies poured. We spent the afternoon siesta writing, snoozing, and planning an evening shopping trip for warmer clothes.

After siesta, Liz was in fine form for shopping. We got to the shopping district 15 min before the stores reopened so we

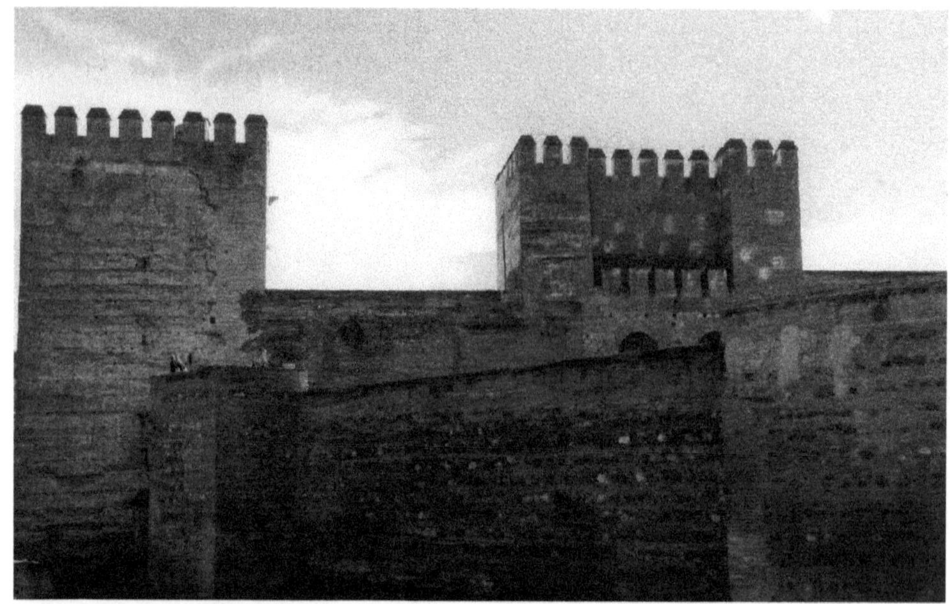

did some window shopping; we had trouble remembering what we saw where. I got into the shopping mood and tried on things with her. I bought a cute black skirt at Zara's and she got the much needed sweater and an adorable black cocktail dress. We stopped in another shop where I bought a youthful black wool jacket (the sales clerk's expression let me know I was too old for it).

We had pizza that was a little overcooked but good. We got the #32 bus at the Plaza Nuvea; the guide book said it was supposed to stop on the Alhambra grounds, well, it didn't ..... the driver was exasperated when he found out he still had passengers! He took a break at the Plaza then took us back. As we approached the Alhambra he made sure we got off, one stop too early! It was quite an adventure.

Sacramonte

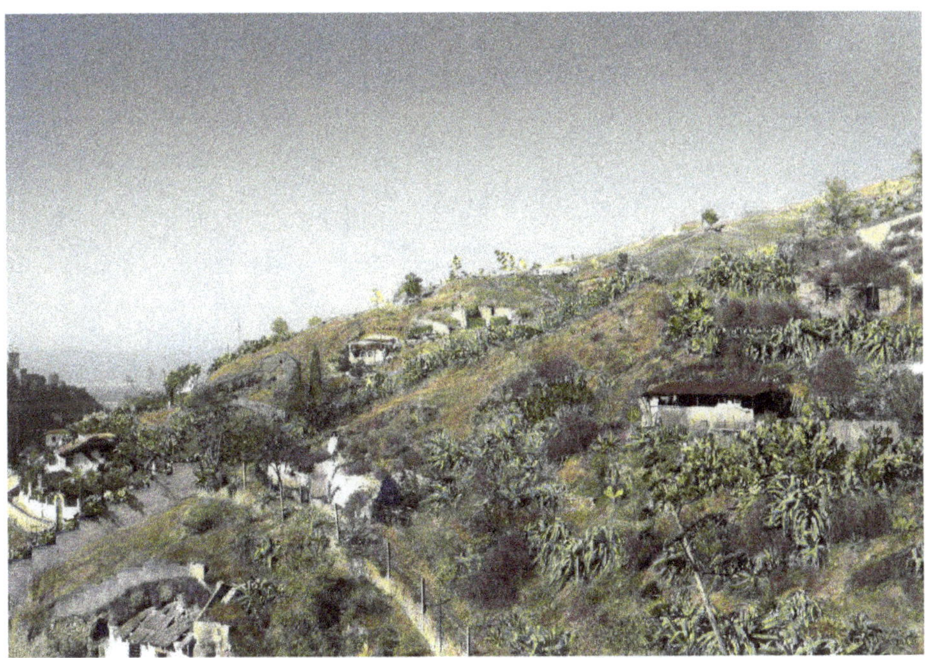

The next morning, we had a leisurely breakfast before heading out. The purchase of warm clothes guaranteed a beautiful day! There is a path behind the Alhambra wall that takes you to Sacramonte, it's all downhill, a steep downhill! Then once you reach the bottom, it's back uphill again to the caves. The cave dwellings we passed en-route seemed to be solitary structures stuck here and there in the hillside. Unlike Gaduix, the 'holiday homes' are missing; all bore the humble façade of poverty.

Across the Darro River Valley is a breathtaking view of the Alhambra. Hard to imagine being forced to leave the beautiful Alhambra grounds and being transplanted into such squalor, much less having that magnificent view as a constant reminder.

Shortly after the publication of Irving's book, the Alhambra was declared a national treasure and restored to its current state. The gypsies were relocated to Sacramonte (translated holy hill), an area of cave dwellings on a hill opposite the Alhambra. They lived there until the area was flooded in 1962.

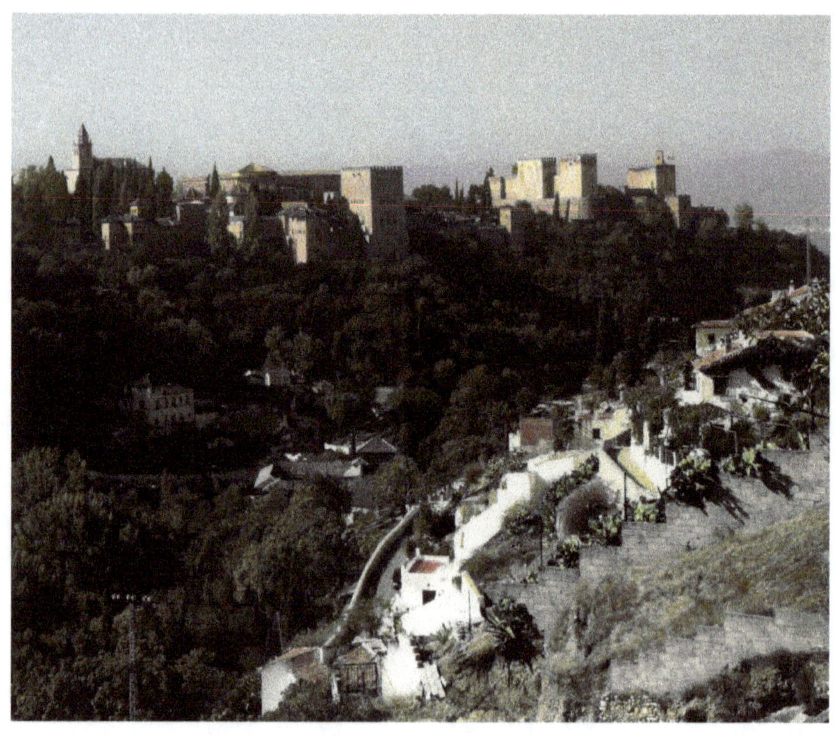

When the gypsies settled into pueblos, the villages, like Sacramonte, became one large extended family. Personal relationships held a high priority. In the evenings, groups of friends met to discuss anything and everything. The men often congregated in the bars. Drinking and swapping stories often lasted into the night and if a cantaor (flamenco singer) was present, a juegra might emerge.

Alcohol is the main ingredient for memorable flamenco and duende. Encouraged with liberal amounts of alcohol, the cantaor is freed from inhibition and able to release pent-up emotions. A juegra could last all night or for several days. Great quantities of alcohol fueled it but the gypsies didn't get drunk or stop for sleep. According to Pohren, their secret was to drink slow and steady and graze throughout the event, taking short naps to refuel.

The gypsy community still lives in poverty. Many families return to the family cave in the evenings where they still enjoy flamenco but now they do it for money instead of as a means of release and renewal. Tourists are warned to be vigilant when visiting Sacramonte at night; during the day there aren't many people around.

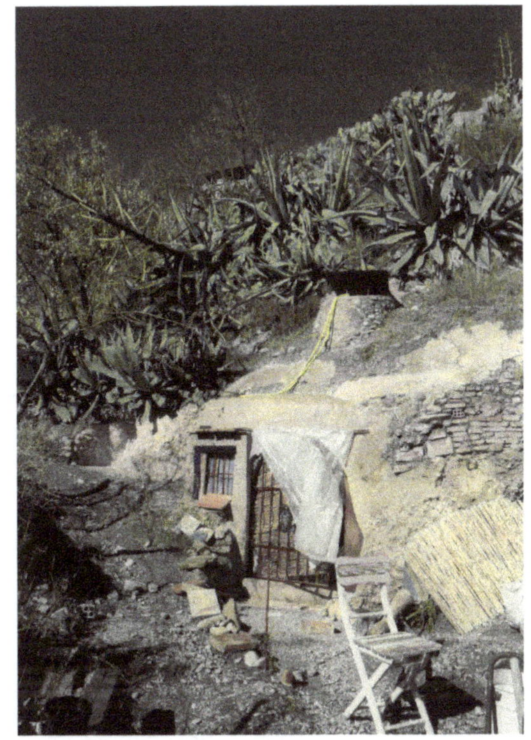

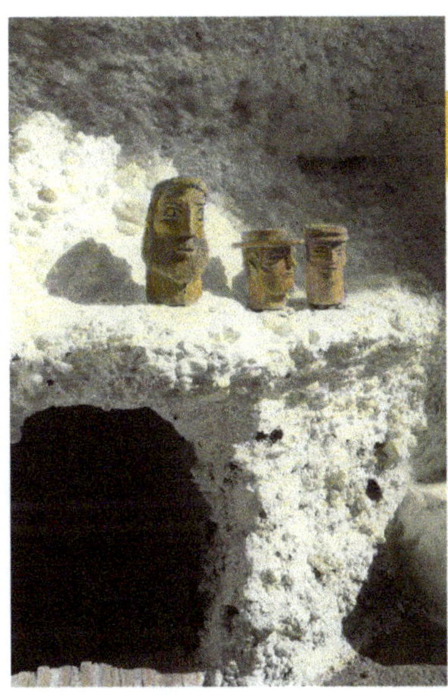

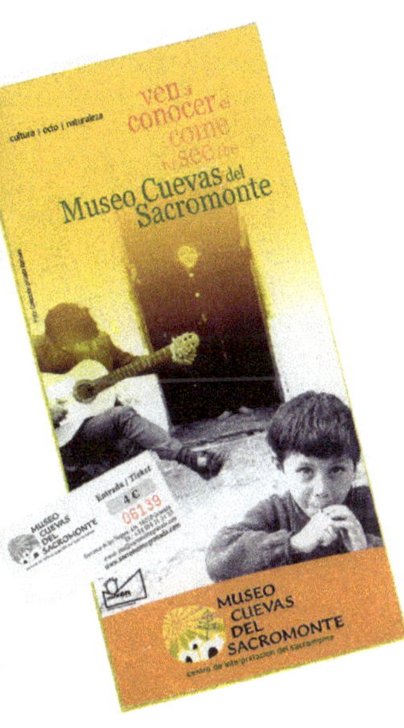

The Museo Cuevas del Sacromonte is a cluster of two room caves that open onto a patio. The rooms were similar to the ones in Gaudix; they are decorated with the tools and basic elements used by the gypsies 100 years ago. The museum focuses on the customs, history, evolution and development of the area.

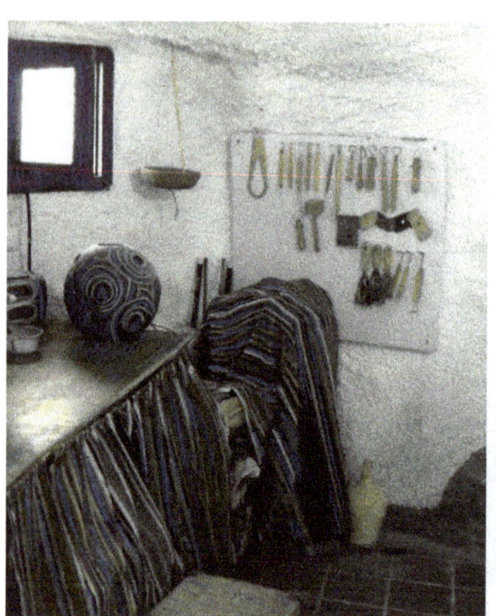

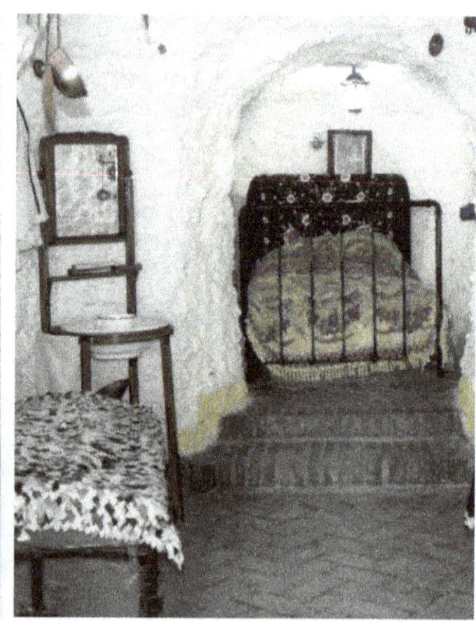

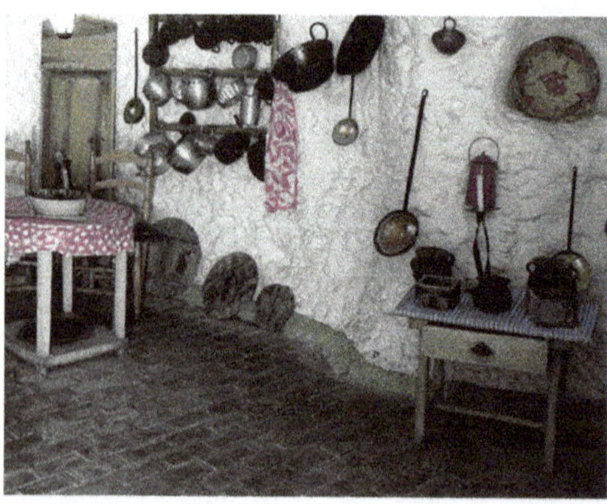

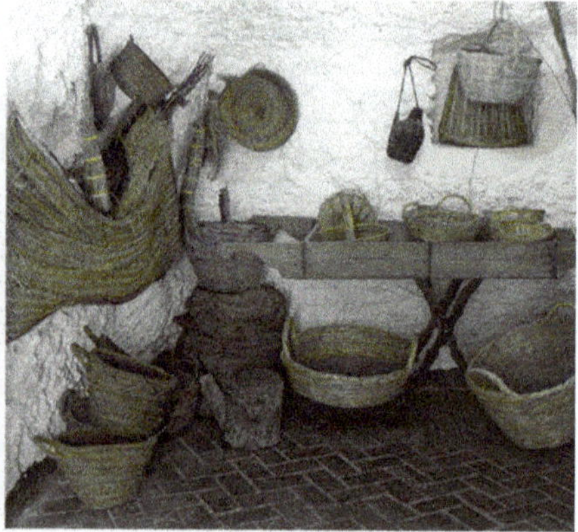

We were able to catch the
#32 bus not to far from the
caves. An older woman
got on the bus with us and
carried on a lively, raucous
conversation with the bus
driver. It sounded rather
naughty but who knows!

Before shopping for sou-
venirs, we had to go back
by the hotel to retrieve
money; I hadn't carried
much with me. We stopped
in the wood-mosaic shop
and bought a few things
including picture frames
and a copy of Washington
Irving's book.

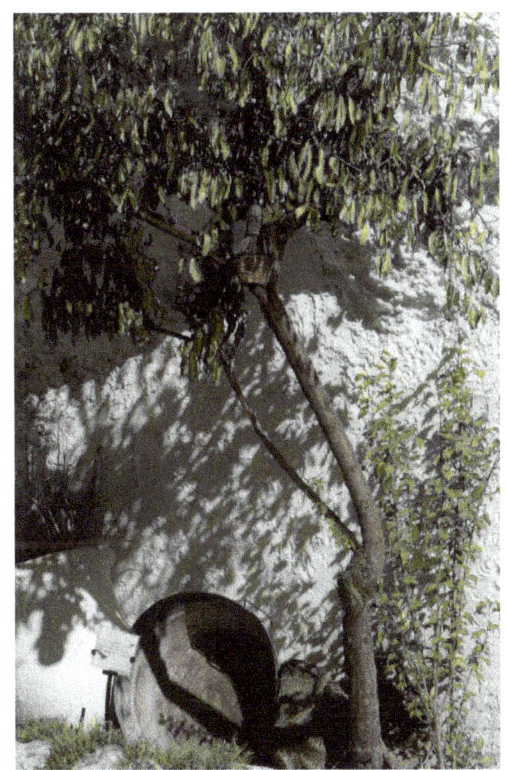

At the car park, we had fun
trying to figure out how to
pay and get out. We had a voucher for discount parking but
couldn't find anyone to pay! Driving through tourists was a
bit daunting but since it was approaching siesta, the crowds
were small and we were soon on our way.

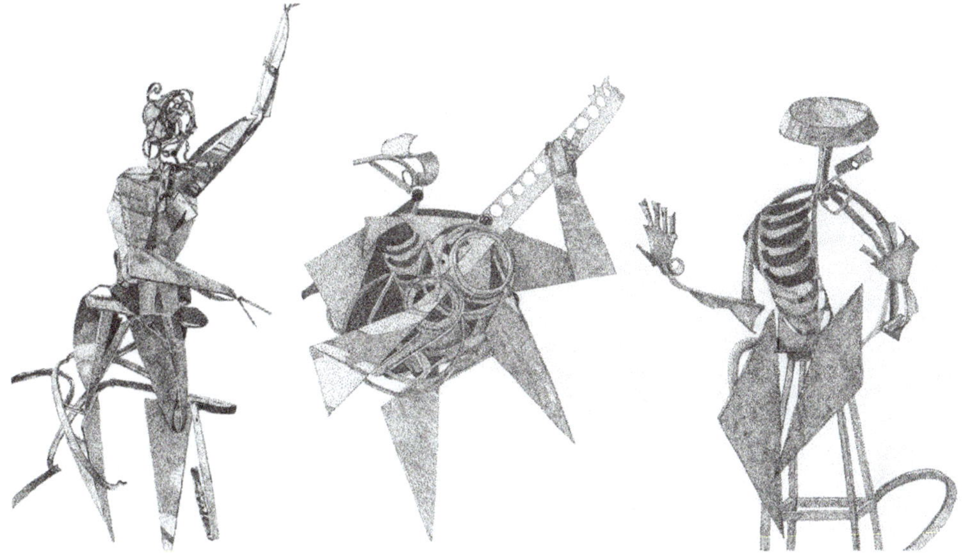

Laguna de la Fuente and El Torcal National Park

The route from Granada passes through several national parks, our agenda for the day. We haven't driven much in daylight so today's journey was a chance to see segments of rural Spain.

Leaving Granada was pretty painless. The first thing I noticed when we reached the highway was the lack of advertising along the roadside. Inside cities there are signs pointing toward hotels, the city center, and attractions; on the highway there are mileage markers and an occasional cut-out of a black bull.

We stopped at a truck stop for gas and lunch. The complex is similar to the stops on the turnpikes in the northern US. Lunch was served cafeteria style; there was a gift shop and a pastry shop but no coffee to go!

Laguna de la Fuente is the largest lagoon in Andalusia and a very important nesting site for flamingos on the Iberian Peninusla. The best time to see flamingos is between February and July. Since it was October, we weren't sure we would see any.

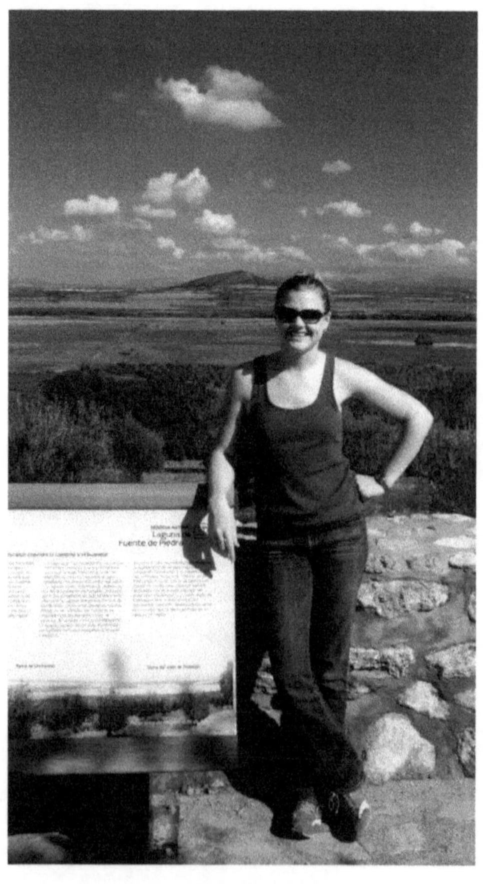

We arrived at Laguna de la Fuente tourist information center during siesta so we were on our own to explore. The large "you are here" map got us started in the right direction but our metric is a little rusty so distances were questionable.

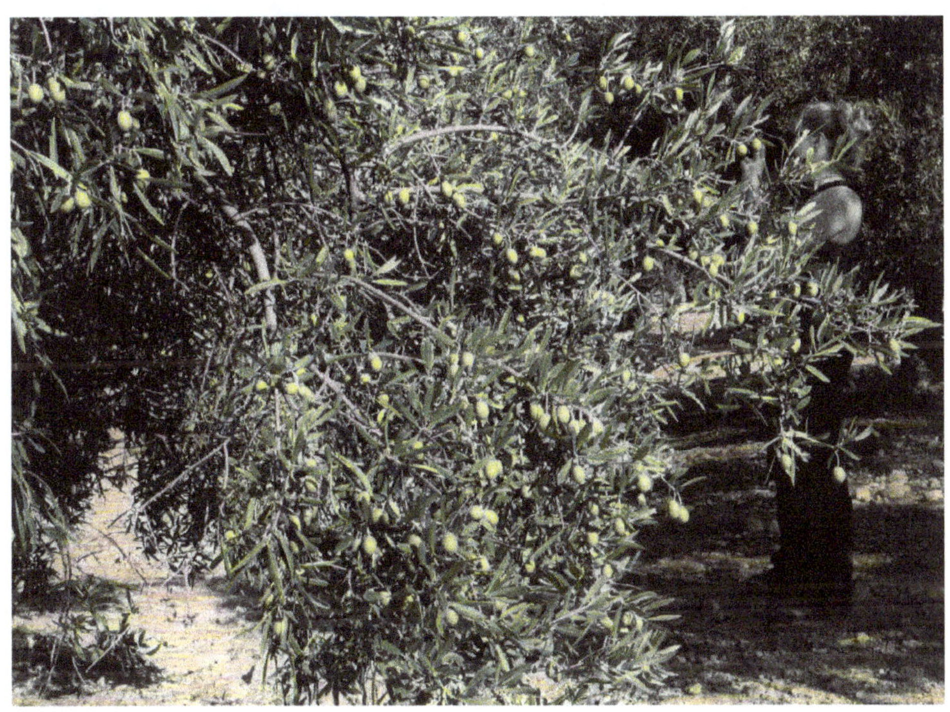

We headed down a trail in search of flamingos or other birds but the trail veered away from the water and all we saw were a few rabbits.

It's discouraging to be hiking along with a deep gully and tall trees between you and your object of desire so we retrieved the car and drove through the olive groves on the other side of the Laguna. The olive trees spread out for miles in orchards of red clay. The fall rains had eroded much of the land and left large standing puddles.

The road was even farther from the water but provided good binocular viewpoints. We finally spotted flamingos, on the other side, not far from where we'd turned around earlier; inaccessible by car.

We went back and once again hiked down the trail, constantly veering away from the water until the trail ended abruptly
at a gate.

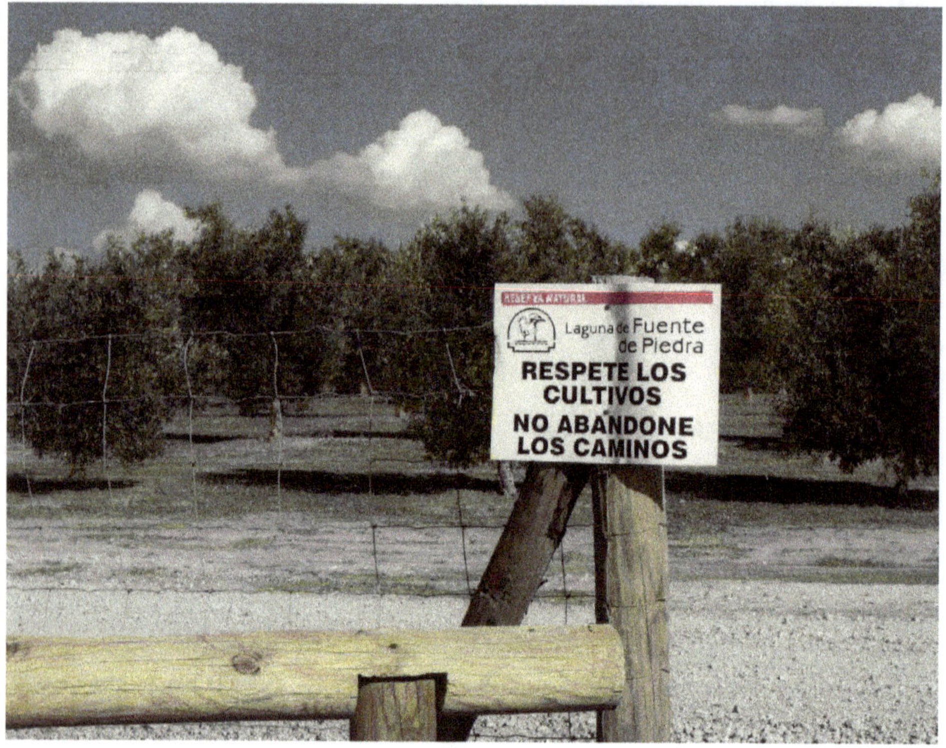

There is a nice sign here that says Respete los coltivos, no
abandone los caminos. We didn't have a caminos to abandon
so we pushed on and headed for a strip of green marked Res-
erva Natural that ran through the furrows.

The furrows ran right up to the fence so we proceeded with
care, stepping between the rows. Our nerve began to falter;
we envisioned a farmer headed out to greet us with shotgun
in hand! Standing up on tip-toe, we could see the pink birds
just a little further ahead.

If we'd known what the sign really said, "Respect the farmers, don't leave the road," I doubt we would have made it this
far, but ignorance is bliss. We got close enough to get a few
shots before losing courage.

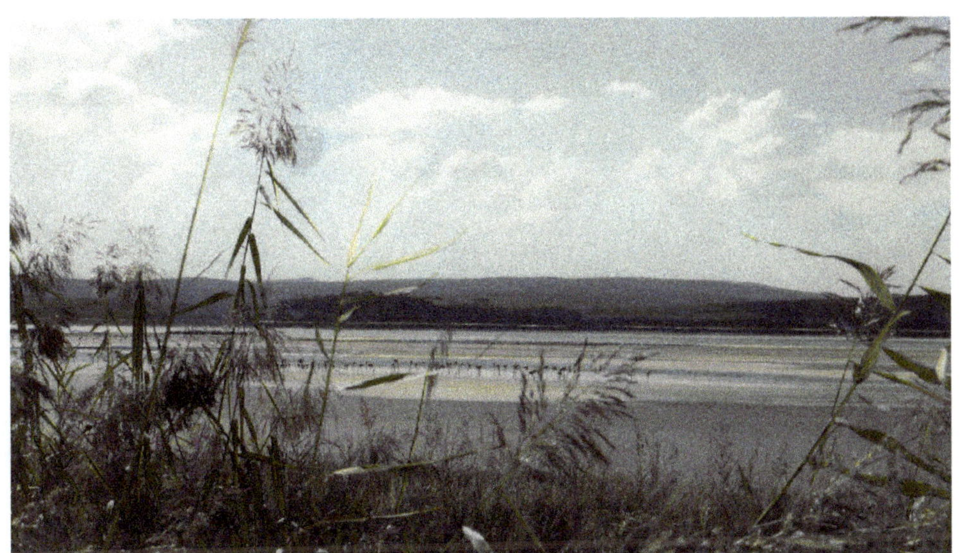

Our next destination was El Torcal National Park, the land of karst. We drove high into the mountains to reach El Torcal. Looking around at the mountains and valleys, it's hard to imagine water ever coming this far inland.

Karst shapes look fragile and unstable in places but they have been here about 150 million years. Karst is created from carboniferous limestone in which the calcium carbonate is washed away leaving a very interesting landscape. The limestone deposits were created when Spain was under the Tethys Sea.

We left before sunset but darkness falls quickly out away from civilization. Our journey was slow going; the road was so curvy that it was easy to outrun the headlights!

I later found a note to myself, "don't approach Ronda from the south, roads winding and dangerous". So much for advanced planning! We arrived safely, picked up Sarah at the bus station, and had another 11:00 dinner.

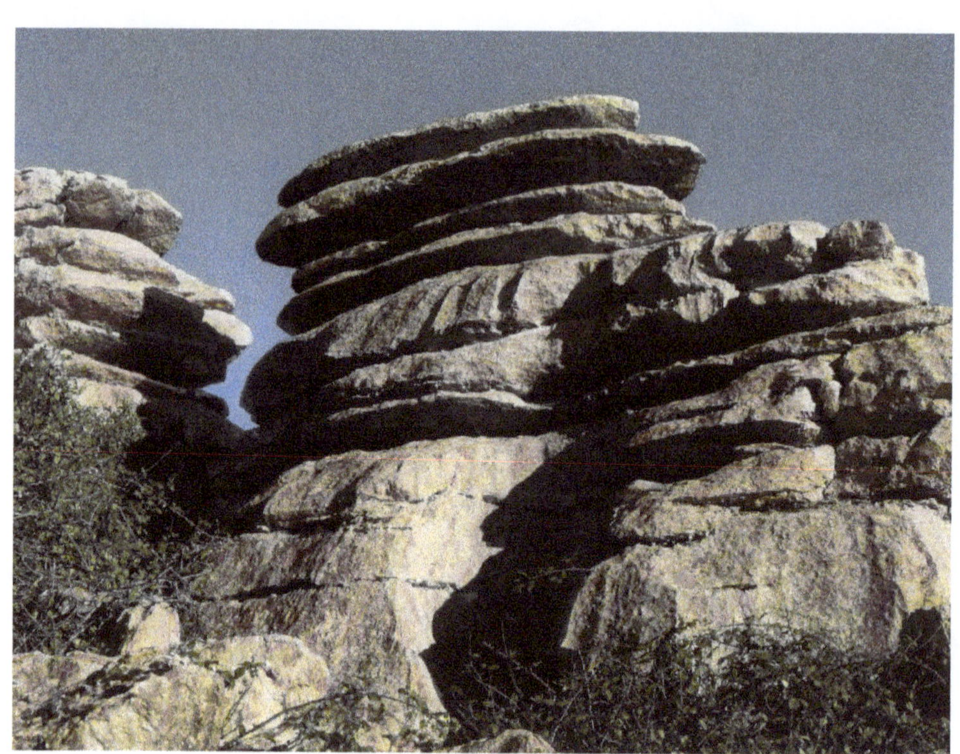

Ronda

Ronda is one of Spain's White Towns, large whitewashed agricultural villages made up of landless laborers that work on the big arable farms of the river plains. The higher the elevation, the smaller and prettier they are. Ronda is known as the Eagles' Nest, perhaps because it is perched so high in the mountains.

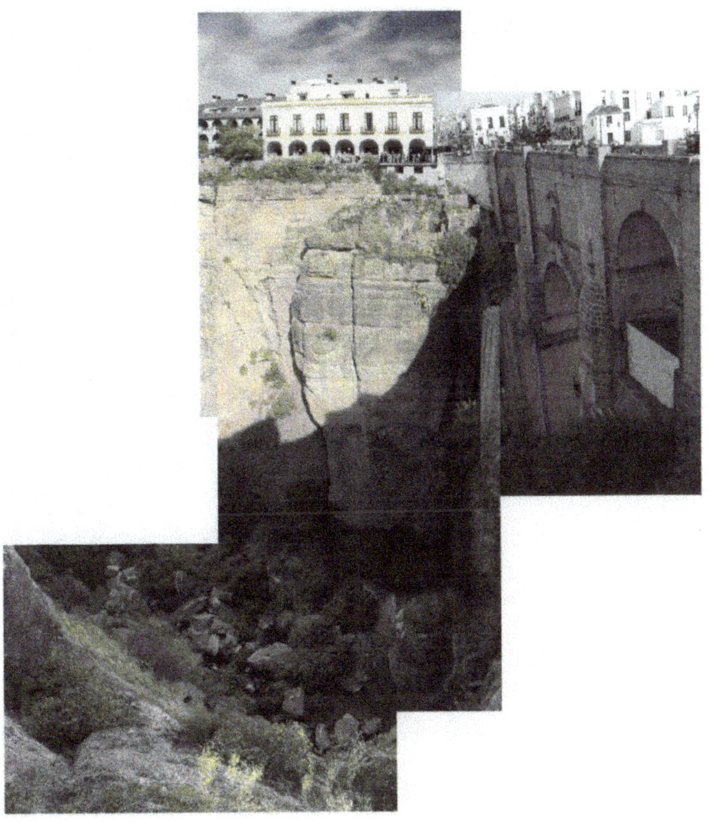

I chose to visit Ronda because of its ties to bullfighting and its proximity to prehistoric caves. Habitation in the area dates back to the Neolithic period.

Once again, we have arrived late and very hungry! We made a lap through town to see what was still open. We found an ultra modern, all white and chrome, tapas bar that really didn't fit the mood of our trip but it was full of locals so we tried it. Turned out to be very good!

We are staying at a new parador that is built around the site of an ancient Andalusian Town Hall that was occupied by the Romans and Moors until 1485.

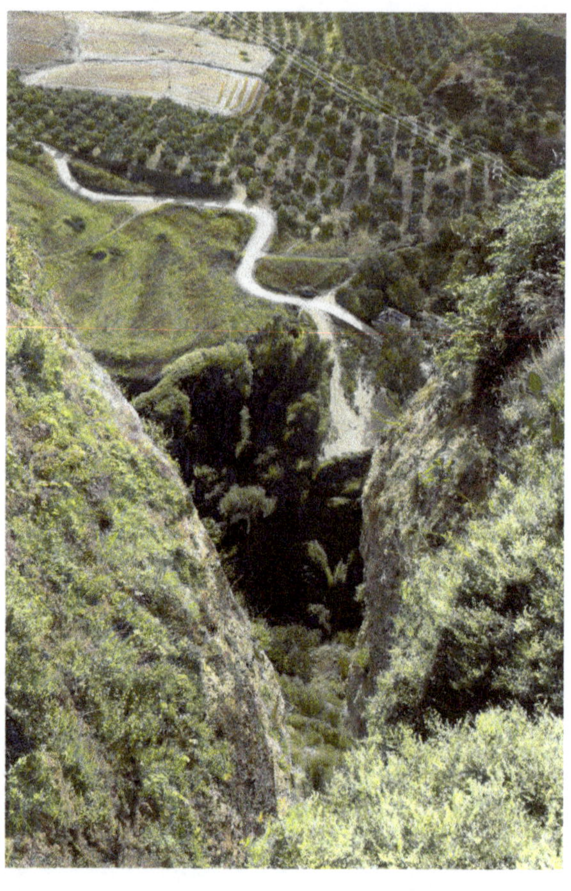

The parador is situated on the El Tajo gorge, a 360 foot deep, 200 foot wide ravine cut by the Tagus River that is traversed by the Puente Nuevo Bridge, the New Bridge, built in 1793. Hemingway once lived in Ronda; he featured the gorge in *For Whom the Bell Tolls*.

We were running out of clean clothes so it was time to do laundry. The hotel had a laundry service so we decided to splurge to save time. Each piece came back in it's own plastic bag - 107 Euros!!

The mountains outside of Ronda have a spectacular cave system. Caves played an important role in Andalusian life; while researching the caves in Andalusia I was excited to find a cave with prehistoric paintings that was open to the public! Most caves with prehistoric paintings are closed to the public for preservation reasons.

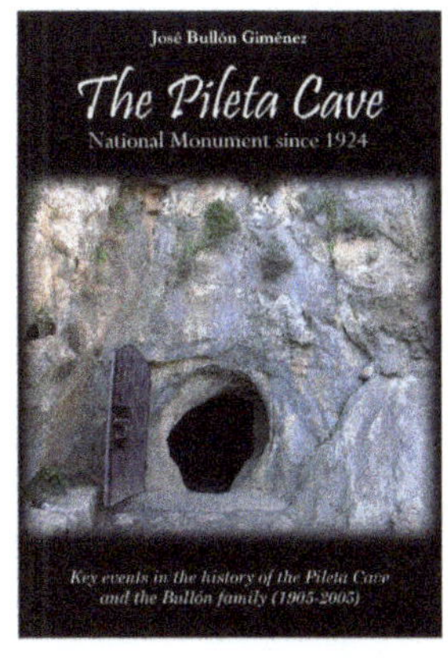

The Pileta Cave is owned and has been run by the Gimenez family since its discovery in 1905. The family were farmers. Bat guano is a good fertilizer so when one of the men noticed a large colony of bats swarming the hillside and disappearing into the mountain, he decided to follow them. The opening was small but it opened into a large cave. He found the guano along with ancient pottery, human bones, and pictures on the walls!

In 1911, a retired British colonel heard about the paintings; when he saw them, he immediately recognized their importance. The paintings are 30,000 years old, dating to before the last great ice age. It's hard to believe that something so magnificent dates from the Aurignacion (upper Palaeolithic) period through the Bronze Age. They are second only to Altamira in significance.

This cave, 670 m above sea level, proves that Ronda has been home to people for a very long time and establishes it as one of the most important crossroads of human migration in southern Europe.

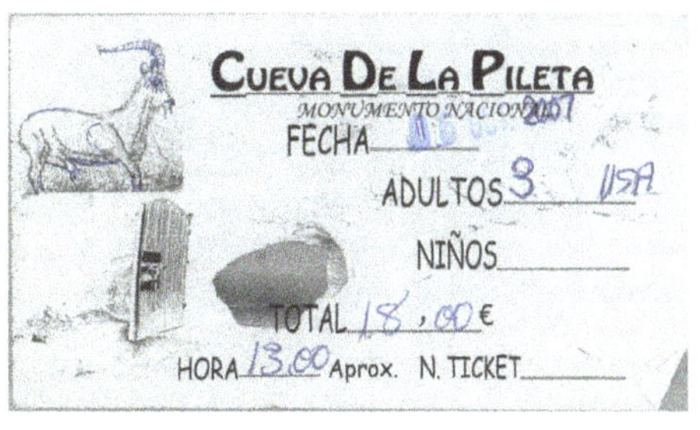

The Gimenez family has managed the microclimate of the cave by fighting commercialization and maintaining a controlled regime of visits. At the time of our trip, tours were given on the hour if enough people show up; I didn't know what to expect.

The cave is in the middle of nowhere with only a small sign to let you know it's there. We reached a dead end with a few parked cars and bikes. A rock hewn staircase led straight up. At the top is a small out-building with a covered shelter for patrons.

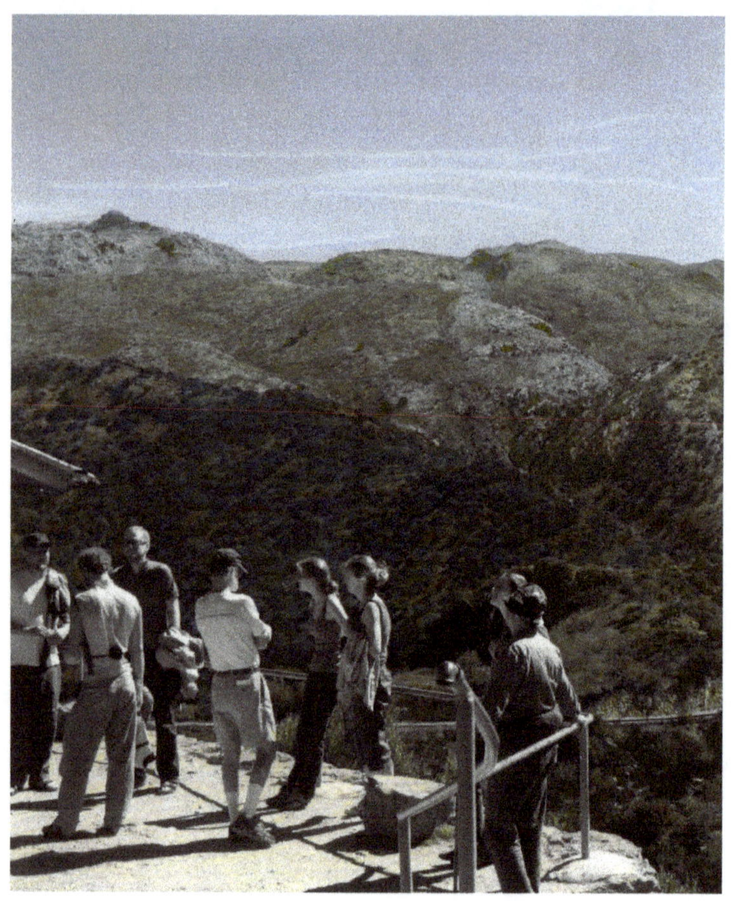

Our group included a few other Americans which was nice. Mr. Gimenez speaks very little English but he has a fine sense of humor. He said that Americans alway say 'Wow!' and 'High'. He's right, no matter how hard you try, it just slips out! Gas lanterns are lit and distributed evenly throughout the group to provide illumination. The family has cut steps in several places and added railings but it's still a slippery journey.

After almost falling several times, I took my shoes off. The floor was cool and somewhat sticky. I received a stern lecture when my bare feet were discovered. I thought he was concerned about hygiene and all the bat guano; turns out that it's unacceptable to show one's feet in public in Spain!

I was surprised at my first reaction to the paintings; they seemed small and insignificant until it registers how they came to be here! The drawings are amazingly proportional and recognizable as fish, deer, and goats. Humans are drawn as stick figures. There are markings that give directions to special areas and fairly accurate maps of the cave layout. Pottery shards and tools are very similar to relics that are found at other sites, just a few thousand years older. Prehistoric man was not that different from us.

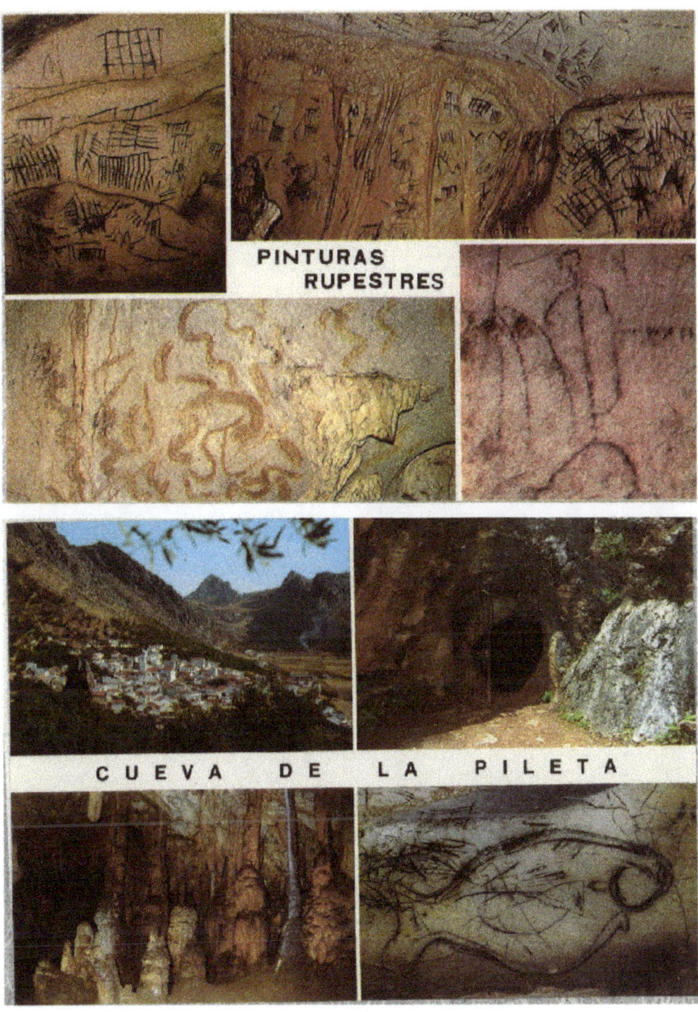

Ronda's Plaza de Toros

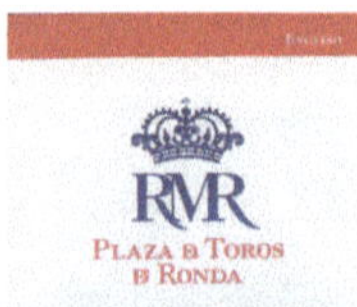

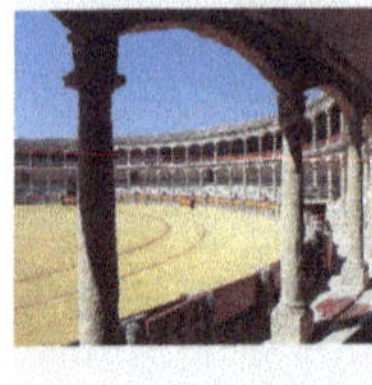

During siesta we explored the Plaza de Toros. Ronda's bullring is one of the oldest in Spain and is considered the spiritual home of bull-fighting. It was built in 1784-1785.

It was here that Pedro Romero developed the modern techniques of bullfighting. Pedro is the most celebrated name in the history of the corrida; he followed in the family tradition that began with his grandfather, Francisco. Francisco introduced the muleta, the modern cape, replacing the short cloak matadors draped over their arm with a cape draped over a stick - much safer. His form of bullfighting became known as the Ronda school, distinguishing it from the more dominant Seville school. Pedro's father, Juan, developed the concept of the bullfighting team known as the cuadrilla.

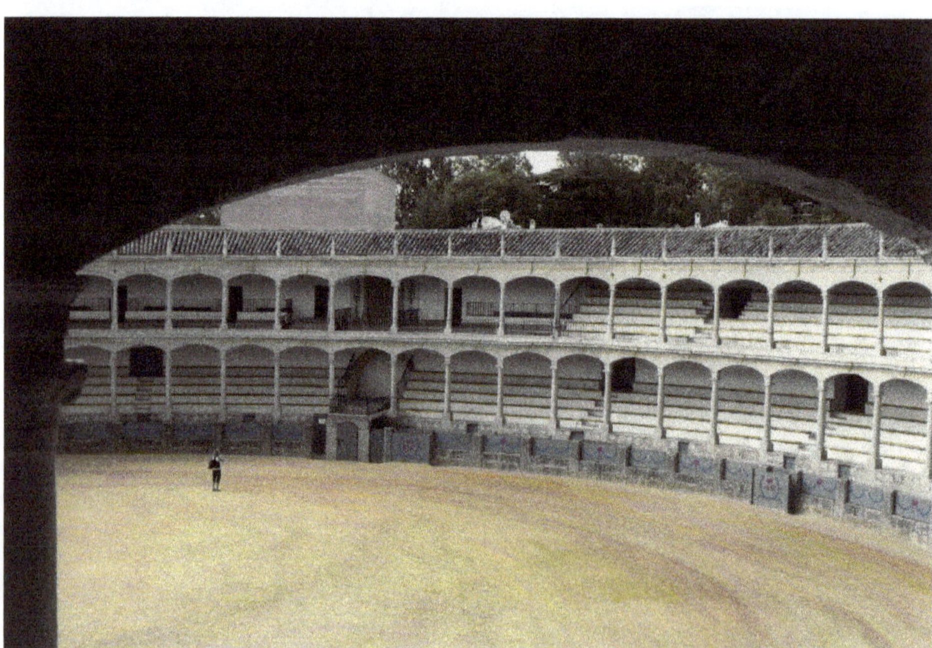

Pedro's contribution was more aesthetic. He was the first matador to conceive of the bullfight as an art that requires great skill. He set the standards and rules still followed today.

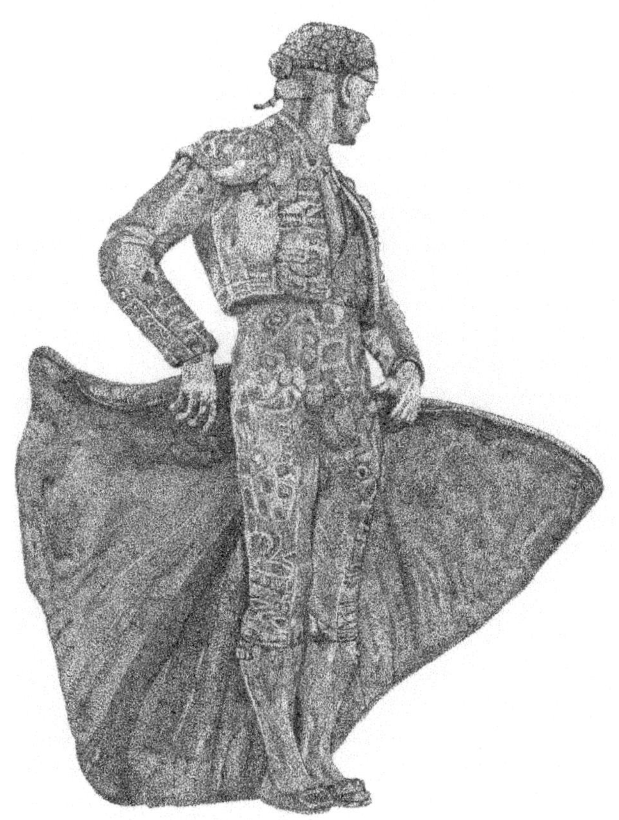

During Pedro's life, it is said that he killed over 6,000 bulls without ever being gored; he was still fighting in Madrid at the age of eighty!

There is a small museum dedicated to the Romero family's illustrative career. Hemingway speaks frequently of the Romero family in his work, *Death in the Afternoon*, which is an excellent source on the rituals and meaning of the bullfight.

Bullfighting, in some form, dates back to the 5th century during the Visigothic era, when young men, out to prove their courage, began taunting bulls. More modern bullfighting has it's roots in the Rejonear, a fight that pitted noblemen on horseback against the bull. It was so popular, small towns and villages scrambled to turn crumbling old Roman amphitheaters into bullrings. When those weren't available, they created makeshift arenas, often in the town square or plaza. Plaza de Toros, the name given to every bullring in Spain, came from this practice.

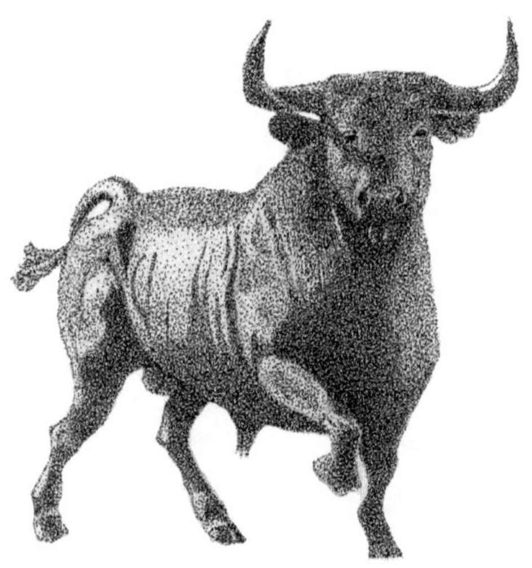

In the 18th century, King Philip V threatened excommunication to any nobleman that participated in this barbarous custom. Thus low-born professionals were hired to fight for them.

Bullfighting is a controversial subject with strong feelings on both sides. Regardless, it is an important part of the culture of Spain and has close ties to flamenco, religion, and the ancient world (the 10th labor of Hercules was to capture cattle of Greyon from Erytheia).

It is an interesting fact that flamenco and bullfighting are closely related and gypsies were leading performers in both professions. Bullfighting and flamenco share many similarities. Outwardly, they are both spectacularly visual in terms of color and movement; swirling skirt and matador's cape. In dance, the male is strong and aggressive, moving towards and around the female whose graceful and quick movements keep him at bay. In bullfighting, the male is strong and aggressive, moving towards and around the bull using graceful and quick movements to wear him down for the kill. A bullfighter can't simply be brave to achieve true artistry and beauty; like the cantaor, he must be driven by the 'force that climbs up inside, taking control of his very being'. He plays to his audience's mood much like the cantaor who embod-

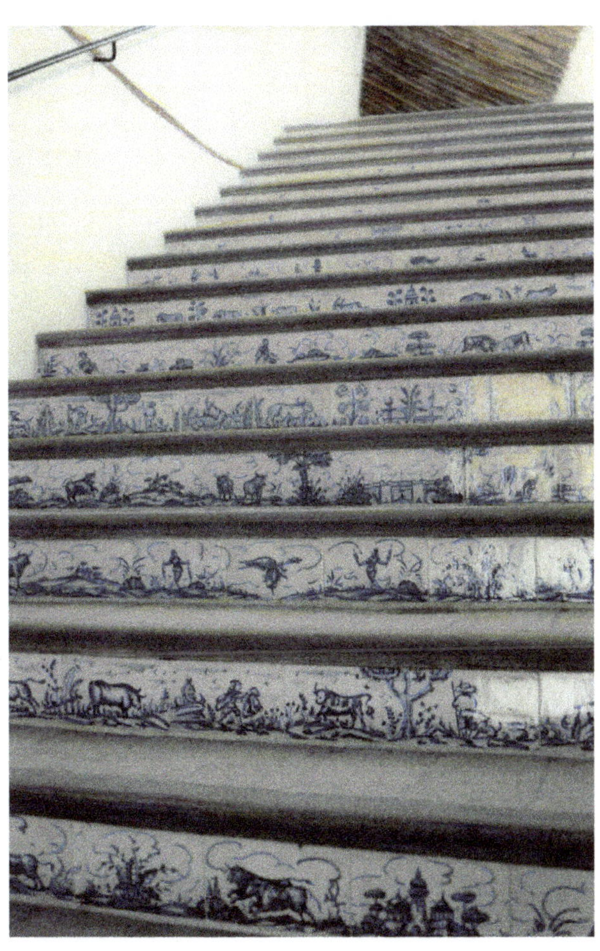

ies the life struggle of his audience. The matador represents man alone against the bull, man alone confronted by fate.

Yesterday, we had breakfast in a small cafe near the hotel.

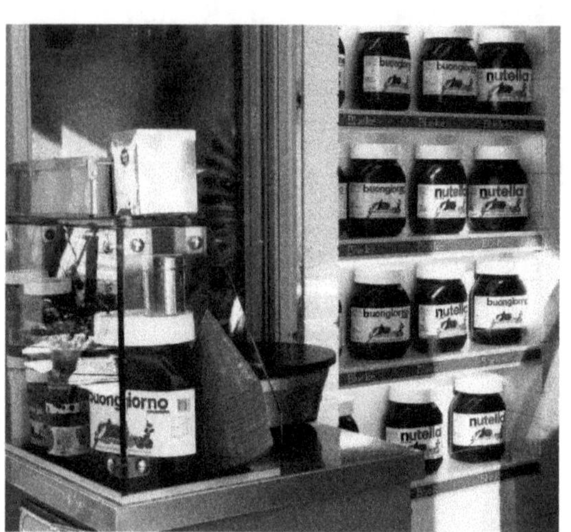

Liz had croissants with a chocolate spread that was yummy. I was looking forward to having them for breakfast this morning but the cafe was out of chocolate filled croissants. To assuage my disappointment, they gave me a jar of Nutella to fix my own. It's exquisite! A great gift idea to take home; that was, until the girls told me you can buy it in the grocery store back home. I believe that is even a better discovery!

The cafe was very crowded with only one waitress so when she began putting our food on the counter to walk around

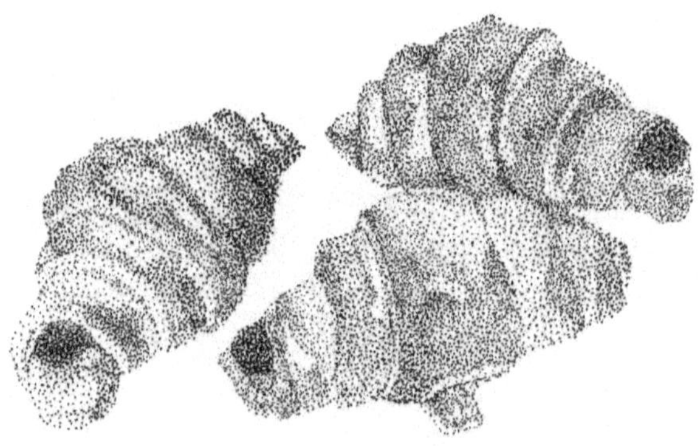

and bring it to us, we decided to risk being rude and carried it to our table ourselves - she gave us a big smile!

To Gibraltar via Estepona

It was another beautiful day and the traffic was light; an enjoyable trip to the coast. We weren't particularly interested in doing more than a drive through; it sounds a lot like Atlantic City and there are more important things to see.

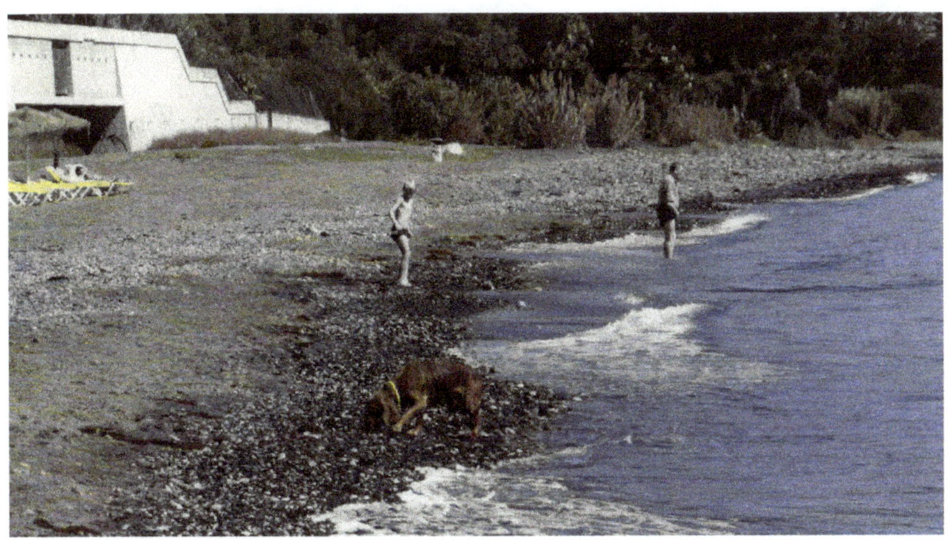

The easiest route to Gibraltar is via Estepona. The highway doesn't encourage visitors; we went for miles with the Mediterranean clearly visible on our left and no exits to get to it! We got off the first exit we found which was the access road to a small posh area of shops, a small dirty beach and an outdoor cafe.

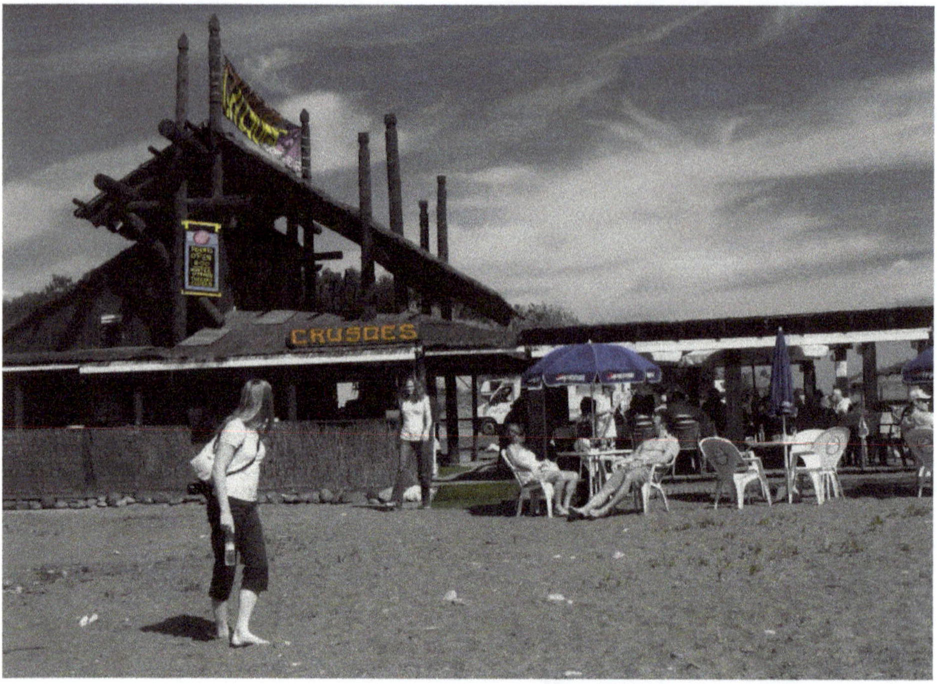

The cafe was British and it served hamburgers and salad, a real treat. Unimpressed with the beach, we ventured into a few shops. The prices were unbelievable! No incentive to hang around or explore further.

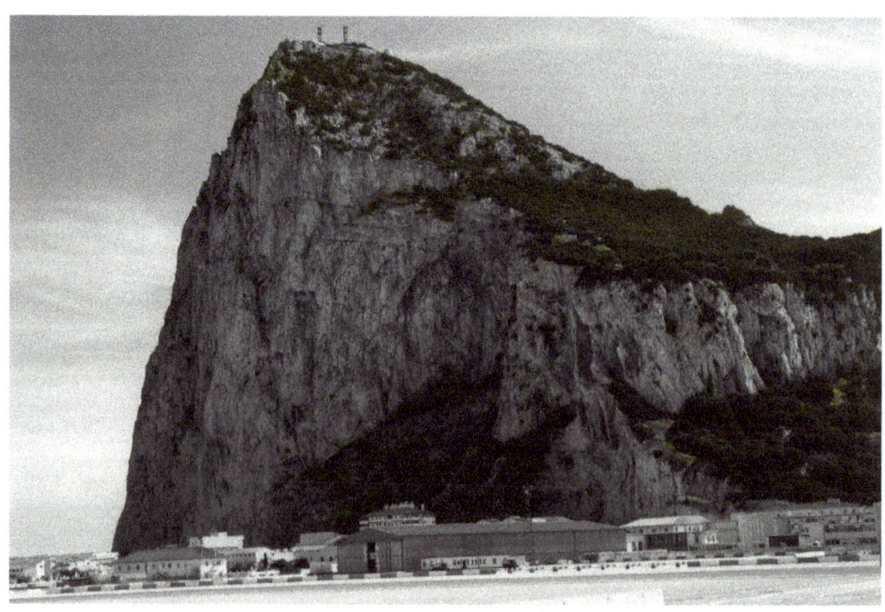

We reached Gibraltar about 3:00, siesta again. We parked in Spain and walked across the border. Gibraltar shares its north border with Cadiz, however it is a British Overseas Territory, ceded to Britain in 1713 in perpetuity under the Treaty of Utrecht.

Spain has tried unsuccessfully to reclaim the Rock several times. On June 23, 2016 when Britain voted to leave the EU, Gibraltar overwhelmingly voted to stay in; the next day, Spain renewed calls for joint ownership.

At the time of our visit, you had to go through customs to enter Gibraltar. After clearing customs, you then walk across a large airfield, keeping a look out for incoming aircraft.

Entering Gibraltar, the first thing you notice is the filth! The territory is only 2.6 square miles, seems like they could keep it clean.

The exchange rate was not favorable, making the ride to the top of the rock very expensive, so we decided to stay at sea level. We chose to walk away from the city center, hoping to walk the perimeter of the rock but ran into a dead-end, due to construction.

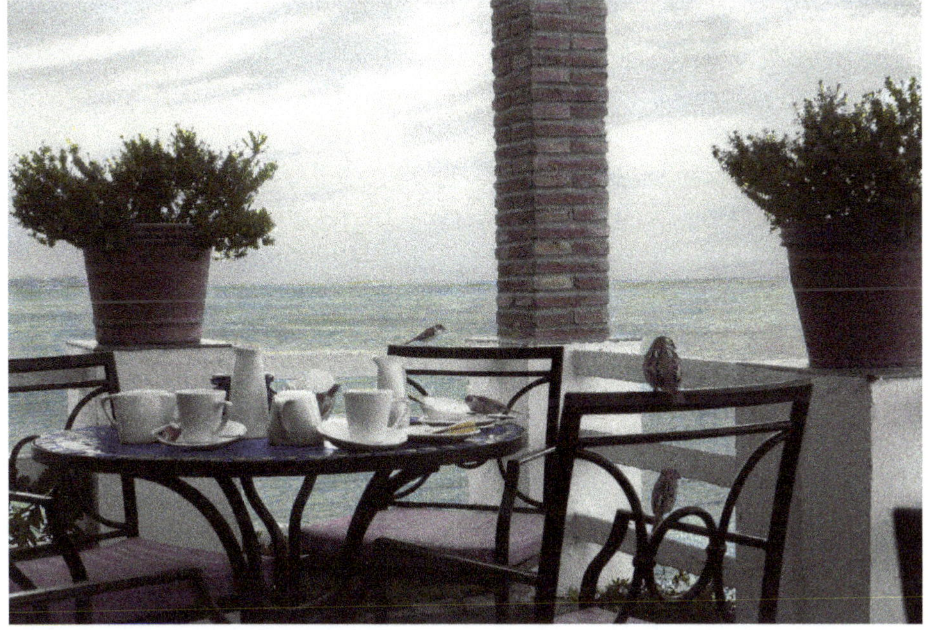

We had afternoon "tea" gazing out at Africa. It was very hazy but you could make out the shape of Morocco, the point of Africa where it is believed that the gypsies crossed the Mediterranean into Spain.

The sides of the rock are steep and pretty bleak. It's very interesting to see all the holes at various levels for cannons and lookouts, suggesting a maze of tunnels for access.

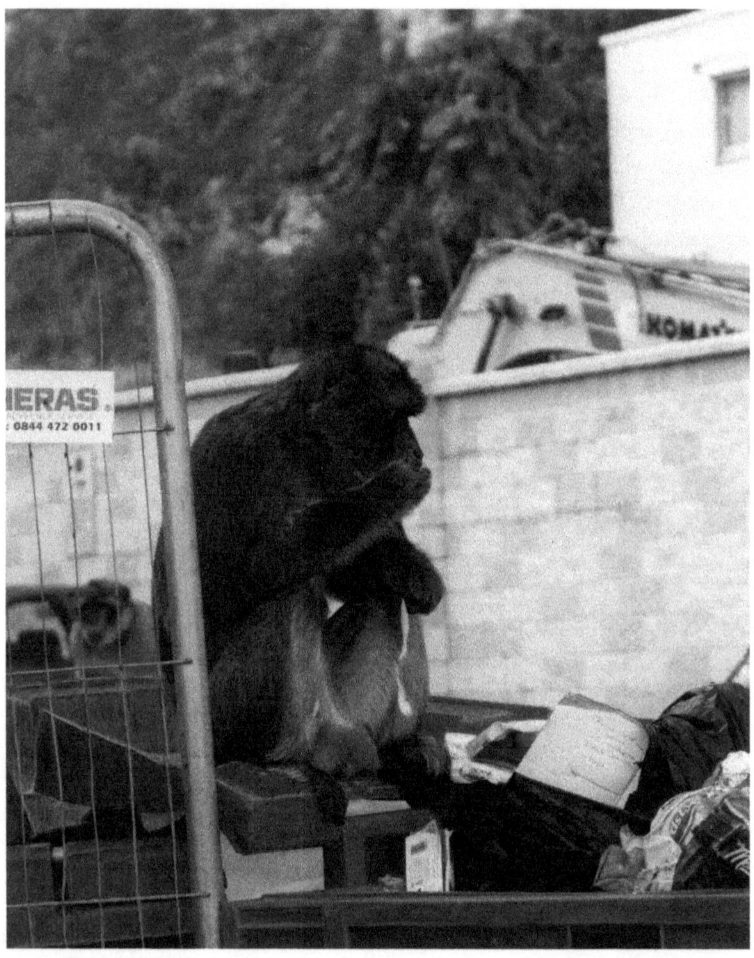

Far more enjoyable were the apes invading dumpsters. The apes are Barbary macaques; they are the only wild apes or monkeys in Europe and they are on the endangered list.

They kept an eye on us but we weren't much of a deterrent to their quest for food. What a mess they made. The apes sit on the edge of a dumpster and dig around looking for food. The non-food ends up on the ground adding to the filth.

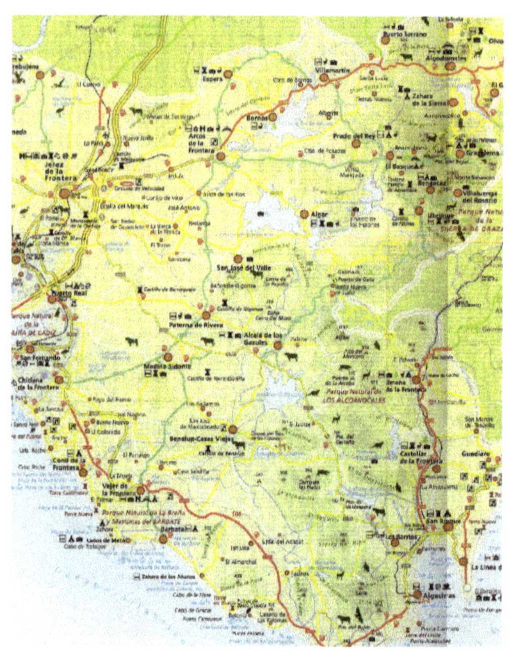

Algeciras is the largest port city on the Bay of Gibraltar and one of the largest in Europe and the world. The port has been important for centuries; it was destroyed by the Goths and rebuilt by the Moors in 711. It has changed hands several times and was part of a war as recently as 1982.

We reached Algeciras a few hours before dinner. This was the least expensive hotel of the trip and easily the prettiest. We had no plans for Algeciras so it was a very relaxed stop.

All Liz wanted to do was nap so Sarah and I sat on the large patio, reading and writing until dinner was served at 8:00 (early!). We chose the dinner buffet for 15 euro a piece and attacked it with gusto. So many things to try. We waddled back to the room, already looking forward to the breakfast buffet with real eggs!

We awoke a bit groggy even though we had managed 8 wonderful hours of sleep! It felt like we were moving in slow motion; sad how dependent on coffee we'd become. The breakfast buffet was included in the room price so we were eager to get started; I had granola with plain yogurt, pineapple, a hard boiled egg and juice. Doesn't sound all that impressive but we'd been living off pastries so this was heaven!

We managed to head out in the wrong direction. The maps have one highway number and the roads have a different number which added to the confusion. Once we arrived in Tarifa, the Point of Tarifa was easy to locate.

Tarifa is an industrialized, major port. The word tariff originated from the fact that Tarifa was the first port to charge merchants to use its docks. It is best known for wind sports; a windsurfing destination. The beach on the Atlantic side is wide and roped off to control the crowds. It was a windy, cool Monday morning - no crowds.

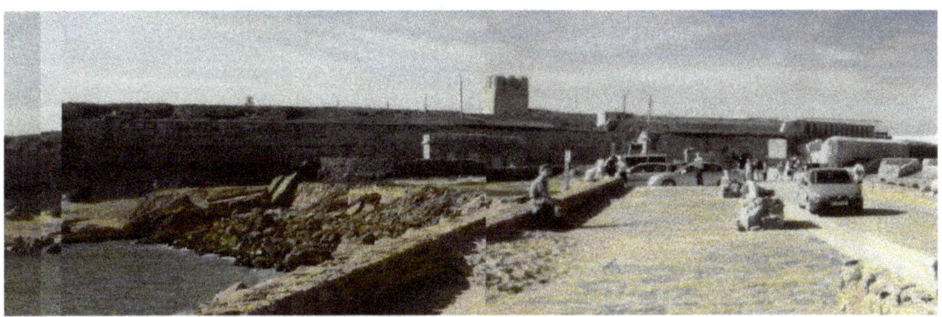

You can drive your car onto a spit of land that divides the two bodies of water. I was disappointed that there is a fortified wall with a locked gate preventing access to the famous meeting of the waters so we had to content ourselves with viewing them separately. I took multiple panoramas showing both bodies of water but it just wasn't quite the same.

Since we've waded in the Atlantic many times, we chose the Mediterranean. There isn't much of a beach on the Mediterranean side; it's more of a rocky cove. The water is beautiful and clear, a deep shade of green. A man was snorkeling just off shore; he came out of the water with squid tucked in his belt.

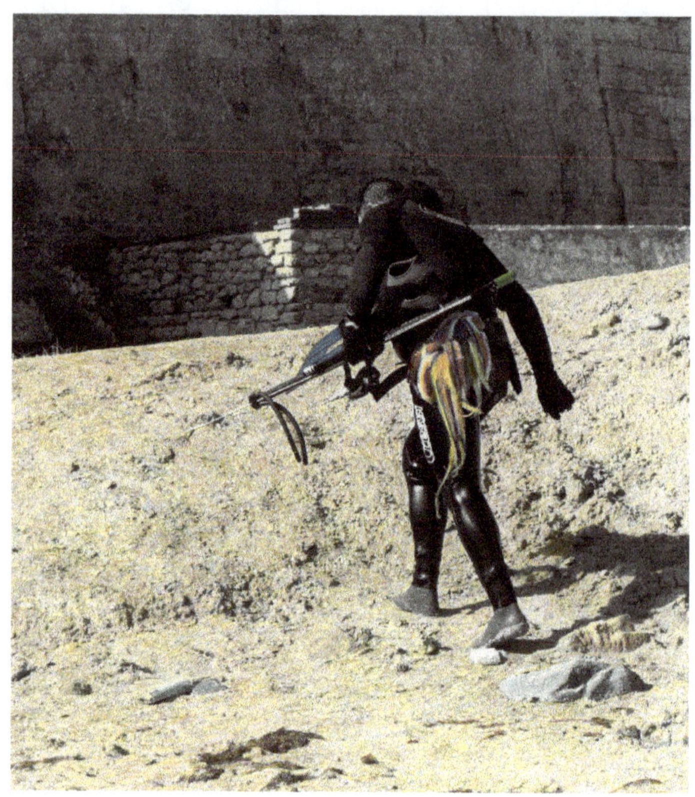

Fishermen lined the rocky Atlantic barrier, sharing the sun warmed rocks and fish heads with beautiful orange cats.

Cat heaven!

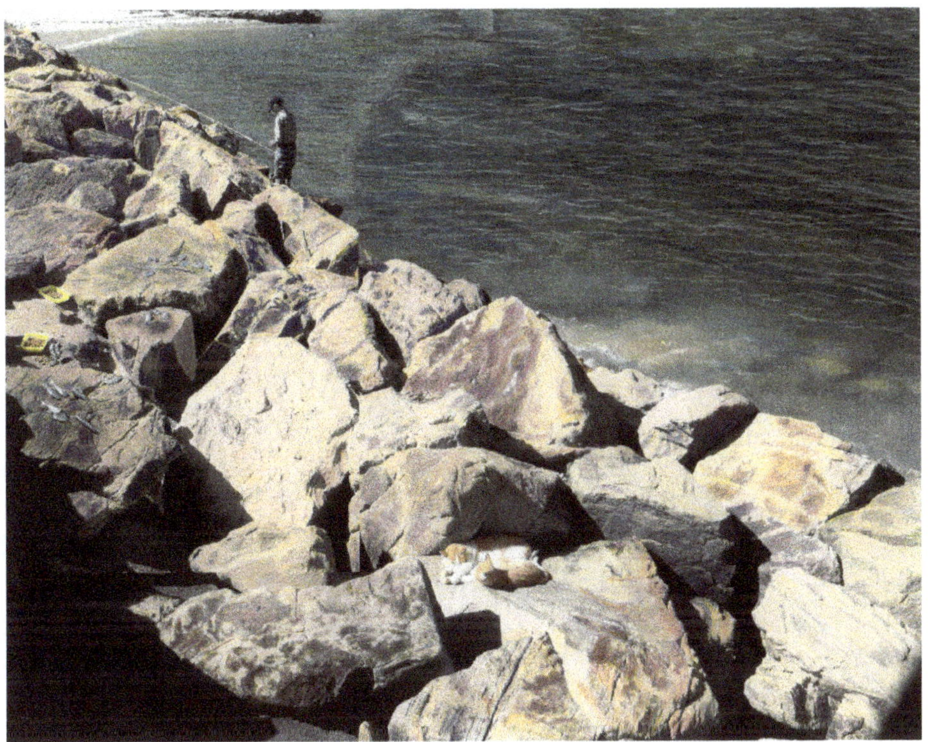

Liz had taken pictures of the cats from the car but the high-lights were a little blown so we decided to go back after our food break. The town was quiet so we had no trouble park-ing. The first cafe we passed was full of old men smoking so we went to the next. We went in and sat at a table; there was a couple sitting at the bar, so we knew the cafe was open but the waitress totally ignored us and left the room! So we left too. After another block, we found a cafe with outdoor seat-ing and friendly service. The coffee and food were excellent too.

It was starting to get more crowded back at the jetty so Liz got out to look for the cats while I turned the car around. They were right where we'd left them!

Arcos de la Fronteria

Inland, between Tarifa and Seville, is an area renowned for its white villages. All of the villages are characterized by whitewashed walls with red or brown tiled roofs. The villages are somewhat isolated so the villagers become like one extended family, just the right environment for tertulias to occur. Tertulia is the term for when a group of friends get together to discuss any and everything; tertulia usually take place in bars and clubs, leading to drinking and flamenco song.

I chose Arcos de la Fronteria to visit. It has a lovely parador on the top of the hill, overlooking the old town on one side and farm land on the other. As was our norm, we arrived during siesta, starving.

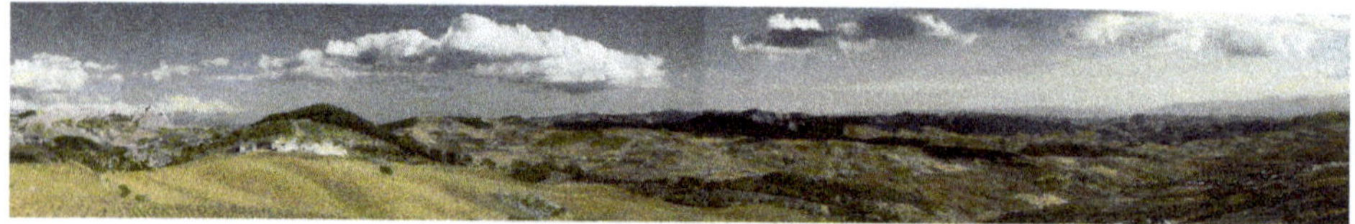

We found one small restaurant open. No tapas and no English. We played it safe and ordered potato omelets since we didn't know what anything else was. Service was very slow and the waitress grumpy. Spanish culture doesn't tip for good service, a lot of wait staff are curt and lackadaisical at best, I wonder if it's related. It took a long time to order and a long time to get our food and even longer to get our check. Feeling restless, we left the money on the table for the tab and included a 1 euro tip. It was the first smile we'd seen!

The old town is a maze of tiny one way streets, climbing to the top of the hill and back down again. The worst part about driving up is knowing you've got to drive back down. Our car is small but we still had to fold the side mirrors in to keep from bumping the buildings on the sides; some of the corners were three point turns. Tourist guidebooks say 'only the brave should drive to the top'!

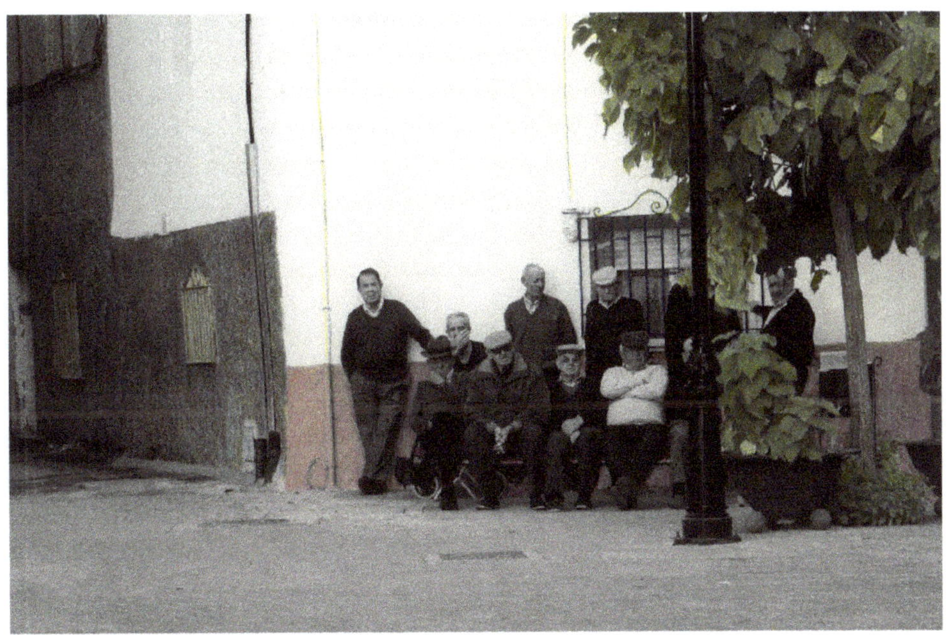

At the top is the Plaza del Cabildo. The only tourist attraction, the cathedral, closed for renovation, shares the hilltop with the parador, a TI, and a small parking lot. The parking lot was watched over by a 'vagrant'; Rick Steves had warned about this. The man ran in front of the car and led us to a parking space, then stuck his hand out for a tip.

The parador is the former house of a local magistrate; it sits atop a 150 m, rocky limestone cliff and overlooks the Guadalete River. The old quarter, which surrounds the parador, is an historical site.

In the spring and summer the white towns are covered with pots of red geraniums; a much photographed sight. In October, there are few flowers left and most of the pots have been taken down.

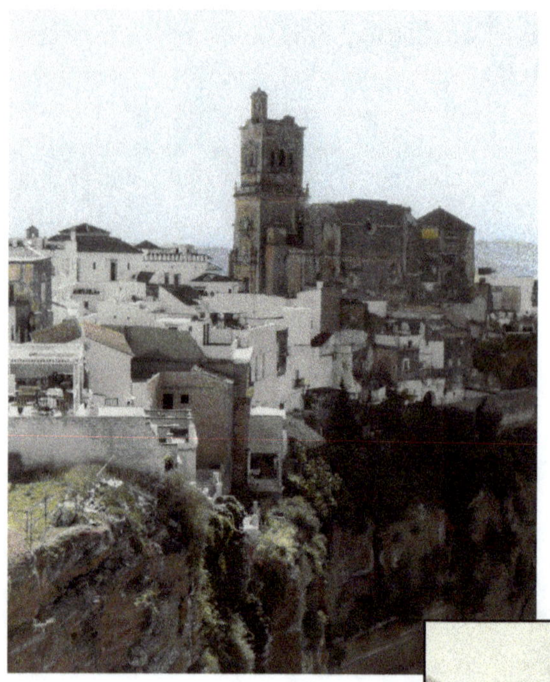

The white washed buildings are enchanting nevertheless and the views are great. There are not a lot of shops, tourist or otherwise. Art galleries and artist studios seemed to dominate, which was fine with us. I always love looking at fellow artist's work; it's so inspiring (or guilt inducing if I've been unproductive).

Jerez

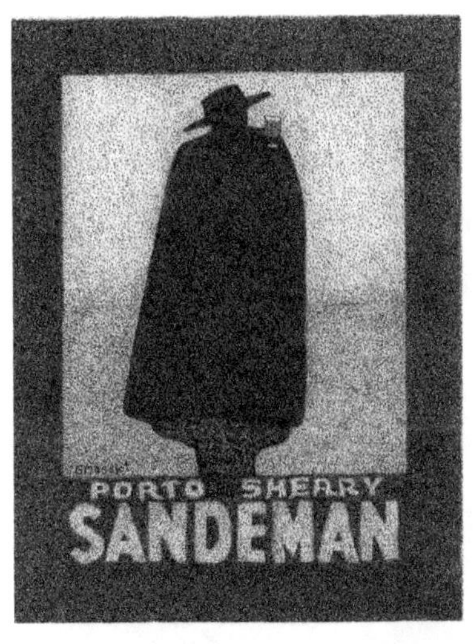

We left Arcos earlier than planned so we opted to pass through Jerez to see the bodegas (wineries) and the famous dressage horses. Jerez is a much larger city than the ones we've been in since Seville but bodegas are easy to find, they are very odoriferous, and closed! Jerez produces over 17 million gallons of sherry a year; it is Spain's most exported wine with 80% sold abroad.

This time it wasn't siesta, it was Jerez's Saint's day; everything was closed or closing. Saint's Days are unpredictable; if you stumble upon one you might get to see processions or like Jerez, most things will be closed.

Jerez is part of the triangle that marks the birthplace of flamenco and is famous for its sherry, horses and flamenco. They proudly claim that flamenco singing began here. In 1993 Spain founded the Andalusian Centre of Flamenco in Jerez to "safeguard and promote the values and standards of flamenco." It houses a library for research, historical documents, and artifacts such as musical instruments, costumes, posters, and postcards; alas closed for Saint's day. In keeping with their long-standing flamenco traditions, they hold an international flamenco festival every winter.

Fortunately, the Real Escueta Andaluz del Arte Ecusestre (Royal Andalucian School of Equestrian Art) was open! The school is "devoted to conserving the ancestral abilities of the Andalusian horse and maintaining the classical traditions"

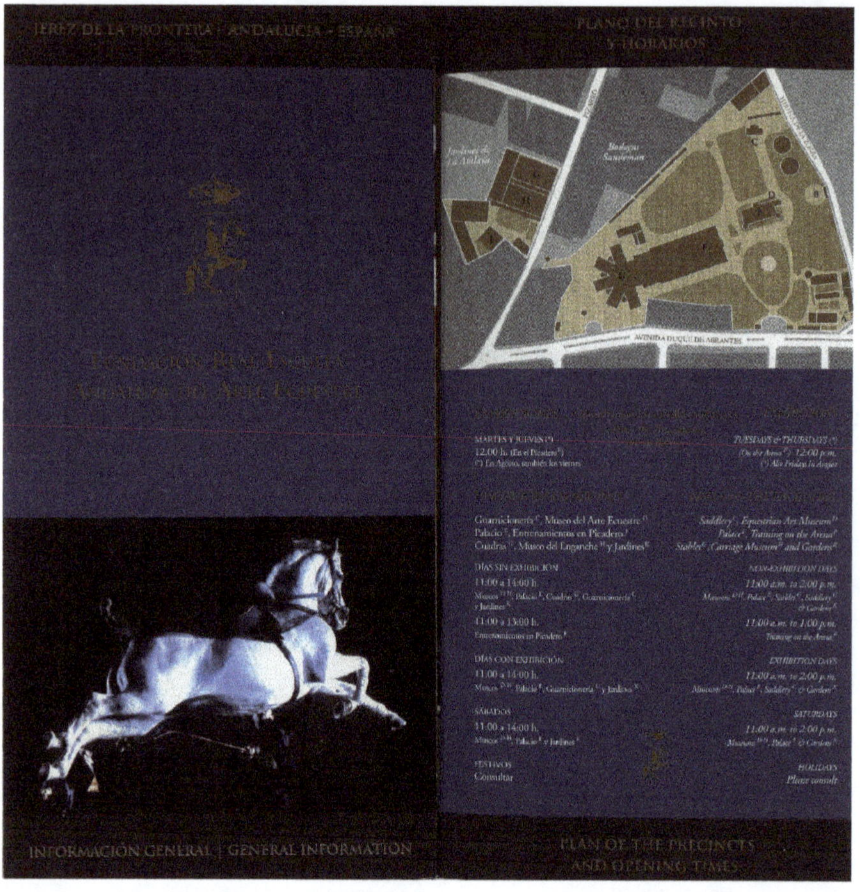

such as dressage and coach driving. These horses are a sub-strain of the Andalusian breed; a bloodline started in the 15th century by Carthusian monks. They are prized due to the excellent nutrition of their marsh pastures.

The school is on the outskirts of town, just beyond the edge of our map. After circling for 45 minutes with no one in sight, I found a man on the street and stopped to ask directions. He knew just enough English to understand that the horse complex was what we wanted to find. We were close but on a one-way street headed the wrong direction from the complex.

The school holds performances based on classical dressage (equestrian ballet), country-style riding, and traditional equestrian chores such as cattle herding and carriage driv-

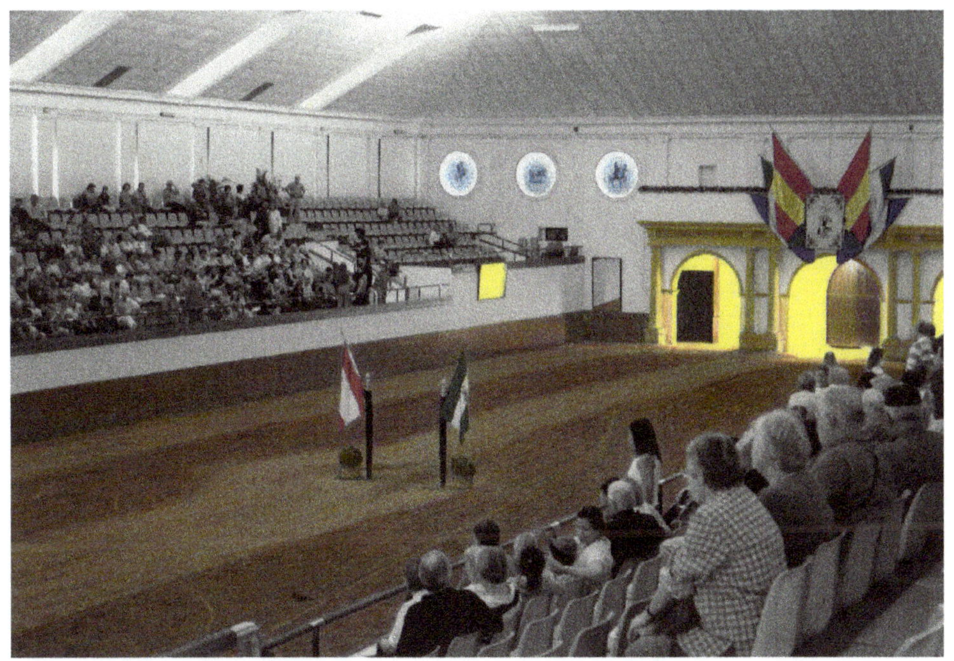

ing. Each segment is choreographed to quintessential Spanish music and the riders are dressed in 18th century style
costumes. We made it to the show with 5 minutes to spare;
they won't seat you once the show has started.

The horses are elegant and the precision is spot on. I've
never seen anything like it. The final performance, called the
Carousel, was the most intricate. The riders were in groups
of 4 or 5 and they performed crossings like a marching band.
That was beautiful to watch.

After the performance was over, we were allowed to wander around the grounds for only a few minutes before they
closed and then it was off to Donana National Park and El
Rocio!

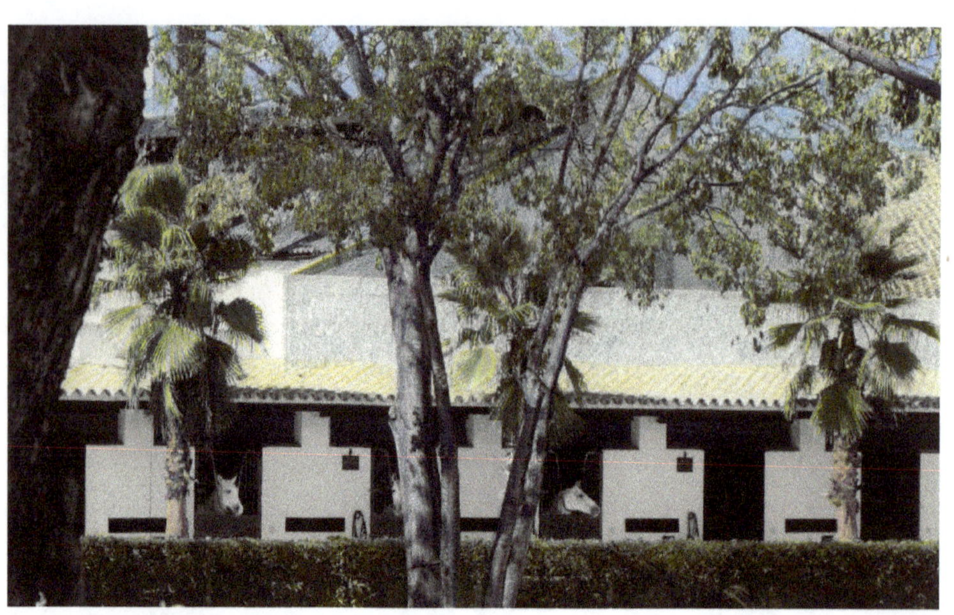

El Rocio

Liz was finishing up her Masters in Wildlife so I thought it would be fun to add a national park to our itinerary. The Donana caught my attention because it has such a unique biodiversity and was close to the areas we were visiting.

Back in the late 1500s, the Seventh Duke of Medina-Sidonia, a commander of the Spanish Armada, bought land in the marshes for a country retreat. He named it Coto Don Ana after his wife, Dona Ana de Silva y Mendoza; the park bears her name. (Wikipedia retraces the lineage)

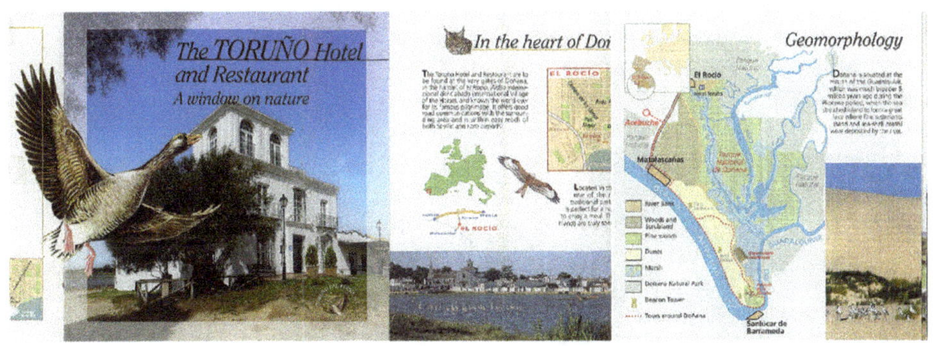

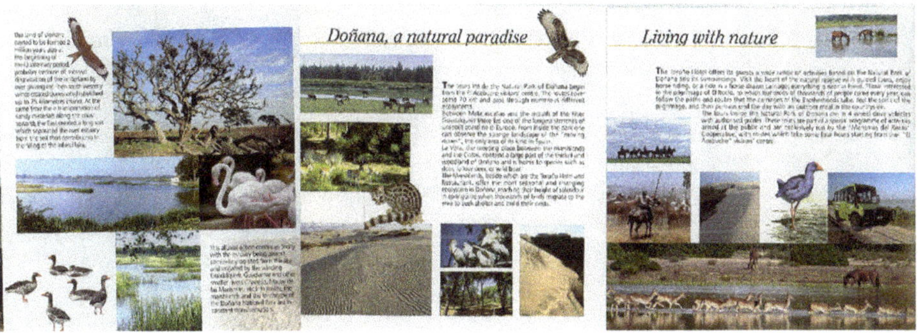

In 1854, a treatise on the birds found in the area created a public awareness of the importance of the area and steps were taken to protect it. The marshes shelter many animals along with thousands of European and African migratory birds; more than 300 species pass through here annually.

In 1969, the World Wildlife Fund joined the Spanish government to purchase a large section of the marshes. Over the decades, the reserve has grown to 255,000 hectares. It was recognized by UNESCO as a World Heritage Site in 1994. Work continues to protect this area from the harms of expanding agriculture, upriver mining, and tourism.

El Rocio is one of the points of entry to the park. It turned out to be a very unique and special village.

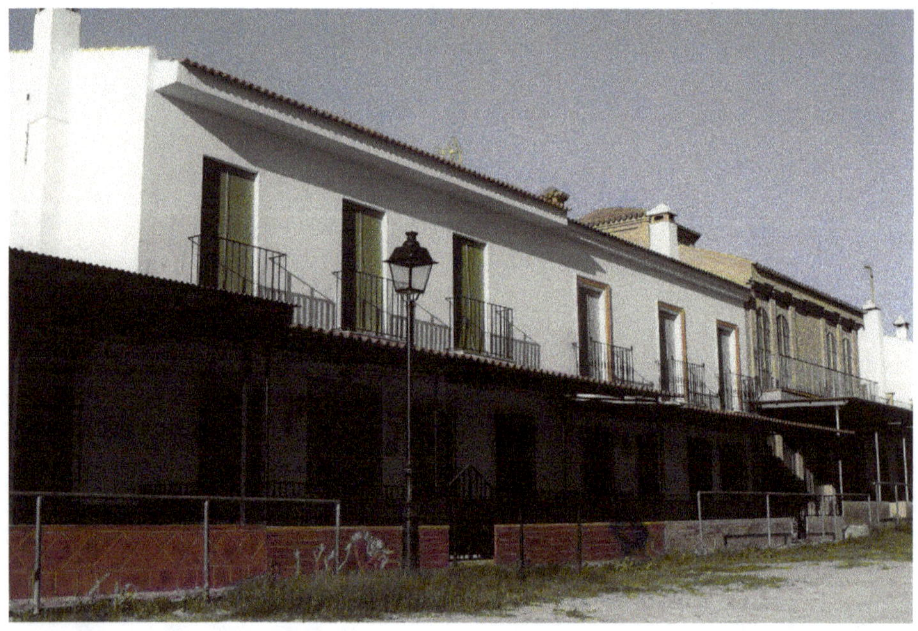

We arrived in El Rocio in the late afternoon. I had chosen El Rocio simply based on its location at the edge of the park. I was totally unprepared for the village.

Driving into town was like driving into a Hollywood western stage set. The roads are sand, no asphalt or concrete anywhere, and no signs. The houses have broad verandas and wooden rails for tying up horses. It didn't take long to realize that the village was deserted, not just siesta deserted but boarded up window deserted, a real ghost town. I expected a saloon to be just around the corner!

Our reservation was for two people; Sarah had decided to join us so we needed to change the reservation. We were flexible, a sleeping bag would have sufficed. As deserted as the town appeared, I didn't think this would be a problem but the hotel was fully booked and the proprietor didn't speak English. When she finally grasped my charades, she became worried and insisted on showing us our room. The room was very tiny and she was afraid we would be too cramped with a cot added. I convinced her that we were okay with the lack of space, we weren't planning to spend much time in the room anyway. We had a narrow path down the length of the room and had to get into bed from the foot! But it was wonderful!

Our room had a small balcony overlooking a small lake that was full of birds; storks, herons, flamingos, ducks and many more. We had an hour to wander around before Sarah's bus arrived. We wandered

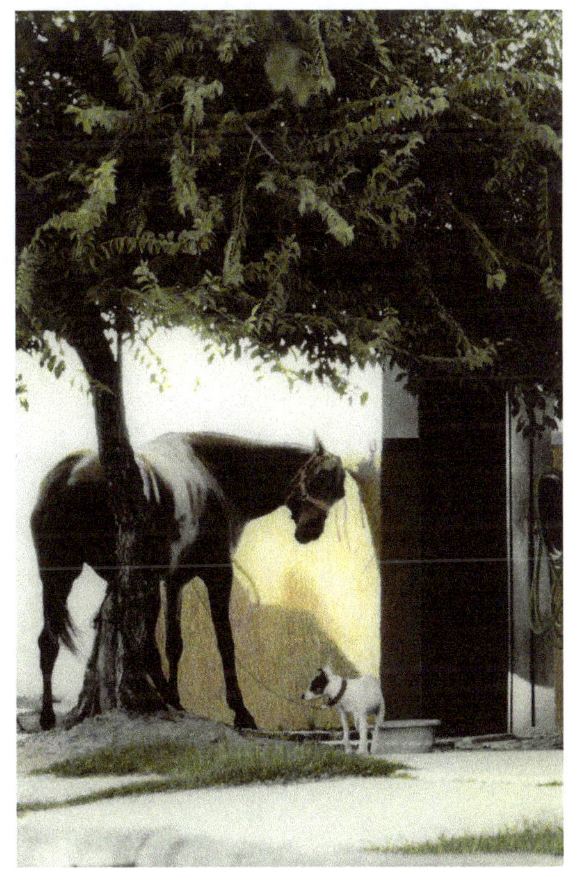

along the lake, Liz with bird book in hand and her binoculars. She was in heaven. We stumbled on this horse with a friend; it's such a different world.

There is a small cafe next to the bus stop. I ordered tinte con lemon (red wine mixed with lemon soda) and received a pastry! My Spanish must be horrendous - that was one of the few things I'd learned to say! After many hand motions, the waitress grasped the wine request and offered me fruit wines. I knew once Sarah got there she'd be able to handle things but the waitress was determined to figure it out. She asked a waiter to try to decipher my request and he under-stood me on the first try - must be the dialect!

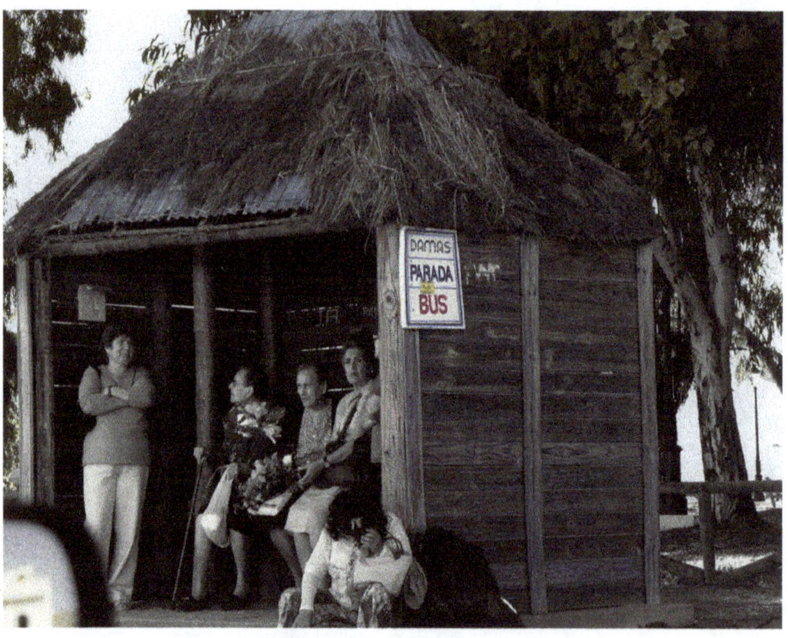

Turns out, there are two bus stops in El Rocio. Sarah called us from the first stop to see if she was at the right one - we couldn't see a bus so the driver brought her to the second one. Life is so very different here; I'm so glad we were on time for this meeting!

The hotel is next door to the church Sanctuario de Nuestra Senora de El Rocio which houses the Virgin known as La Blanca Paloma (White Dove). The chapel is centered on the Virgin, from the minute you walk in, she is all you see. She's immense and awesome to behold; covered with gold, surrounded by silver bull's horns. La Blanca Paloma is thought to cure infertility and mental disorders; in 1653 she was credited with saving the village of Almonte from the plague.

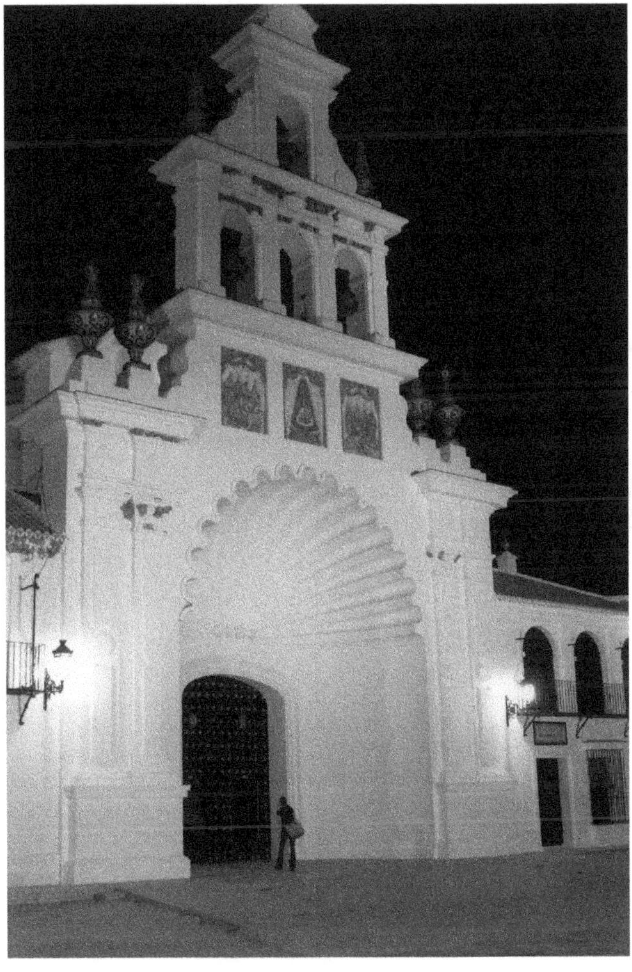

In the 14th century, a hunter discovered a statue of the Virgin in a tree trunk near the Donana. He carried it into the village but when he stopped to rest, the Virgin went back to the tree. This happened several times. The village took it as a 'sign' and built a chapel where the tree stood; it has become a place of pilgrimage.

A cult following has grown over the years centered on this Virgin; during the week of Pentecost (7th weekend after Easter) pilgrims make their way to El Rocio to worship her. They come on foot or on horseback with covered wagons pulled by cattle or horses. They follow age-old cross country tracks. These days participants come from as far away as Barcelona and the Canary Islands - not to mention tourists who travel from abroad. Everyone sings rocieras (flamenco-style songs about the pilgrimage) as they travel.

The pilgrims wear traditional Andalusian dress including broad brimmed hats and flamenco dresses. Large sections of housing belong to more than 100 hermandades (brotherhoods); other houses belong to families. For one week a year, El Rocio is filled with one million pilgrims celebrating the Virgin with one long party; nights of flamenco and romance fueled by alcohol.

In the early hours Monday morning, Pentecost, the Virgin is brought out of the small church and carried around to each hermandades building before returning to the chapel in the afternoon. After Pentecost is over, El Rocio returns to a small village of population 700.

Coto Donana National Park

The next morning was gorgeous! The Coto Donana National Park lies at the mouth of the Guadalquivir River. Over the years large sandbars have blocked all the river's outlets to the sea except for one which makes the Guadalquivir delta unique. There is speculation, based on soil samples and aerial studies, that this area was home to the semi-mythical city of Tartessus. Researchers are examining the area for signs that the 3000 year old city was here and was destroyed by tsunamis that plagued the area.

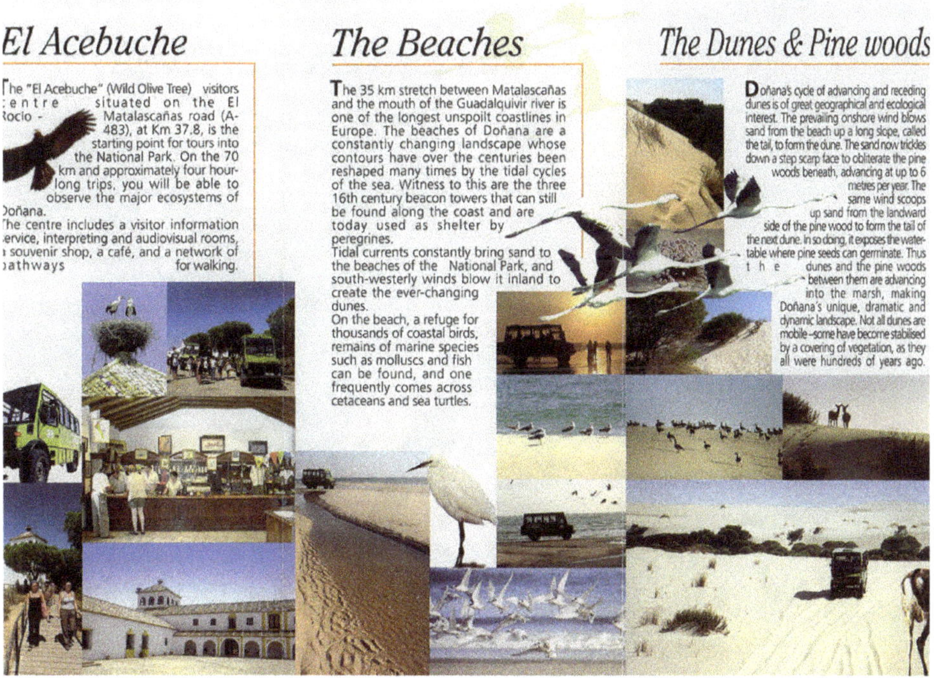

El Acebuche

The "El Acebuche" (Wild Olive Tree) visitors centre situated on the El Rocio - Matalascañas road (A-483), at Km 37,8, is the starting point for tours into the National Park. On the 70 km and approximately four hour-long trips, you will be able to observe the major ecosystems of Doñana.
The centre includes a visitor information service, interpreting and audiovisual rooms, a souvenir shop, a café, and a network of pathways for walking.

The Beaches

The 35 km stretch between Matalascañas and the mouth of the Guadalquivir river is one of the longest unspoilt coastlines in Europe. The beaches of Doñana are a constantly changing landscape whose contours have over the centuries been reshaped many times by the tidal cycles of the sea. Witness to this are the three 16th century beacon towers that can still be found along the coast and are today used as shelter by peregrines.
Tidal currents constantly bring sand to the beaches of the National Park, and south-westerly winds blow it inland to create the ever-changing dunes.
On the beach, a refuge for thousands of coastal birds, remains of marine species such as molluscs and fish can be found, and one frequently comes across cetaceans and sea turtles.

The Dunes & Pine woods

Doñana's cycle of advancing and receding dunes is of great geographical and ecological interest. The prevailing onshore wind blows sand from the beach up a long slope, called the tail, to form the dune. The sand now trickles down a step scarp face to obliterate the pine woods beneath, advancing at up to 6 metres per year. The same wind scoops up sand from the landward side of the pine wood to form the tail of the next dune. In so doing, it exposes the water-table where pine seeds can germinate. Thus the dunes and the pine woods between them are advancing into the marsh, making Doñana's unique, dramatic and dynamic landscape. Not all dunes are mobile –some have become stabilised by a covering of vegetation, as they all were hundreds of years ago.

The park is internationally recognized for its ecological wealth; there are three ecological habitats contained in 1300 sq km. At the delta, the winds have created a barrier of large sand dunes. The next area is known as the marismas (marshland). The rains begin in October, flooding the marismas with fresh water that reaches a uniform level of 12-24 inches.

For centuries this area was uninhabited by man creating an ideal space for wildlife and a major site for migrating birds. Birds from north and central Europe pass through on their way to Africa in the winter and geese and flamingos from Africa arrive in the summer. There are a few resident species but most are migratory. Beyond the marismas is the cork oak woodland, home to 37 species of mammal.

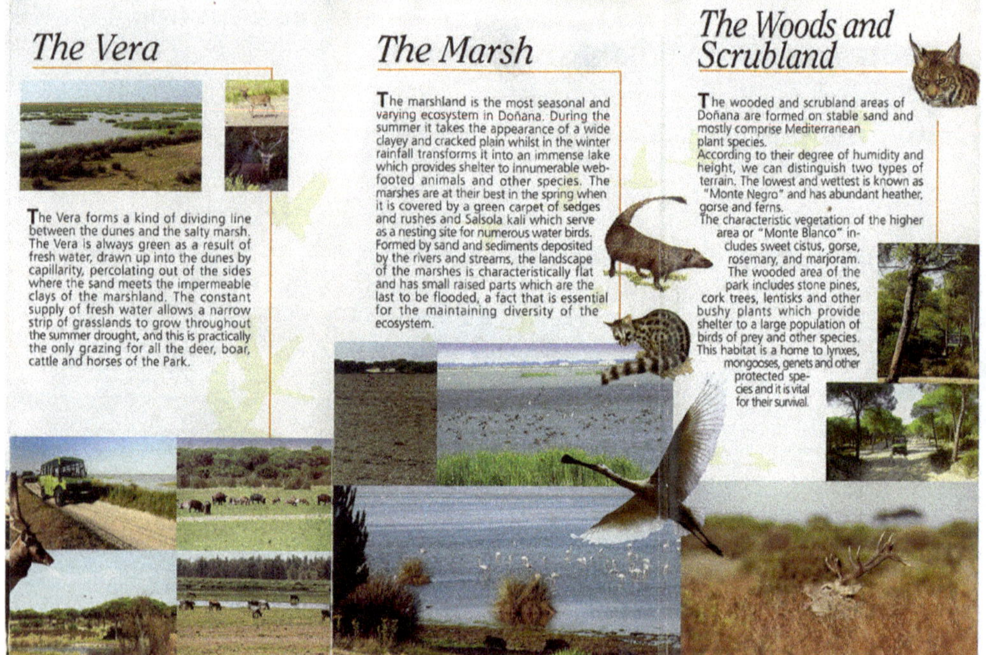

Access to the park is limited to a few private guides whose permits are limited to small areas; it didn't take long to see the area our guide was permitted to drive through. After visiting Yellowstone, I envisioned driving through remote areas and seeing all sorts of mammals; we only saw deer and 2 Egyptian mongoose.

Liz had informed us that she was going to be in high gear this morning and if we were running late, she would not be a very pleasant person so she was apologizing in advance! Luckily we were ready on time, no panic ensued.

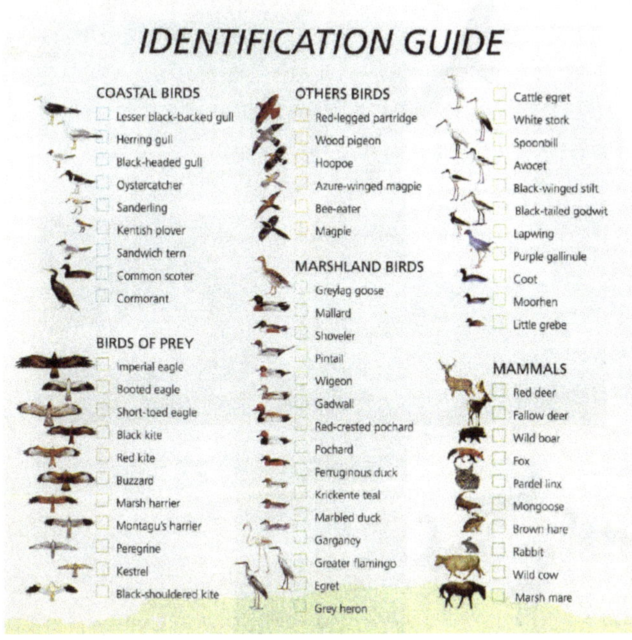

Armed with her bird book, binoculars, and list of questions, she hopped in the front seat and started chattering. Our guide enjoyed having someone that was interested in bird identification and spent his time pointing out things in her book and trying to find new birds to add to her list.

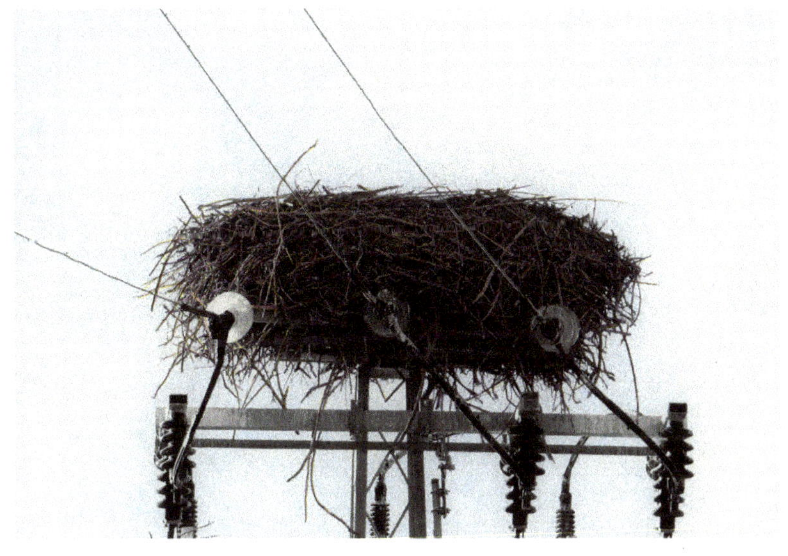

We spent most of the day in the nearby rice paddies bird watching. Our guide knew which areas were being harvested, thus where the birds would be en mass, gleaning. We saw 60+ species of bird; flamingos were always too far away to get a good shot.

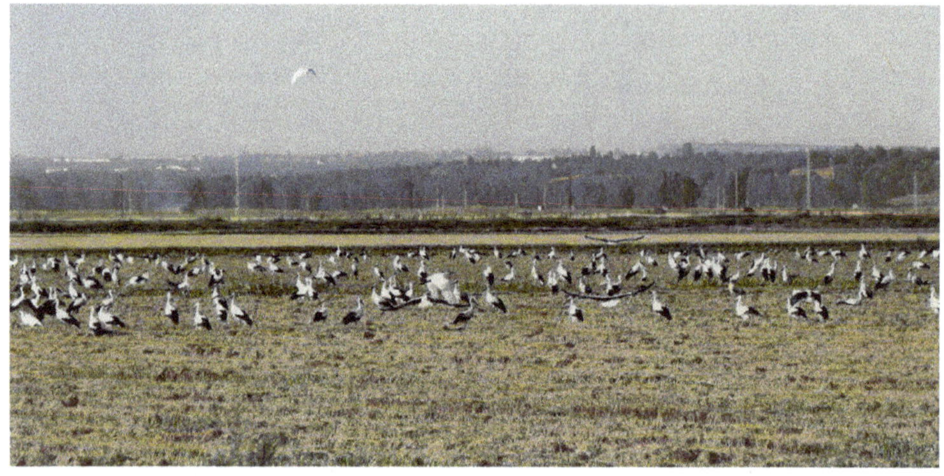

We had a late lunch of tapas in a small village near the rice fields; I have no idea what we ate but most of it was good - another adventure!

The afternoon was hot and the AC didn't work very well at our slow pace so the only air we got was from the front windows unless we were going slow enough to have the sliding doors open!

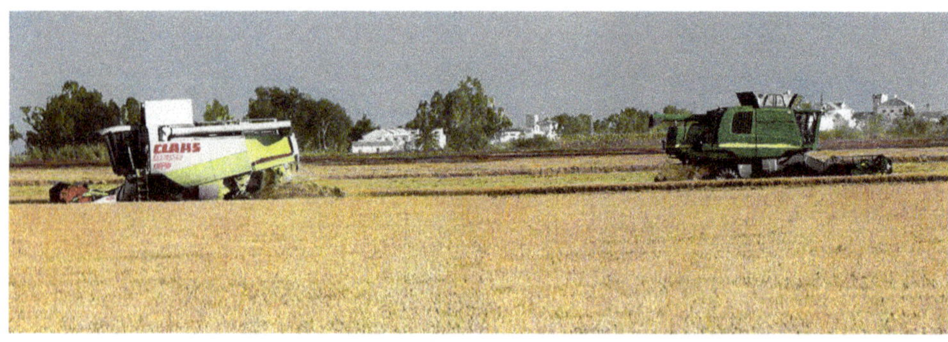

Spain is the second largest producer of rice in the EU and the area around the park is a great location for cultivation. Rice production is limited by the availability of water and this area has plenty during the growing cycle. Rice can be grown in salty soil and it's the best way to keep sea salt away from the land.

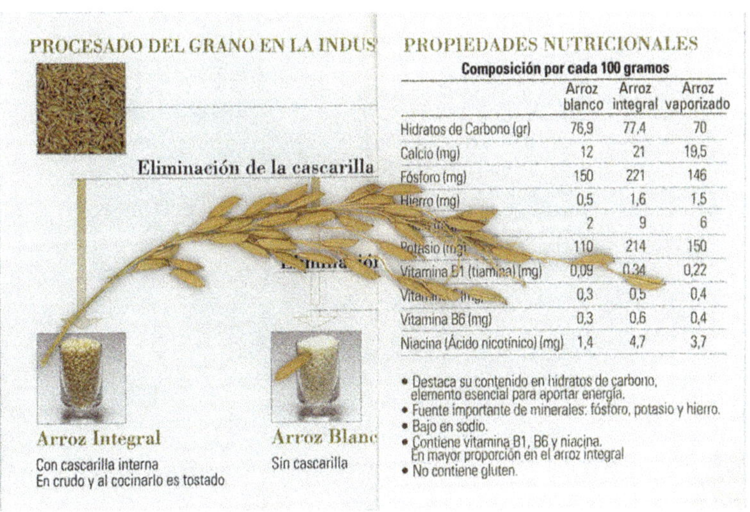

	Arroz blanco	Arroz integral	Arroz vaporizado
Hidratos de Carbono (gr)	76,9	77,4	70
Calcio (mg)	12	21	19,5
Fósforo (mg)	150	221	146
Hierro (mg)	0,5	1,6	1,5
	2	9	6
Potasio (mg)	110	214	150
Vitamina B1 (tiamina) (mg)	0,09	0,34	0,22
Vitamina (mg)	0,3	0,5	0,4
Vitamina B6 (mg)	0,3	0,6	0,4
Niacina (Ácido nicotínico) (mg)	1,4	4,7	3,7

Rice farming reached Spain most likely in the 6th century, coming from Byzantium. The first known fields were planted by the Muslims of Al-Andalus in the river deltas of Guadiana and Guadalquiver. In the 13th century, after the Christian re-conquest, rice became unpopular because it was considered a Muslim food; Christians wanted to plant more tradition-ally Christian crops. Then in the 14th century, rice became associated with disease because the wetlands were more prone to deadly diseases. In recent time, rice has once again become an important crop with Spain producing 30% of the EU's rice.

For not doing much of a physical nature all day, we were exhausted. We dined at the small restaurant next door to the hotel and had le menu. The food was okay; the enter-tainment was superb. We ate outside. Across from us was a

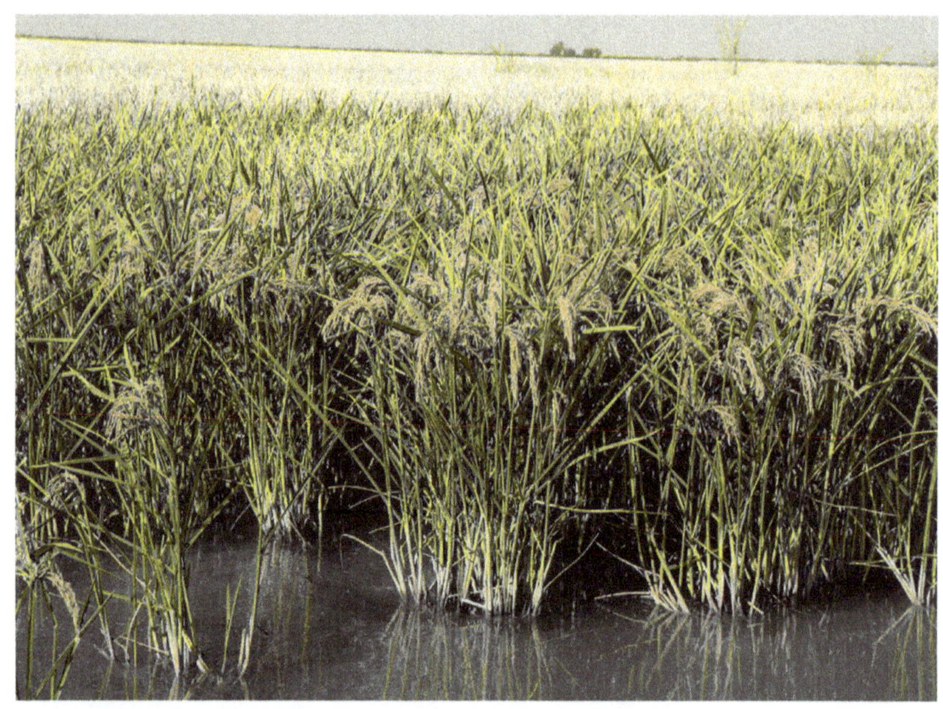

group of young men at a long wooden table. They had one guitar that they shared; mostly the music came from beating time on the table. The cantaor was passionate. No dancers, just authentic, spontaneous flamenco. A perfect end to a special day; if only I'd had my camera.

When I woke up the next morning, it was cold and dark; as the sun rose, I was delighted to see flamingos right outside our bedroom window, caught in the sunlight!

Breakfast this morning was much better than yesterday's, maybe because I was starving! I managed to order my food and coffee, Sarah only had to help me get a cup of coffee to go.

We began our journey by heading south to the dunes of the Donana. The gigantic dunes (called mobile or transdunes) are constantly shifting, burying the boardwalk and benches.

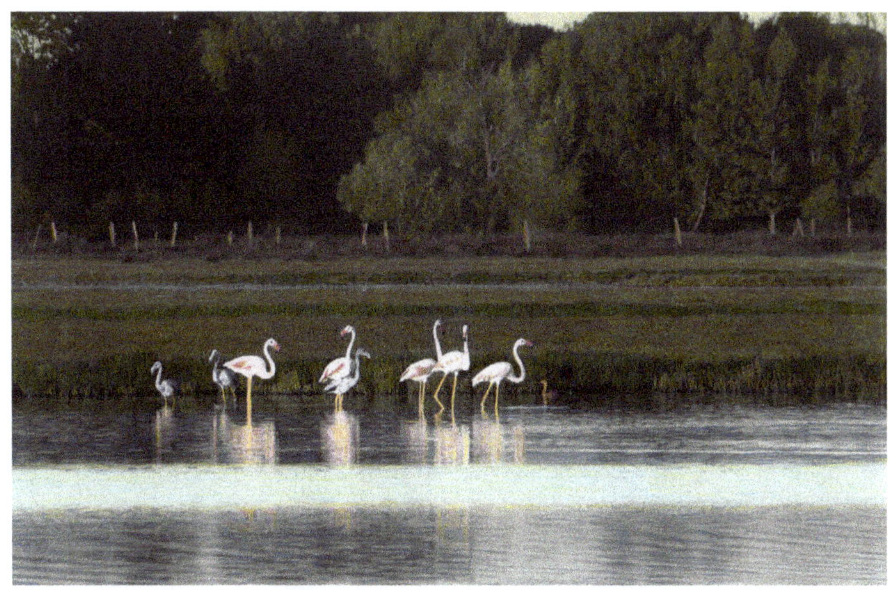

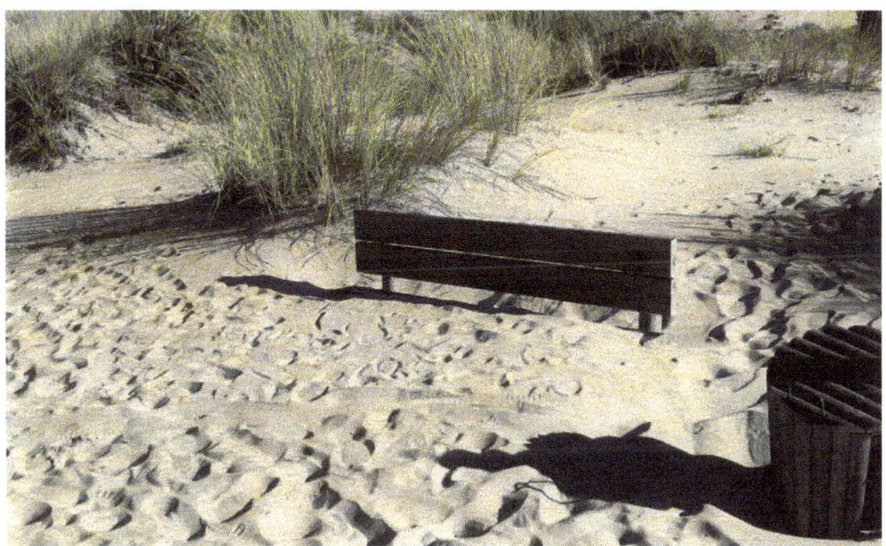

It's funny to see a sign asking you to stay on the path when there's no path in sight!

We listened to a radio station playing American music as we drove to Seville. They don't censor the lyrics like they do in the US; some of the lyrics were surprising.

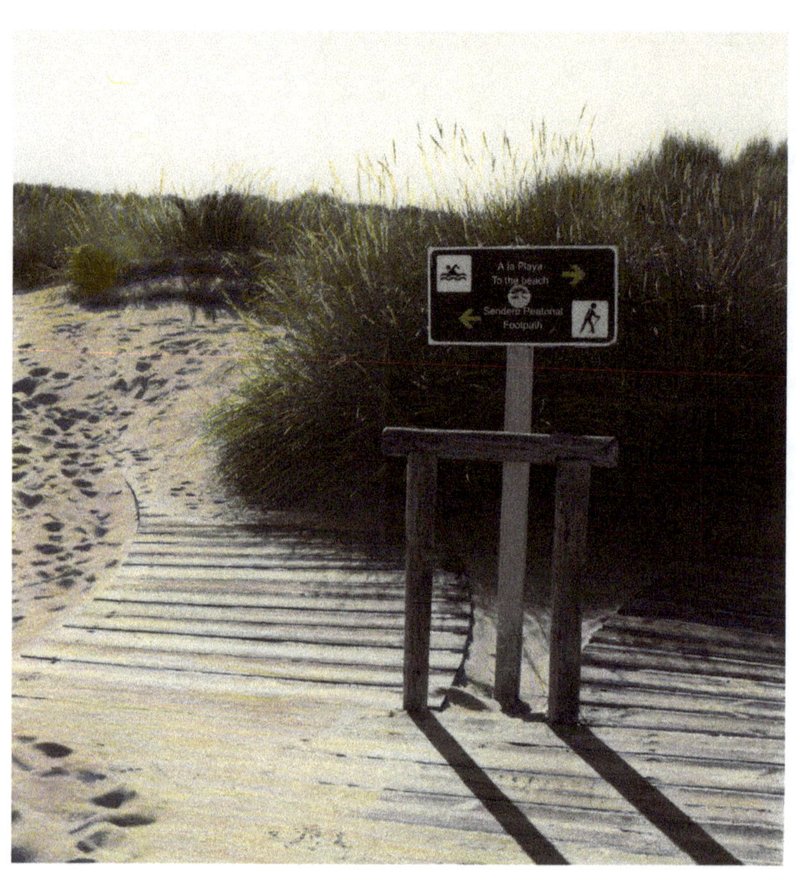

A la Playa
To the beach
Sendero Peatonal
Footpath

Passing through Seville

We passed through Seville, to drop Sarah off, on our way to Jerez airport to catch our plane to Barcelona. We spent the morning in the Reales Alcazares de Seville (founded by the Moors in 712). It is one of the oldest European Royal Palaces still in use.

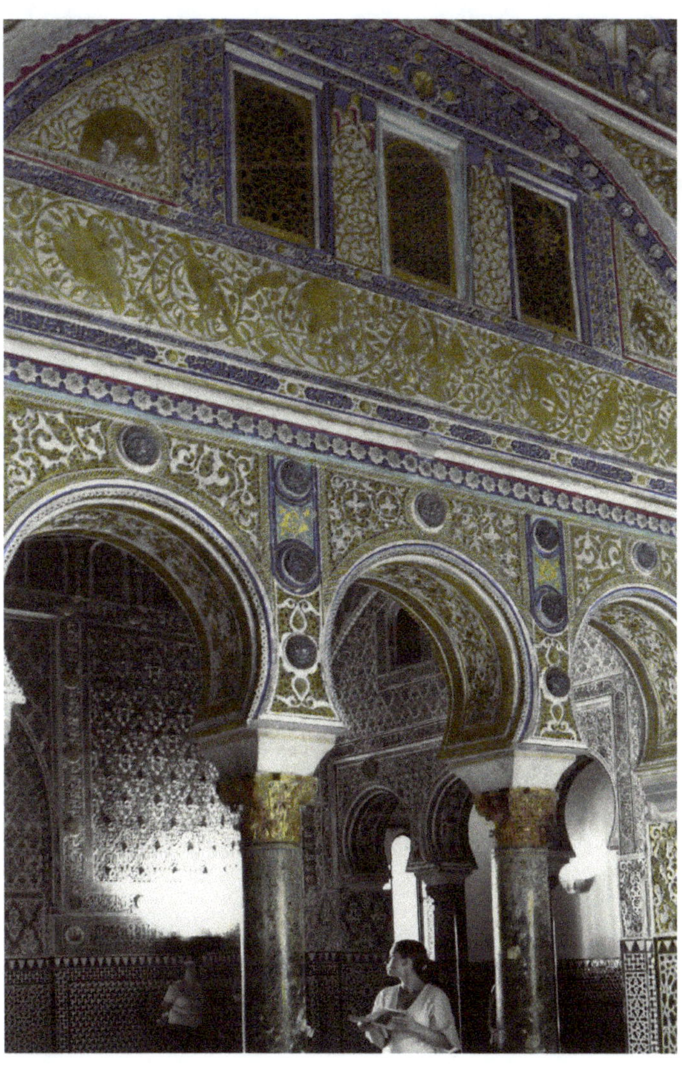

The Alcazar is much the same style as the Alhambra, on a smaller scale. It is decorated with plasterwork, tiling, coffered ceilings, gardens, and water in the form of irrigation channels, runnels, jets, ponds, and pools. The sky was clear and bright, lighting the rooms with the rich quality of light Spain is known for.

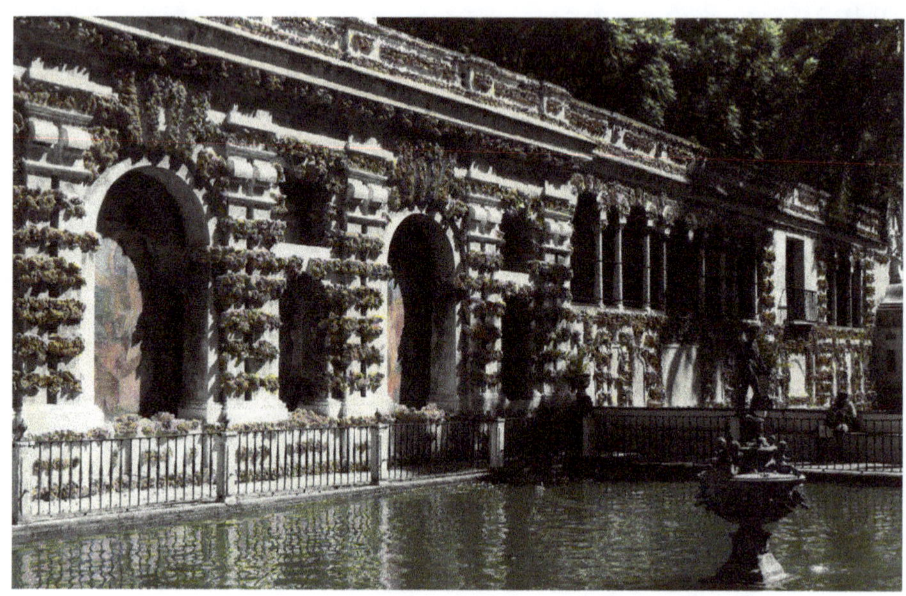

There were few tourists milling around, allowing us to enjoy the Alcazar immensely. The gardens were lovely; it was nice to be able to sit and enjoy them, something we hadn't found much time for so far.

There is a high wall that separates the garden from the city, creating a cozy space. Artists were set up throughout painting en plein air.

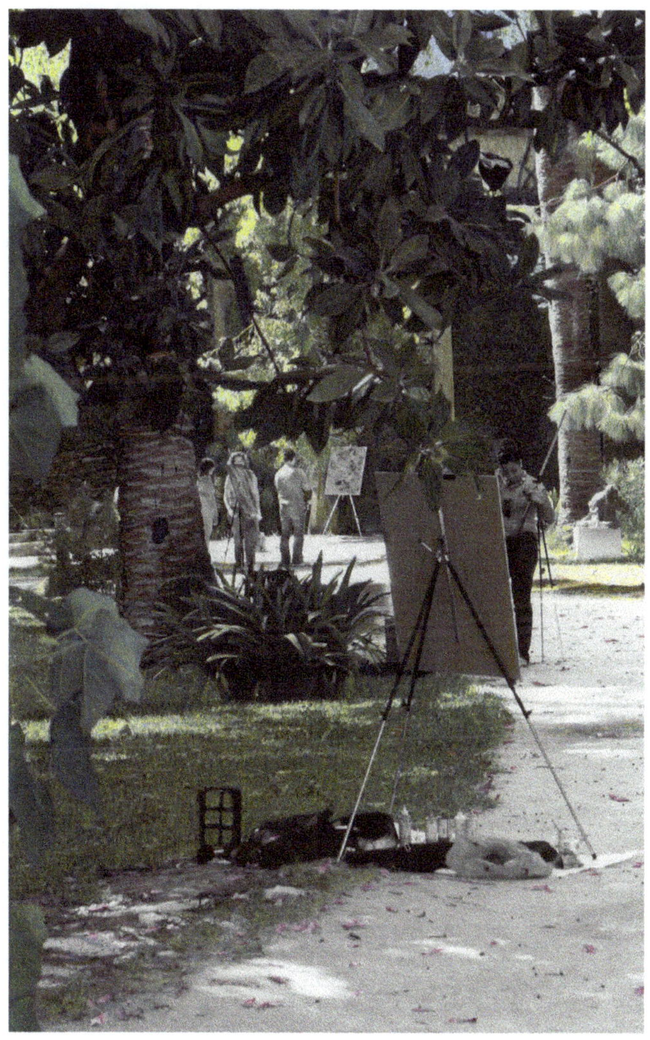

Since we'd seen most of the sights on our first visit, the only thing left to do in Seville was shopping! But of course it was siesta. The flamenco museum was nearby, and open, so we ducked in to check on the mantilla that I'd admired.

Department stores stay open through siesta so we wandered through the Ingles department store. It is huge with a wide variety of everything. I found the perfect gift for the guys, a winter coat wired for all the techno gear one might want to carry. Alas, it was 400 Euro. Then we discovered a floor called Opportunities; pay dirt! The whole floor was clearance merchandise. We bought some very Spanish styled clothes at great prices.

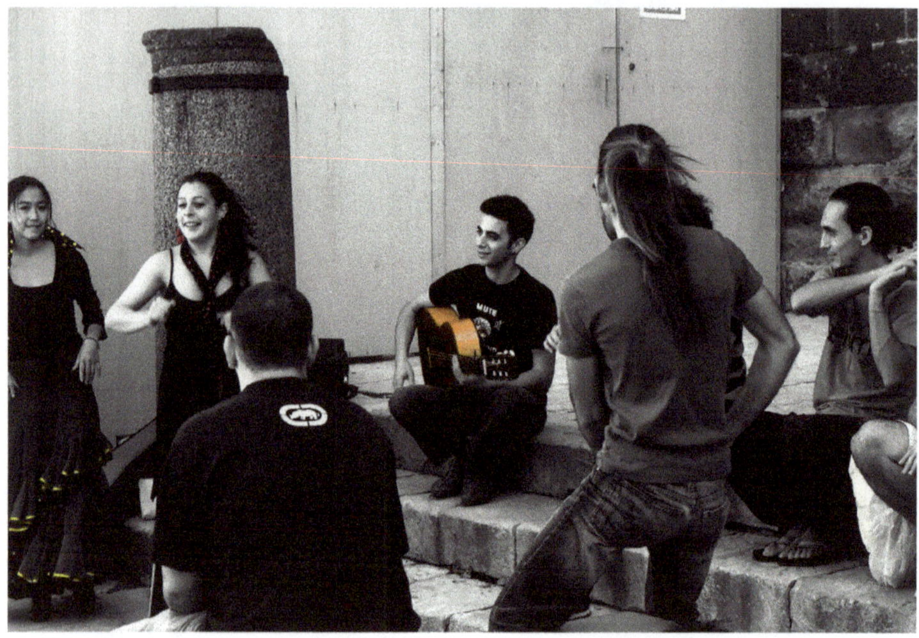

We had time to wander around Seville before heading back to Jerez. We found the cafe with the tiny sub sandwiches and had lunch. We ran into a group of flamenco students enjoying the day too.

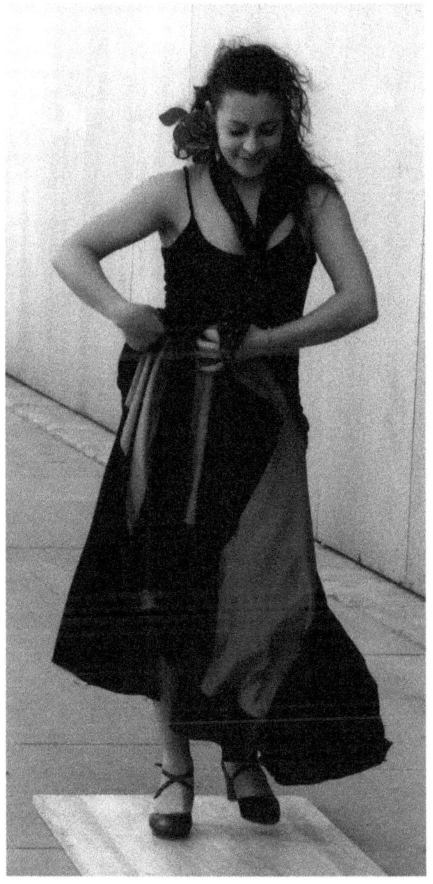

Returning to the car, I broke my resolution to avoid American chains; I needed coffee for the road and there sat a Starbucks. It wasn't as good as the local cafes but it was portable.

We arrived at the Jerez airport with plenty of time. Cleaning out the car and shuffling our gear was challenging. We began to realize that we needed another bag to get everything home. I hated giving up our car. Our flight to Barcelona left at 10:25 pm, Sarah was on a later flight; we met up with her at 12:30 am and arrived at our hotel at 2:00am and collapsed. The joys of traveling...

Barcelona: Salvador Dali in Figueres

We woke up starving! No food had been served on our flight so dinner had been a pastry and orange juice at midnight. We slept until 11:00; the breakfast buffet was over. While the girls were getting ready to go out, I wandered down to the lobby to get brochures. The breakfast buffet was still set up and nobody was around so I ducked in and got a cookie; I felt like a thief but boy was that cookie good.

October 12th is Columbus's birthday; a national holiday so most things are closed in Barcelona. We made plans to go to Figueres and visit the Dali Museum. Salvador Dali was a friend of Fredrico Garcia Lorca; he created the stage sets for one of Lorca's plays. While Dali isn't directly connected to flamenco, he is a part of the art movement that embraced

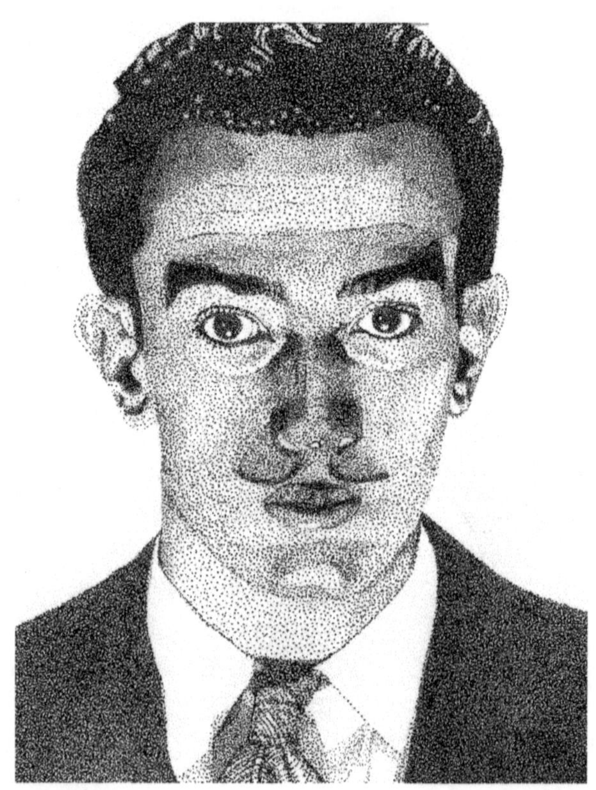

contemporary flamenco; installations and flamboyant theatre.

The concierge gave us directions to the train station but we ended up in the metro. On the wall by the metro map was a red information call box, what a great idea. In polite Spanish, Sarah inquired where the train station was. A disembodied voice replied "You are in the metro". I repeated the request in English with the same results so I got pushy. It took a bit of patience until we finally learned that the train station entrance was across the street!

We made our 1:30 train only to find out we were headed in the wrong direction! We back tracked and waited for the 2:30 train. We ducked in the little shop on the platform and

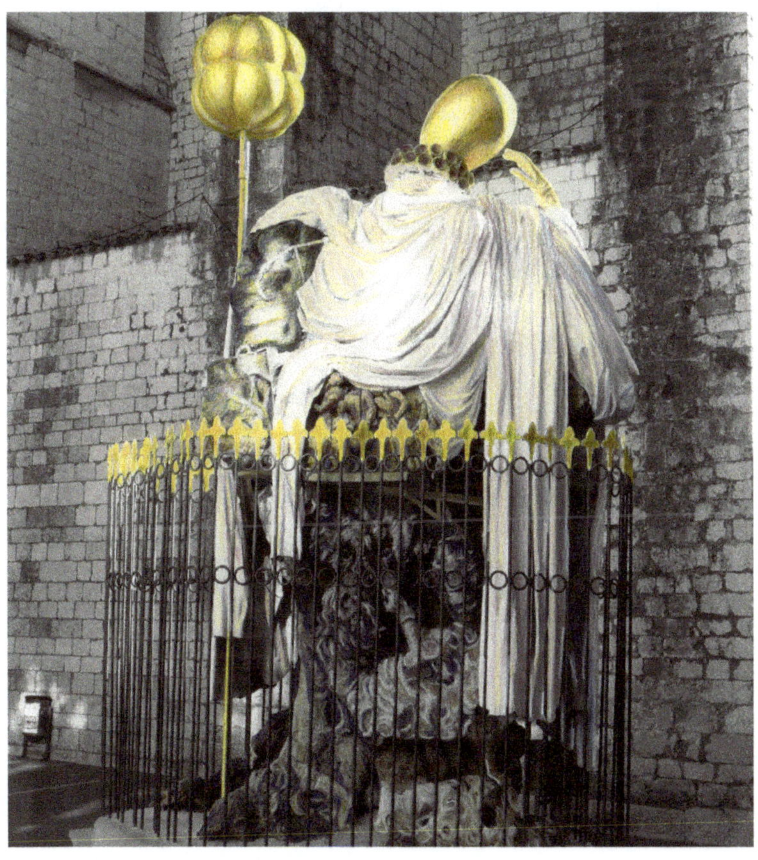

bought sandwiches, snacks, wine and a can of lemon soda. It was a very relaxing trip; it pays to go with the flow.

Salvador Dali went to Madrid University with Fredrico Garcia Lorca. They became good friends and both had a strong influence on the artistic experimentation reaching Spain and the art movement that embraced contemporary flamenco.

When I think of Salvador Dali, I think of melted watches, bizarre and fantastic images. For some reason, I think of his art as being large but most of his canvases are small and his attention to detail is remarkable. His wife, Gala's face is photo-realistic and a woven basket with a chunk of bread looked so 3-d it took a moment to convince myself it was flat. Dali's work is serious but to the casual observer it looks simply playful.

Lorca defined Dali's art as being "muse oriented with occasional angelic touches", no duende. Dali had very different ideas about the roots of creativity. He focused on the psychological and visual perception of symbols.

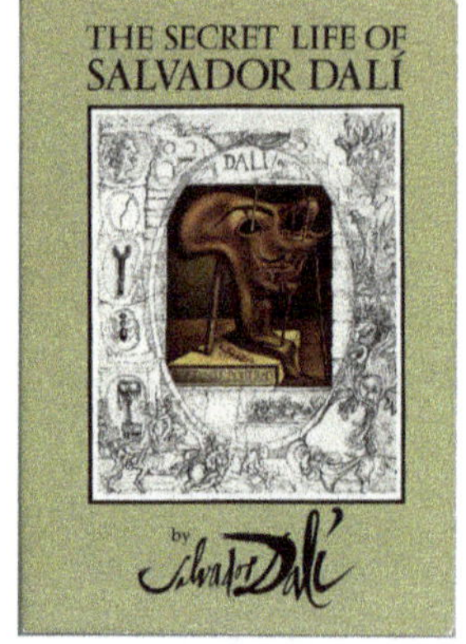

Dali published his autobiography in 1942, covering his life up through the 1930's. The New York Times rated it one of the most irresistible books of the year; the book shows Dali is crazy as a fox! There are questions as to the veracity of the book with George Orwell commenting that "no one can have all the vices but Dali seems to have as good an outfit of perversions as anyone could wish for."

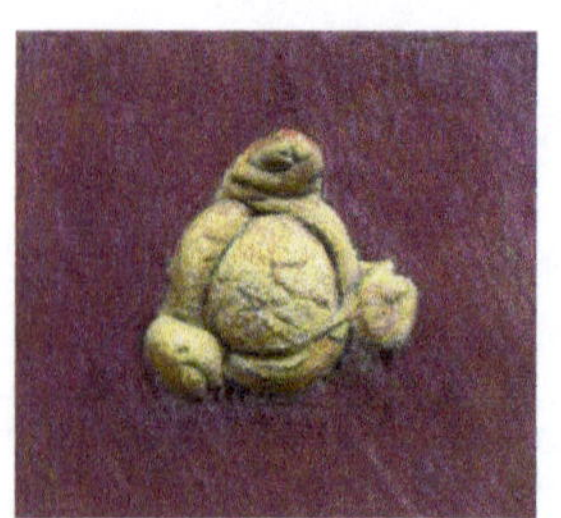

"Great art springs from courageous confrontations and reactions against overwhelming uncertainty, terror, fear, pity, and dread."

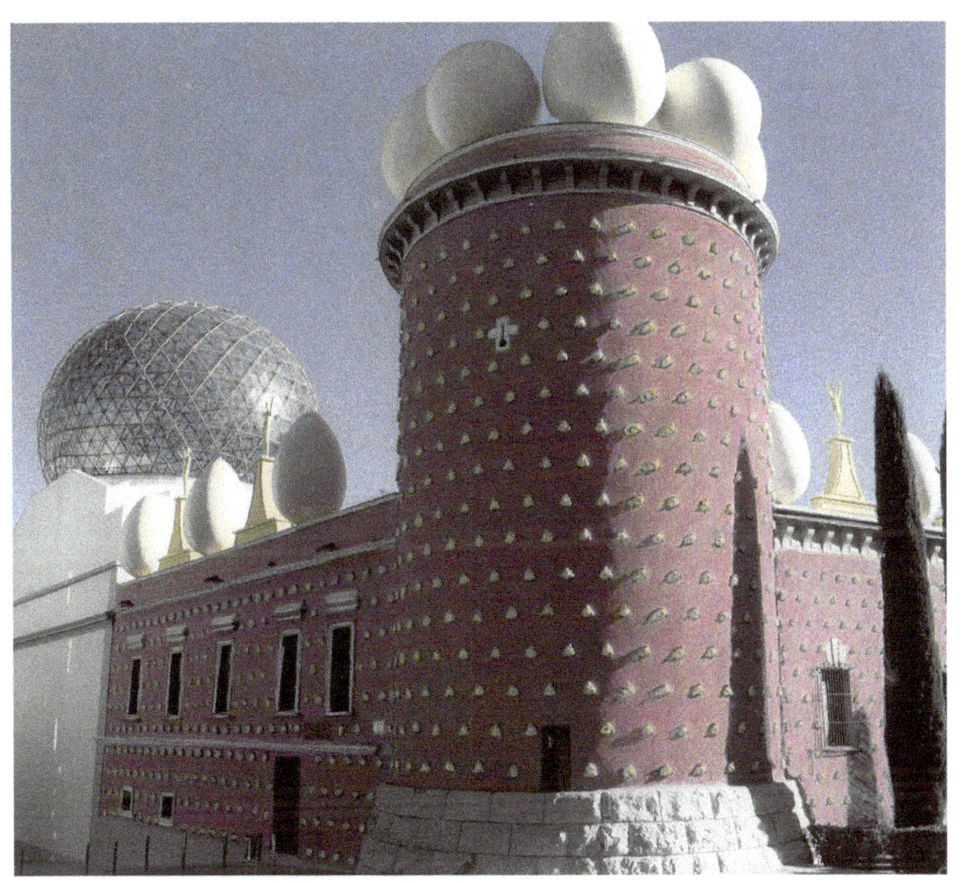

When Dali set out to build a museum to house his legacy
he decided that the most natural choice of location was his
home town of Figueres. He converted the town's theatre into
a visual experience.

The Dali Museum is not just a museum; it's a gigantic surrealist object.

It is the most fun museum I've ever been through; a surrealist fun house. Dali designed and oversaw his creation. The installations and art he chose to display give an intimate view of his personality from the Mae West living room to the Rainy Taxi which greets you in the foyer - his personal black Cadillac, his wife Gala's boat, and blue condoms that look like giant raindrops. You can insert coins to have it rain inside the car!

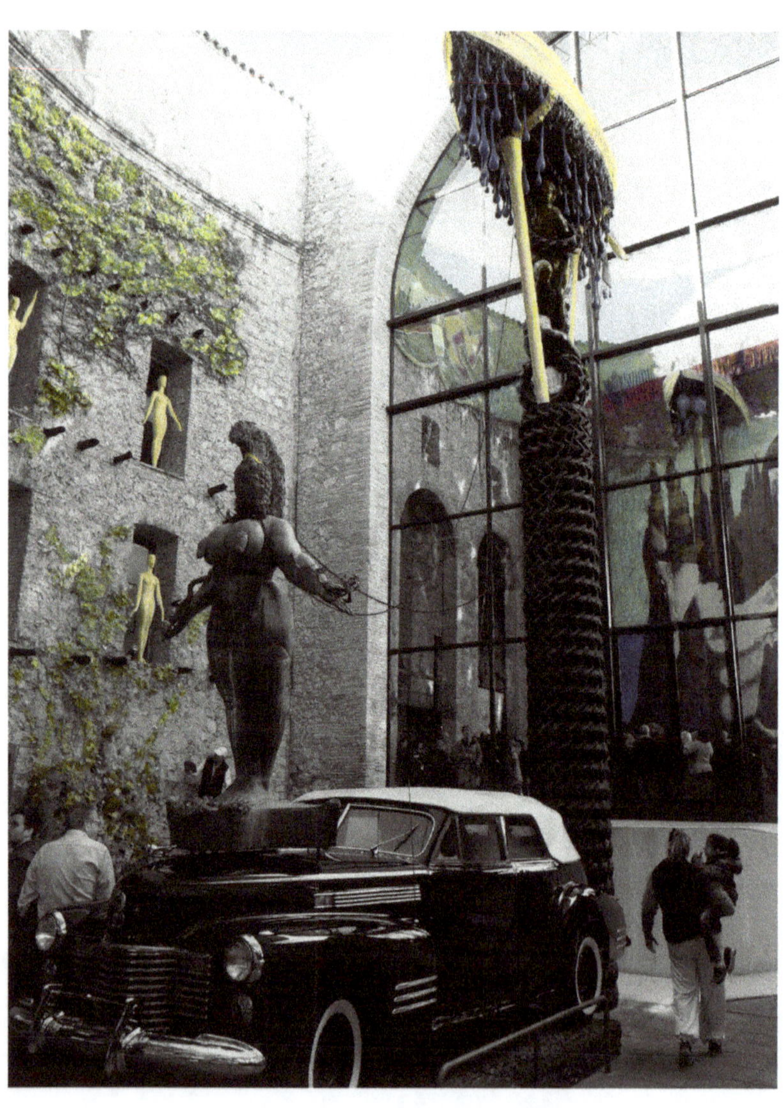

The museum houses the single largest and most diverse collection of his works. Not all of the art in the museum is by Dali; it contains his personal collection of contemporary artists too. Dali also chose to share the work that went into his creations before he began painting.

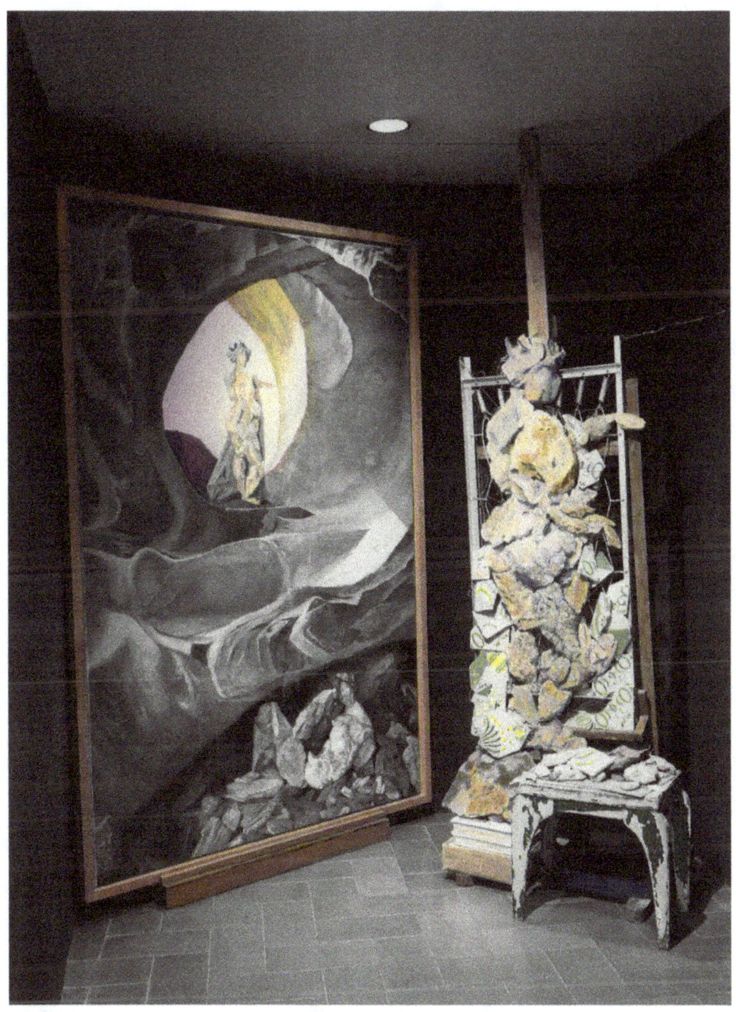

Of special note is the geodesic dome over the stage which is directly above the crypt where Salvador Dali is buried. The dome was designed to resemble a fly's eye.

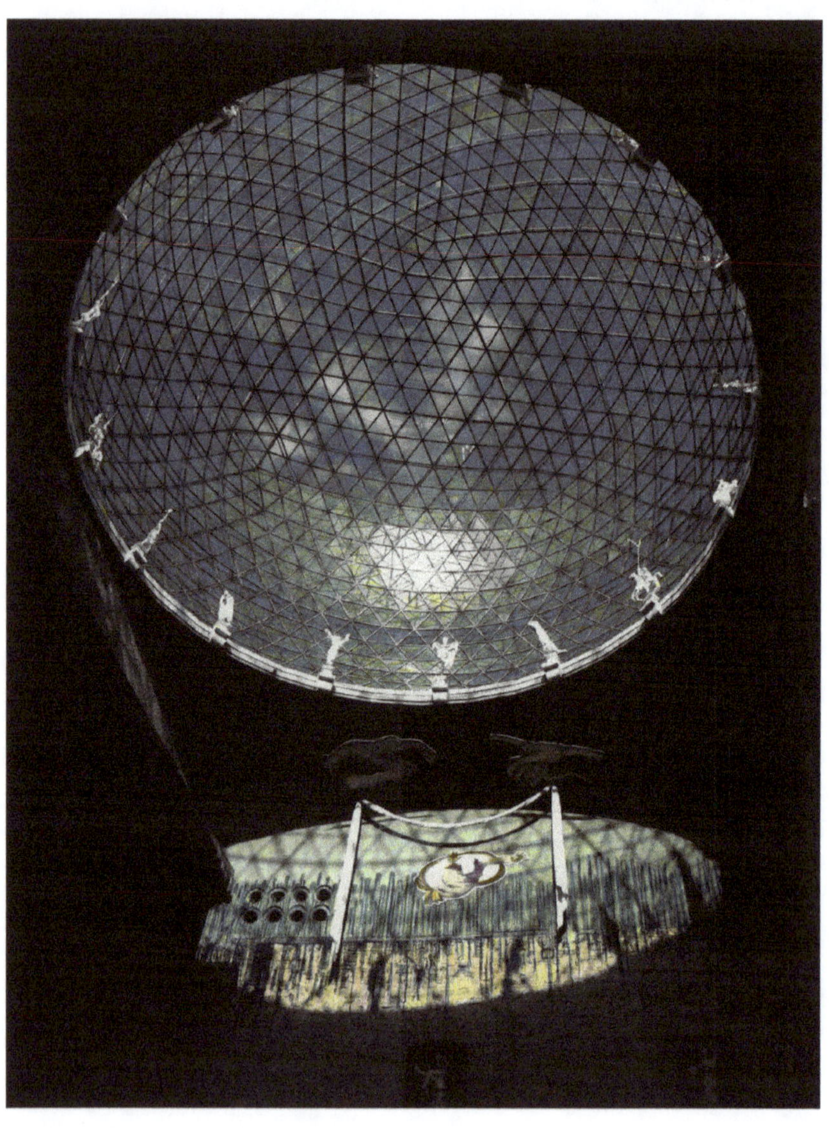

Antonio Gaudi

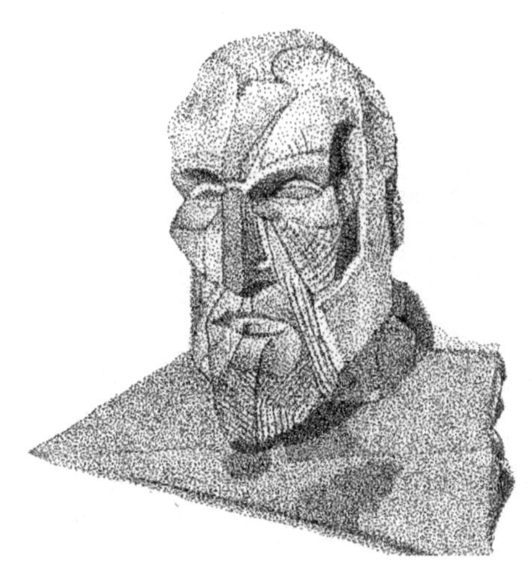

Barcelona is the home of
my favorite architect, An-
tonio Gaudi, and the mod-
erniste movement. Gaudi's
work is colorful and playful; it embodies his interest in shapes, color, the
geometry of nature, and
religion. All of his buildings are topped with an
off-center cross.

Lorca applied the theory of
duende to Gaudi's work as
the:

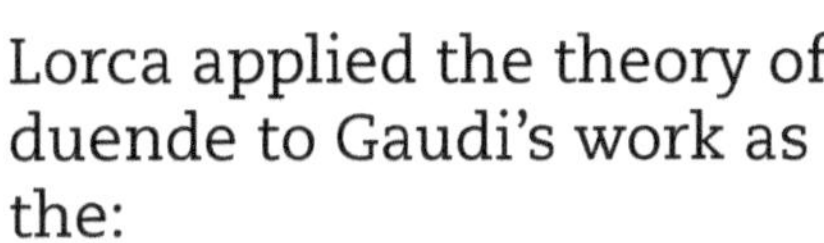

"radical change of all forms based on old structures which results in religious enthusiasm."

Like Dali, his space is distorted, imaginary.

I studied Casa Mila in art history; it's always fascinating to
see textbook entries in situ.

The facade of the building is very organic, curvy and round,
wavy or rippled; its roof line has been compared to ice
cream. The carefully sculpted iron rails on the balcony look
like a pile of used ribbon or adding machine tape about to
pour over the edge.

The iron grille at the entrance drew inspiration from spider
webs while the courtyard's soft colors and organic shapes
feel very aquatic. Stepping onto the roof, there is a feeling of being watched. I had never noticed the faces on the
chimneys and ventilation ducts.

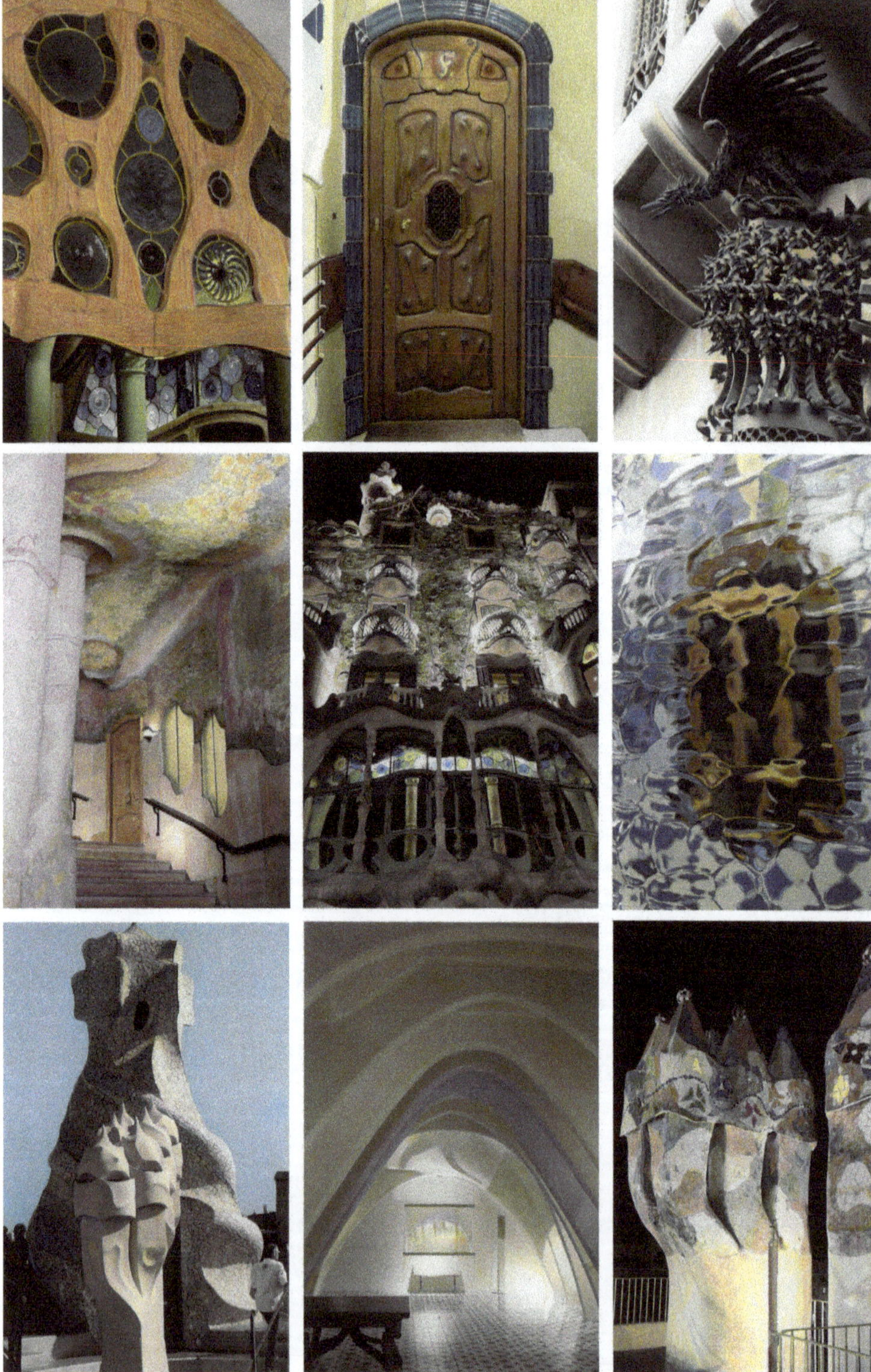

Close by is Casa Batllo whose exterior is more colorful; the glass and ceramic mosaics look like it was splatter painted. The roof of this building looks like a dragon's back; theory states that the rounded portion on the left side represents the lance of St George, patron saint of Catalonia.

The interior is all about the sea; the tile around the elevator shaft is seen through wavy glass which enhances the feeling of water. Casa Batllo was built using a method referred to as beehive construction, very much like the Alhambra.

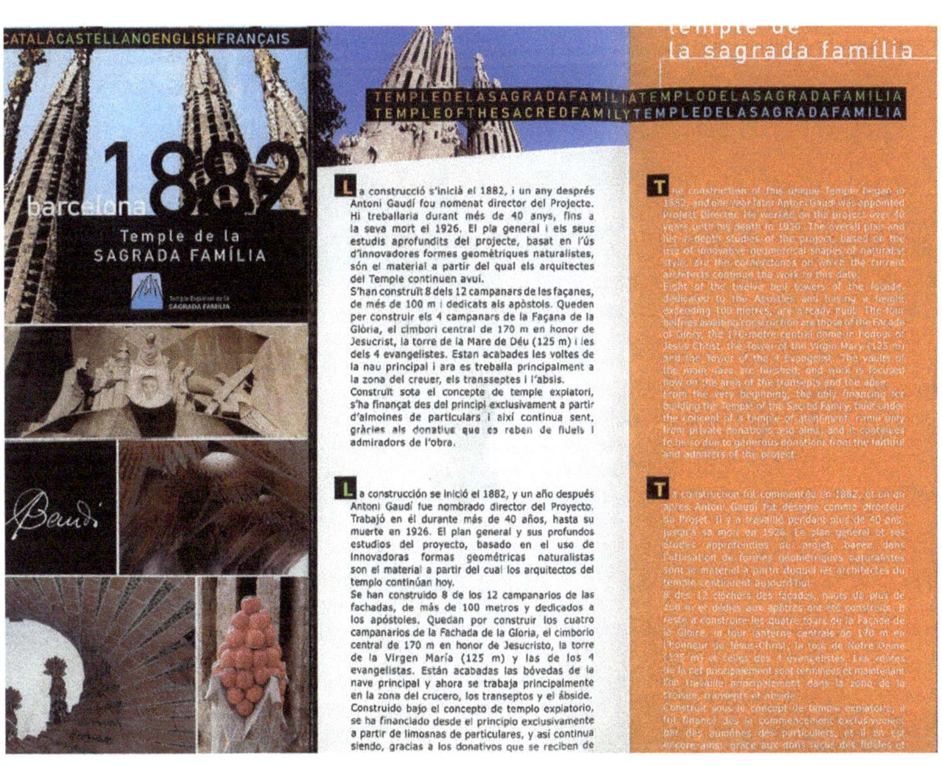

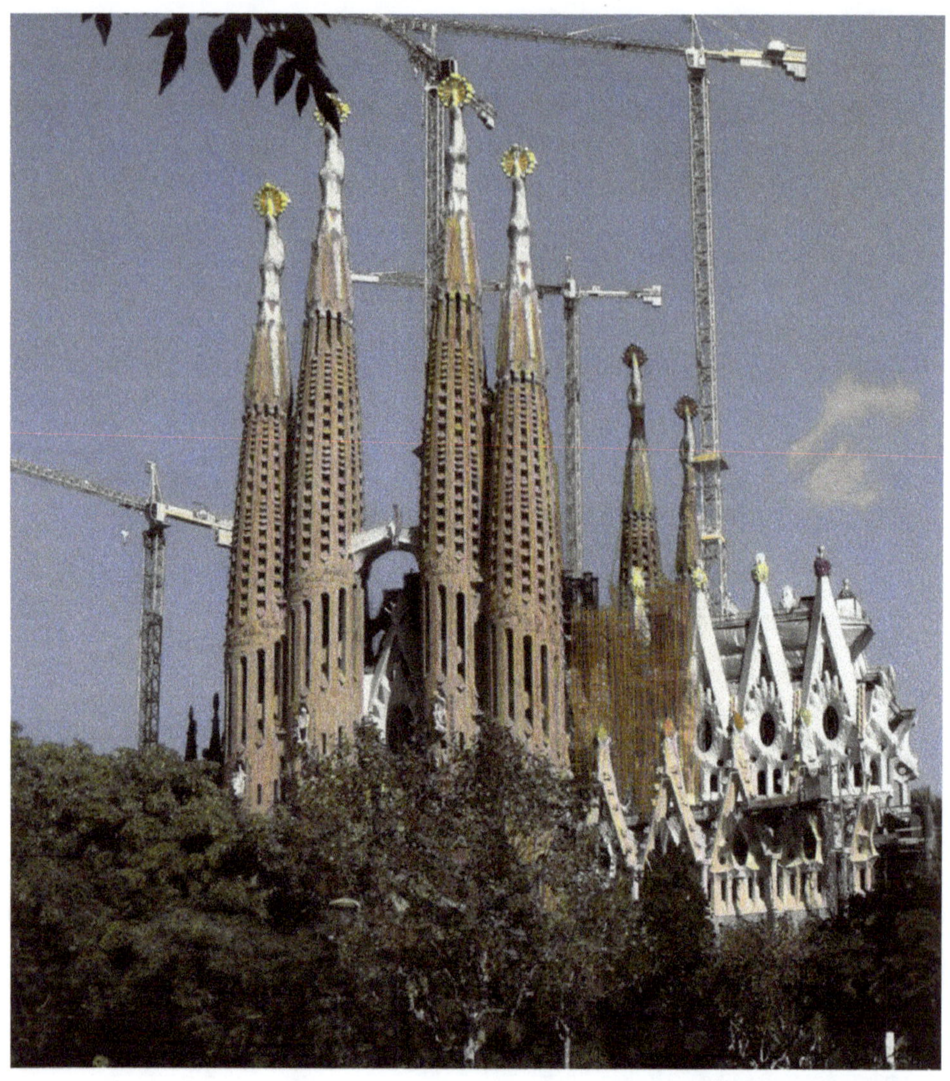

Hands down, Gaudi's most wonderful creation is the Sagrada Familia, the most visited monument in Spain. Construction was begun in 1882 and continues today, completely funded by donations.

At the time of our visit, the interior was full of construction material, leaving only a path around the circumference. It was interesting to see the forms that will be used to create the interior and inspired us to imagine how the light from the stained glass windows will fall.

When I returned 10 years later, the interior was bathed with color. A wonderful experience!

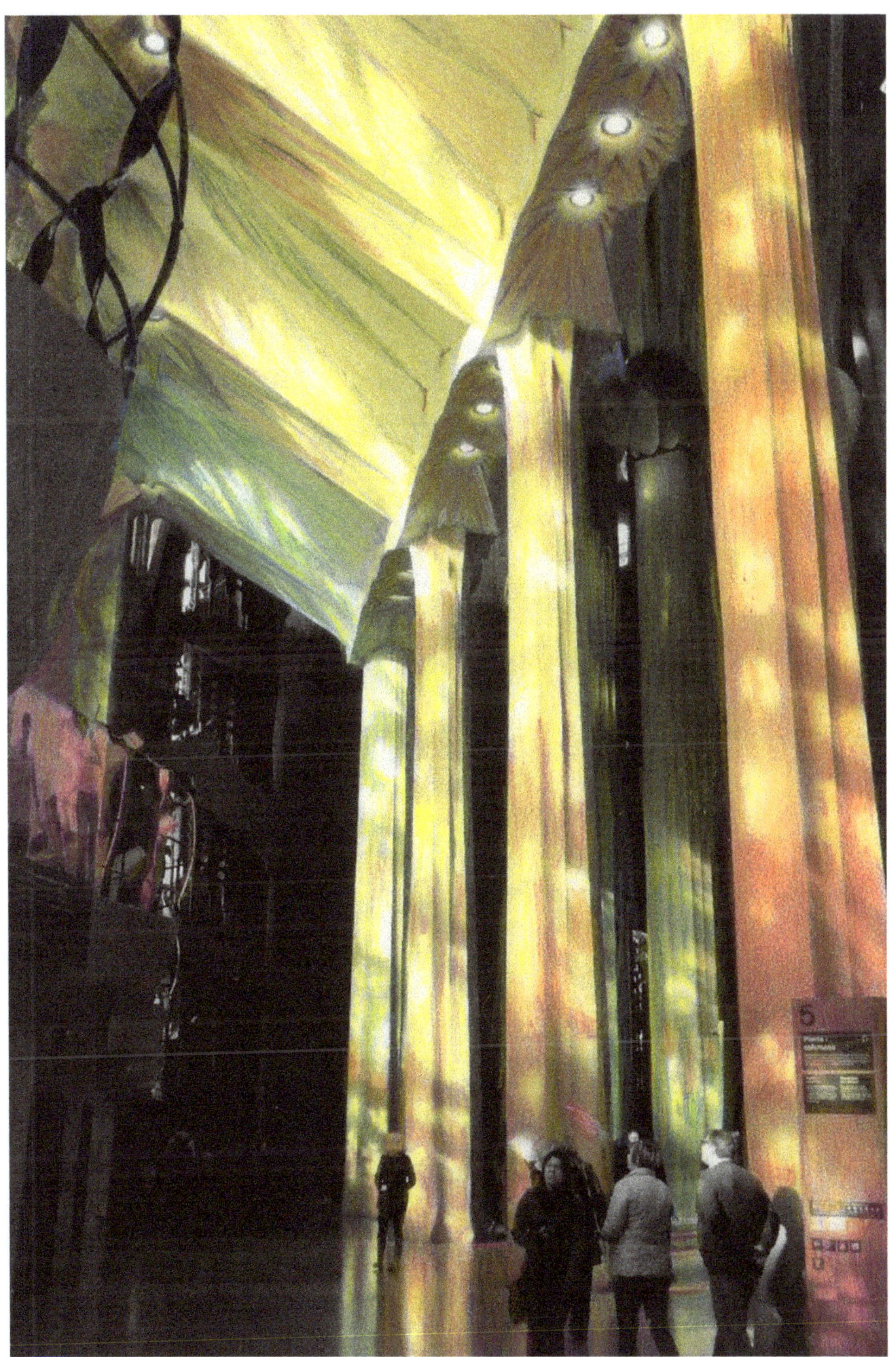

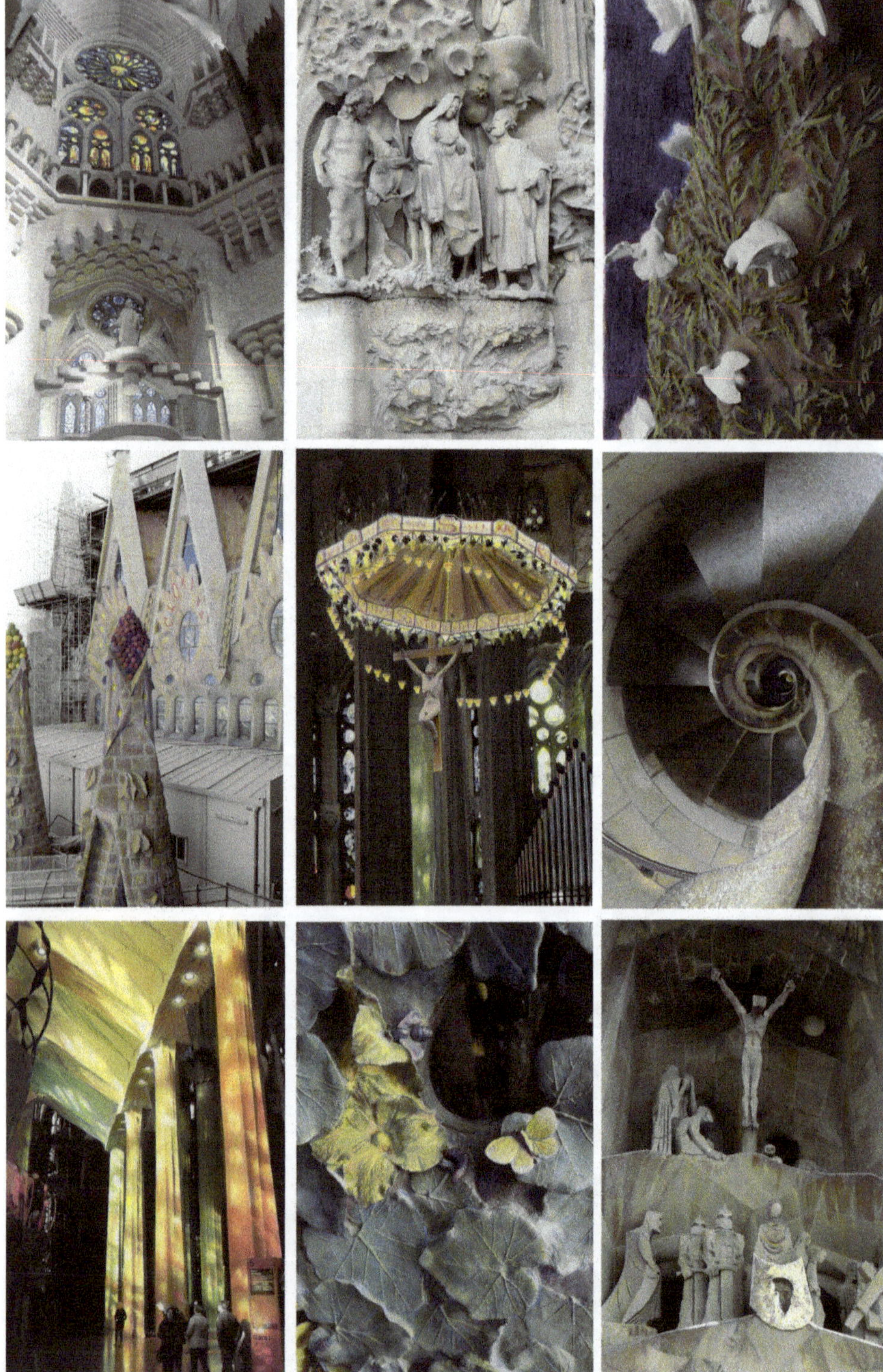

Two of the exterior facades are complete, the Nativity Façade and the Passion Façade. The figures on the Nativity Façade are very traditional in appearance, the whole face is highly decorated and there are many symbols portrayed through nature. The Passion Façade is a stark contrast. It is bare of decoration, the sides are angular and flat, the figures carved with harsh straight lines.

The church was consecrated by Pope Benedict XVI in 2010; video of the event was striking. In 2015, I was able to return to Barcelona and revisit the Sagrada Familia. It is the most beautiful church that I have ever seen! The light through the stained glass takes your breath away. I didn't want to leave. Construction is projected to be complete in 2026, the centenary of Gaudi's death – I plan to return!

Dali wrote in his autobiography that when Lorca saw the Nativity Façade, he:

"claimed to hear the 'griterio' – a cacophony of shouts that rose stridently to the top of the cathedral, creating such tension in him that it became unbearable. There is the proof of Gaudi's genius, he appeals to all our senses and created the imagination of the senses."

Imagine what he would say today!

In the basement of the church is a small museum filled with construction models, photographs, plans, and decorative objects. It provides information and history of the church's construction as well as Gaudi's life and some of his other projects. It explained the Christmas decorations! Gaudi hung chain to create the shapes he used for arches.

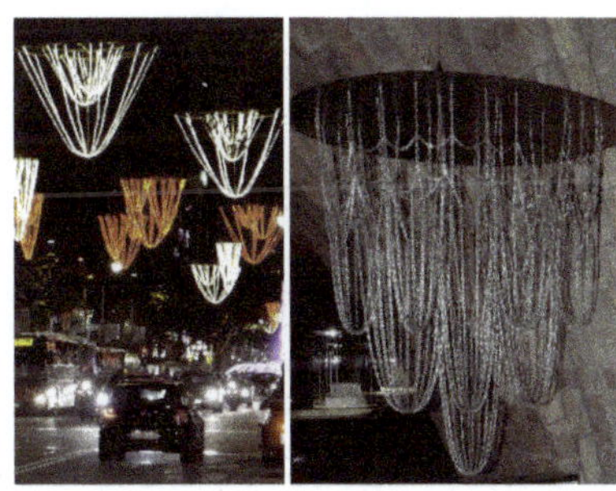

Another must see is Parc Guell, a public park designed by Gaudi, built between 1900 and 1914. The area is high above the city and was designed to provide a peaceful space to escape the pollution and busyness of the city.

The area was originally a planned neighborhood for the well off families of Barcelona in the early 1900s. The developer, Eusebi Guell, hired Gaudi to help him create his vision but due to the exclusive nature of the estate and the lack of proper transportation, the project was not viable. Gaudi worked on the park until 1914; after his death, Barcelona City Council purchased the land from Guell's heirs in 1922. It opened as a public park four years later. It is a much treasured leisure area for the people of Barcelona; UNESCO declared it a Cultural Heritage of Humanity in 1984.

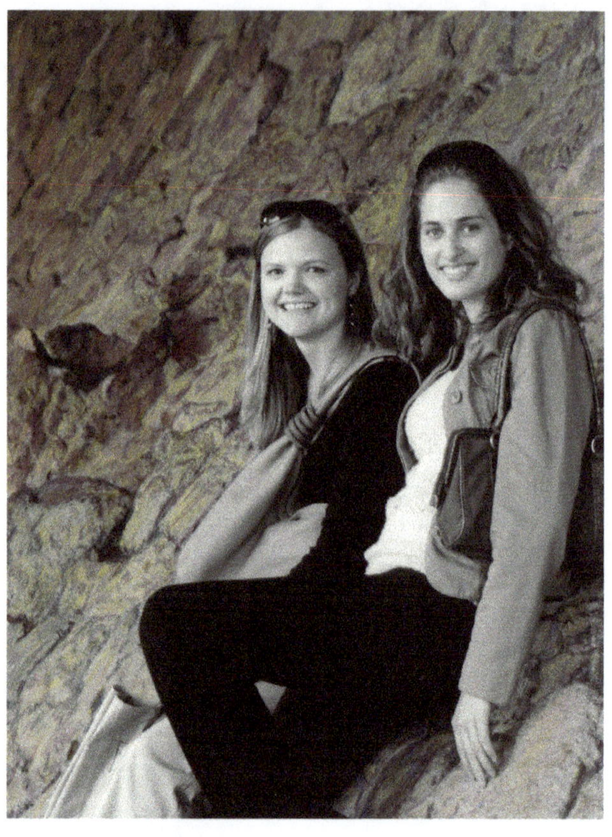

The best place in the park is the main terrace that has a mosaic bench that undulates around the perimeter, looking like a sea serpent while providing a wonderful social atmosphere. And in keeping with Gaudi's love of dragons, the main entrance boasts 'el drac', a colorful mosaic salamander fountain which has become the icon of the park. The park was also a setting for a shoot of America's Next Top Model. We all have our priorities.

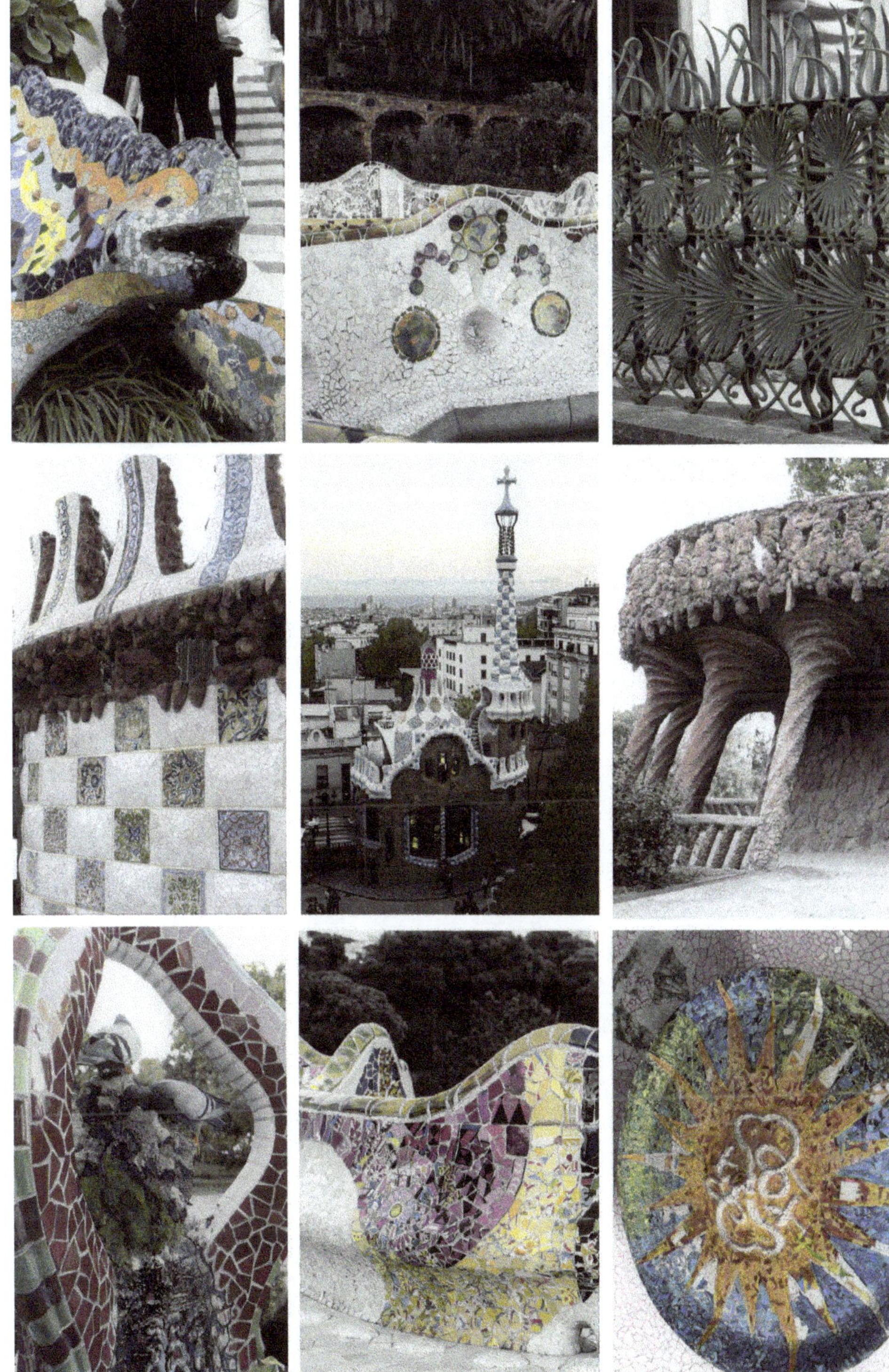

Modernista Architecture

Gaudi is not the only architect of renown in Barcelona. The central part of the city is full of interesting and unique buildings, light fixtures, park benches and even sidewalks thanks to the Catalan Renaissance.

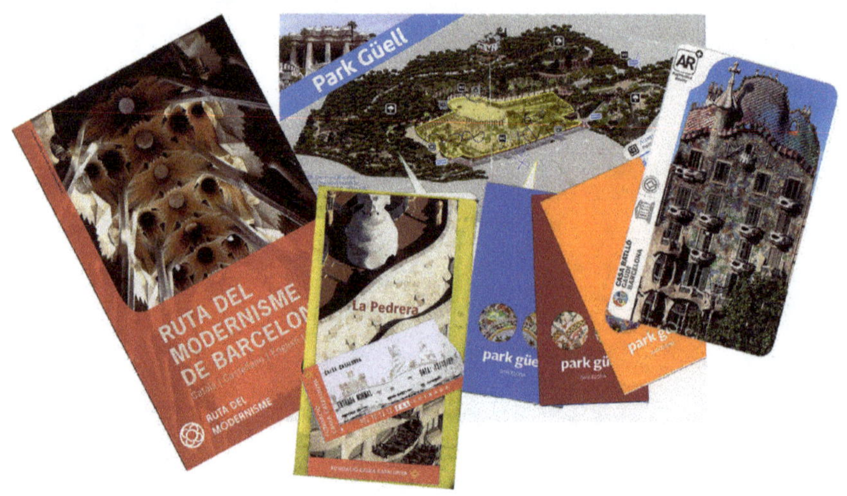

Catalonia has been an independent region off and on through the centuries with its own language and customs. In the mid-1800s, the region was emerging from 150 years of oppression, and the Catalonians were seeking a way to re-establish its identity. With their growing wealth and power, they were looking for a way to invigorate their community to become as progressive as Europe's leading countries. Thus the Catalan Renaissance was born.

Modernisme, a wide-scale movement across all the arts, became the vehicle for change and with rapid urban growth, architecture was at the forefront. Barcelona is the capital of Catalonia so it was the natural center of the movement. Its preeminent architects, Montaner, Cadalfach, and Gaudi created a unique style that reflected the Catalan soul. Today there are still more than 2000 examples that attest to the popularity of the style these men created.

Beginning in the 1850s, Barcelona expanded out from Old Town to accommodate the growth and the Eixample was born. This large area became the playground of the Modernista architects. Wealthy aristocrats became patrons of the Modernista architects and they were given much freedom in their creations. The most elite street in the area is Passeig de Gracia where, in one block, you can see masterpieces by Montaner, Cadalfach, and Gaudi side by side; this block is called the Block of Discord.

Everywhere you look, you will see something interesting. The ordinary flats throughout the area are adorned with Modernista style balconies, ironwork, ornamental door-knockers, ceramic plaques, Arabic style crenelations, and so much more!

Modernista architecture is characterized by curves, organic and botanical shapes, rich ornamentation, bright colors, asymmetrical shapes, and symbolism which includes traditional Catalan rural life and mythology along with Arabic patterns and decorations. It also stands apart due to the materials and construction methods used including ceramic work on the facade, creative brick work and decorative ironwork. The results are often absurdly over-the-top but they are bright, colorful, and human. When I was designing my house, I was inspired to implement a playful use of color and space; the mosaics are coming!

If you are interested in the modernisme movement and get to visit Barcelona, stop by the Modernista Society. They have a great book that gives you historical information on all the properties; laid out in the order that they appear on the accompanying map.

The Modernista Society is in a large office building, just off Las Ramblas, down near the waterfront. They must not get many visitors because they seemed surprised to see us. The Modernista route came about as a result of an endeavor of the city council of Barcelona to protect its Modernista heritage. This project is a collective project involving all the entities directly related to Barcelona's Modernista heritage, incorporating three decades of research, rigorous restoration, careful maintenance, and cultural management. Profits from the sale of the book are devoted to the preservation and promotion of Barcelona's Modernista architecture.

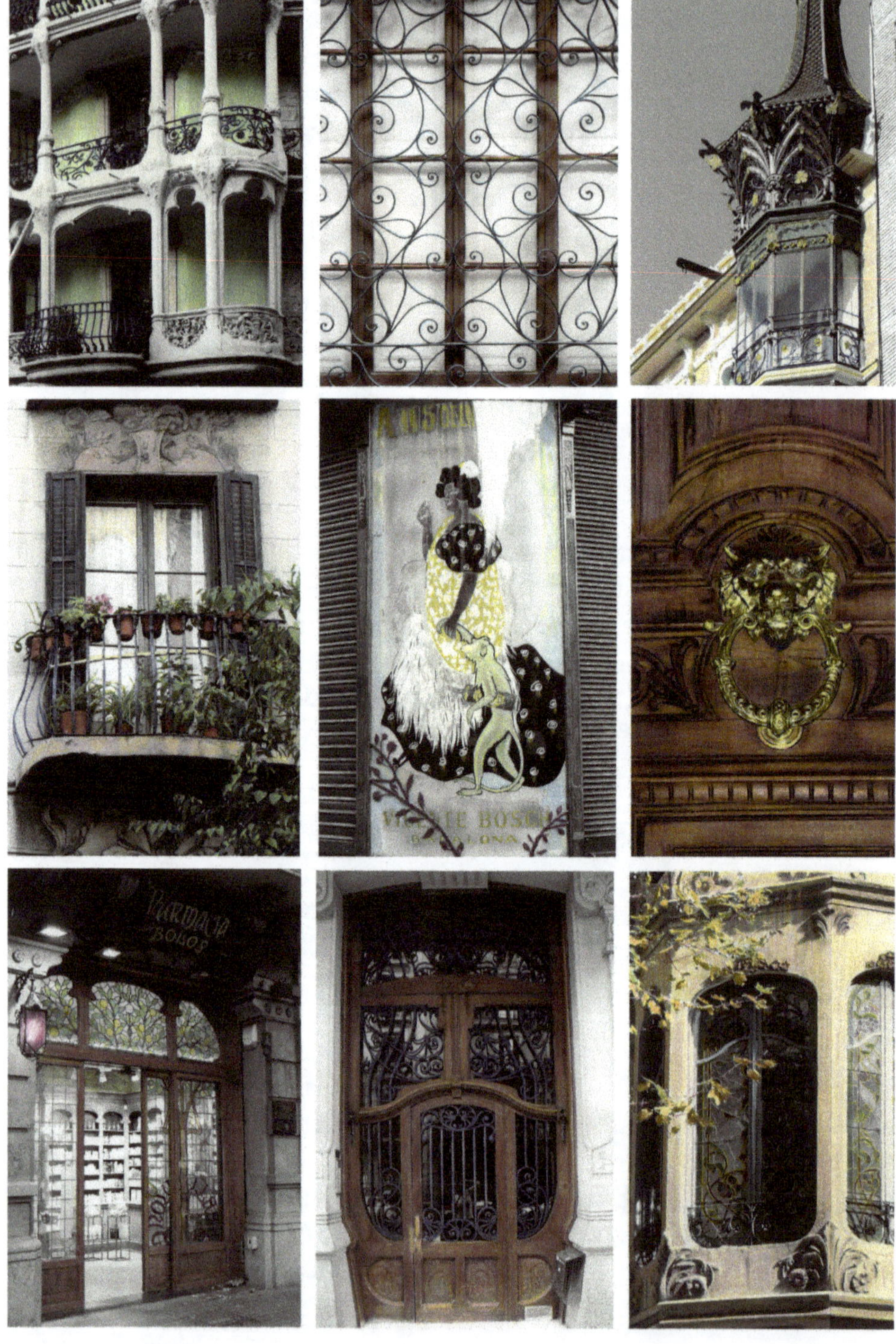

Flamenco arrived in Barcelona at the same time as the Modernista movement. Barcelona's money attracted good theaters and cafe cantantes, flamenco followed. In short time, flamenco became integrated into Catatonian society. Many famous flamenco performers are from this area including Carmen Amaya who was from Somorrostro Shanty town in Barcelona.

Some of the neighborhoods are a maze of streets that meander in all directions making it easy to get turned around. If you see something you like, better stop because you might never find it again! We were looking for espadrilles and stumbled on this fun shop. And of course, the buildings were amazing!

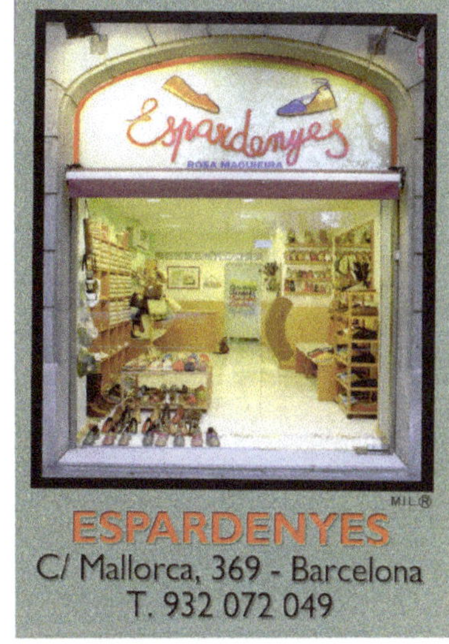

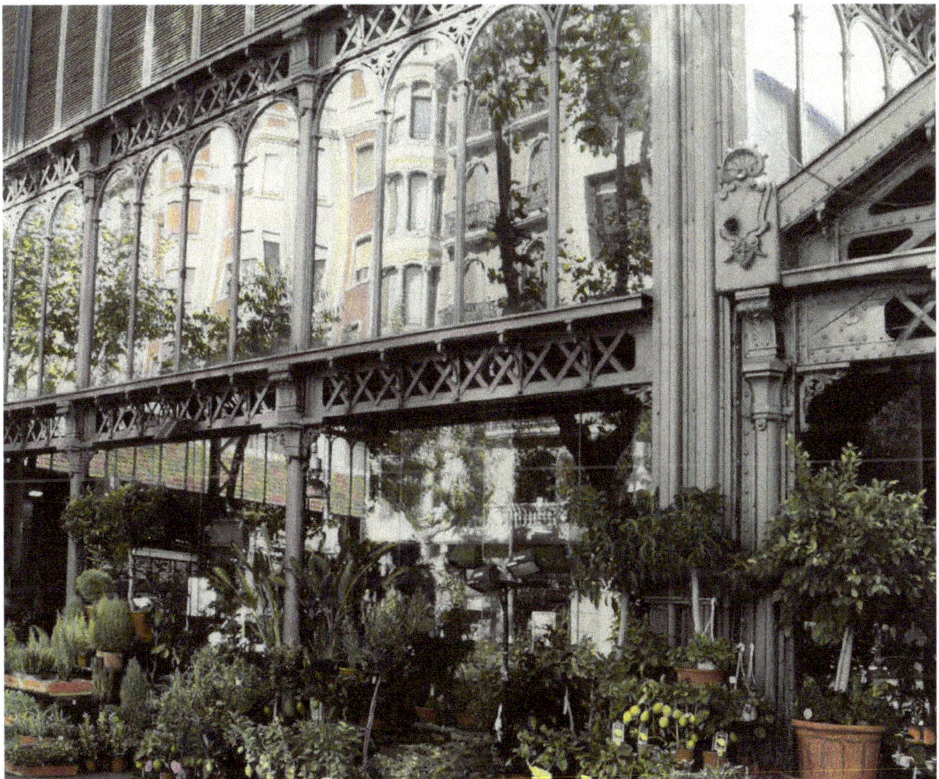

Winding down after a long day, we decided to make dinner simple, we ate at Hard Rock. We've been listening to John Grisham's *Playing for Pizza* which had us craving Italian food! It was the best meal of the trip!

We wandered Las Ramblas after dinner which is famous for shopping and people watching. La Rambla is the main street; it has a large tree-lined pedestrian walkway in the median filled with stalls, restaurants, entertainers, pick-pockets and ladies of the night. Best to beware of your surroundings but don't miss it – it's a wonderful adventure.

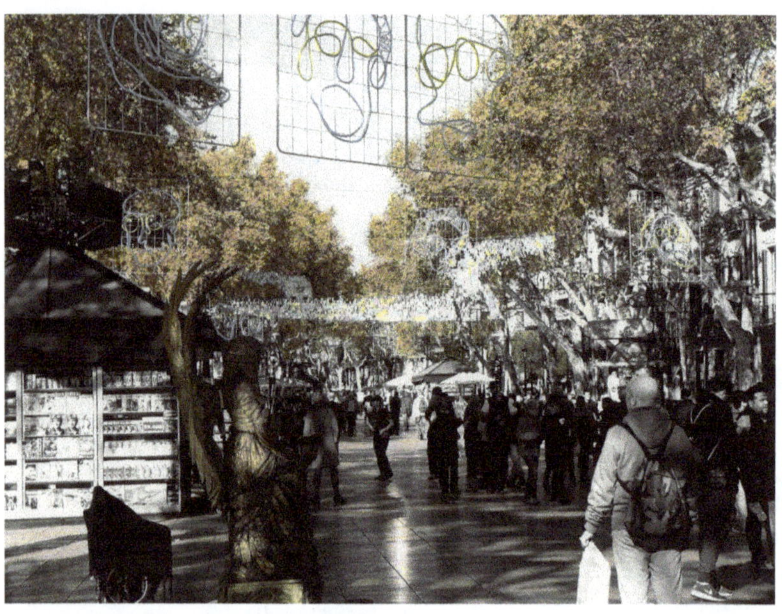

Rick Steves lays out several walking tours of the area; the one that caught my fancy was the Sweet Tour - chocolate shops! Of all of the chocolate boutiques, only one was open late. The chocolate seemed watered down and thickened with cornstarch; not very good so I guess this means we'll just have to try this again!

Madrid

Madrid has a different feel to it. There are old buildings and monuments but something is different. Wide streets with lots of traffic take over the city center similar to Paris or Milan. The cities we've visited seem to confine traffic to the perimeter of the city center, leaving the pedestrian friendly atmosphere intact. Once you enter into that protective haven you leave modernity and its problems. Madrid definitely feels more modern.

Our hotel turned out to be a room in a hostel. The main hostel was full so we were ushered across the street and down an alley that reeked of urine, to a very desolate looking facade. It didn't get much better once you got inside. The hostel is on the third floor of the building. There is a wide marble staircase that spirals upward around a caged elevator. The elevator only had enough room for the luggage which would have been okay but it wouldn't budge without pressing the button to go up from the inside. I don't know how I got the job; I climbed inside and straddled the bags for the ride up and unceremoniously fell out when the door opened. I was ready to head elsewhere, but the price was right and the hostel is situated between the art museums and the palace near the Plaza Mayor and shopping.

This area is known as the Golden Triangle of Art; it is one of the most important concentrations of art in the world. Our room was sparse but spacey, the mattress firm and the bathroom, full service. The place was immaculate, there's free internet and a vibrant, youthful feel. Young people live here while they go to school or work in addition to the backpackers so there are very strict rules especially about noise. We felt comfortable right away.

It's Sunday afternoon and we had two museums to visit and a bullfight to attend!

Our first museum is the Thyssen-Bornemisza Family's Collection housed in the Palace of Villahermosa. The museum is relatively new; it was opened in 1992 to house the collection of Baron and Baroness Thyssen-Bornemisza de Kaszon. The relocation of their collection was the largest move of art in the history of the 20th century.

The collection dates back 3 generations, beginning with August Thyssen. In 1910 he commissioned Rodin to create seven pieces, four are in the current collection. His son, Heinrich, began exhibiting the family collection to the public in 1930, opening a gallery in his Villa Favorita in Lugano in 1936.

"A painter does not work for the eyes of a single man. My legacy as a collector is to share, and I can only return this gift by making it possible for as many people to see his work as possible and to understand the talent of the artist."

It is an interesting collection of minor works by major artists and major works by minor artists from the 17th century to the 20th. The Baroness Carmen Cervera, Baron Hans Heinrich's wife, contributed 429 works to the collection. Her collection emphasizes 19th and early 20th century with a special emphasis on Spanish artists.

I had never heard of any of the minor artists, they haven't made it into the art history texts, but their work is beautiful and often their style is similar to the more famous painters.

Makes you wonder what other overlooked artists are out there. The Thyssen-Bornemisza is a small collection, very vibrant and uplifting.

The Prado, which was established in 1819, is a small museum with a fantastic collection. It can display around 1300 works from its over 22,000 pieces. It is one of the most visited places in the world and one of the greatest art museums in the world. Michener gives a great history of the building and its renovation in his book *Iberia*.

We saw Ruben's Three Graces, Velazquez's Minos, multiple masterpieces by Caravaggio, Titian, Poussin, Goya, El Greco and my favorite, Hieronymus Bosch's The World of Earthly Delights.

I'm always intrigued when I see how writers and artists of earlier centuries portray a world that is so familiar; Bosch's painting could just as easily have been about the 21st Century.

It was also interesting to see cheerful pieces by Goya and El Greco; art history dwells on their dark, depressing, historical pieces. I could have spent hours in the Prado absorbing the Masters but the bullfight started at 5:00.

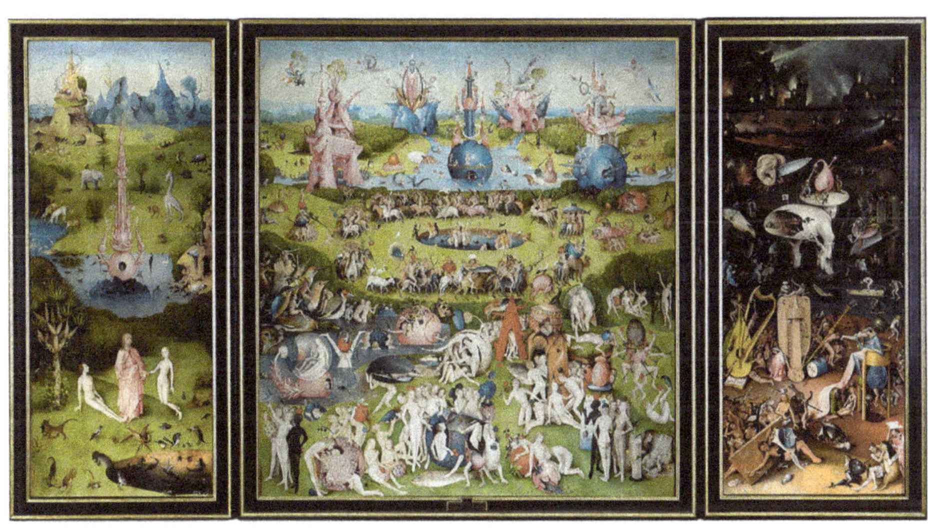

The Bullfight

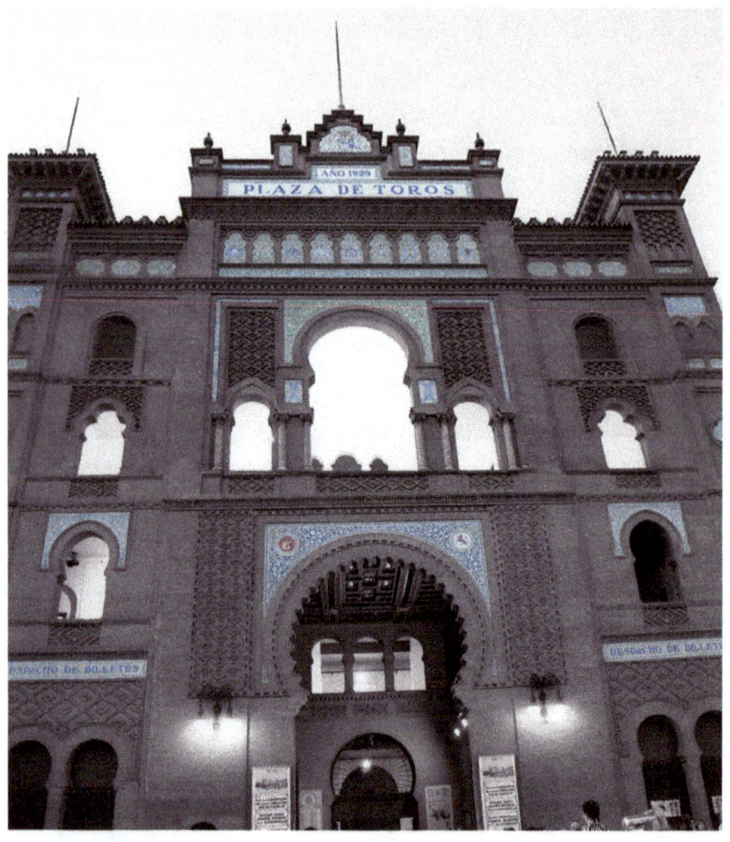

The Palza Toros Las Ventas Bullring, one of the largest in the world, was built in 1931. It's 196' in diameter and holds 23,798 fans; it is one of the most important arenas in the world. The complex was constructed using hand-painted tiles in the Neo-mudejar style of 12th century Arabic Moors.

The complex houses an important bullfight museum, two chapels - one devoted to the Virgen de Guadalupe (Mexico) and the other one devoted to the Virgen de la Paloma (Madrid), an infirmary with the latest technology and two operating theatres.

Bullfighting isn't for everyone. We weren't sure we'd make it through the first bull! As I noted before, bullfighting has close ties to flamenco, ancient history and religious iconography and is a big part of Spanish culture. Some of the best matadors are/were of gypsy decent so I had to go!

I read Hemingway's *Death in the Afternoon* which is a wonderful history of the bullfight with a thorough explanation of the importance of each part or ritual. And, according to Hemingway, Madrid is the best place to see your first fight and it should be a novillada.

Just so happened that the only bullfight to take place while we were in Spain was a novillada and it was in Madrid. I was psyched! I was afraid that I would be going alone but curiosity got the better of the girls and they consented to go with me. I thought it was a great way to celebrate Liz's birthday.

I saw my first bull fight on closed circuit TV because I'd stopped by the bathroom and the fight started before I could get inside the arena. I'm not sure why it mattered, all the action was far away; no way would I have distracted that bull. But rules are rules…and there was the language barrier!

Bullfights are held in the afternoon. It was a beautiful day. The crowd was small, perhaps because it was a novillada fight. We had cheap seats. Wish I'd known that the cheap seats were in the sun; turned out all the action takes place on the shady side where the officials sit. I discovered that I

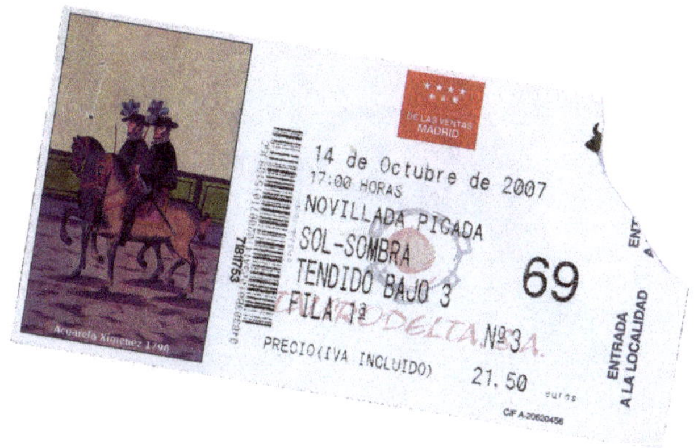

had left my heavy telephoto lens at the hostel so I was very disappointed when none of the action happened close by. Luckily, since it wasn't crowded, no one seemed to mind my going down closer to the bullring to take pictures; all was not lost.

The Corrida

Bullfighting is a sport full of rituals; even without Hemingway's dissertation, the rituals were easy to figure out. The fight proceeds in stages; a brass band marks the shift to the next stage. There are three matadors and six bulls that make up a corrida; each fight takes 20 minutes.

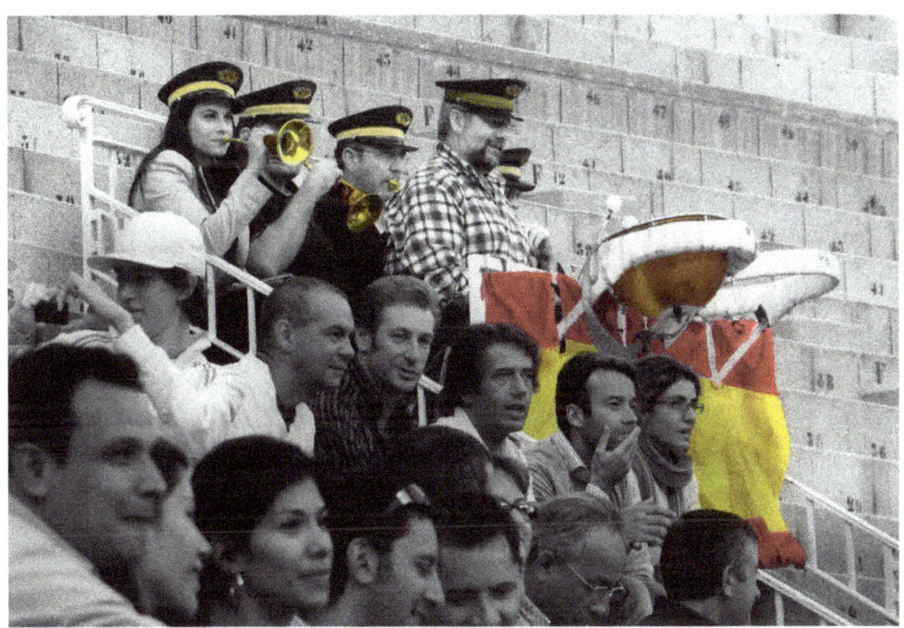

Stage 1: Tercio de Varas (third of lances)

Before a matador steps into the ring, he gets a preview of how the bull will perform. His group of banderilleros come out and take the bull through a series of passes letting him see which side the bull passes con, how it charges and how ferocious it is. If the bull meets the matador's approval, the picadors come out with their varas (lances). If the matador rejects the bull, another bull is sent out and put through the paces.

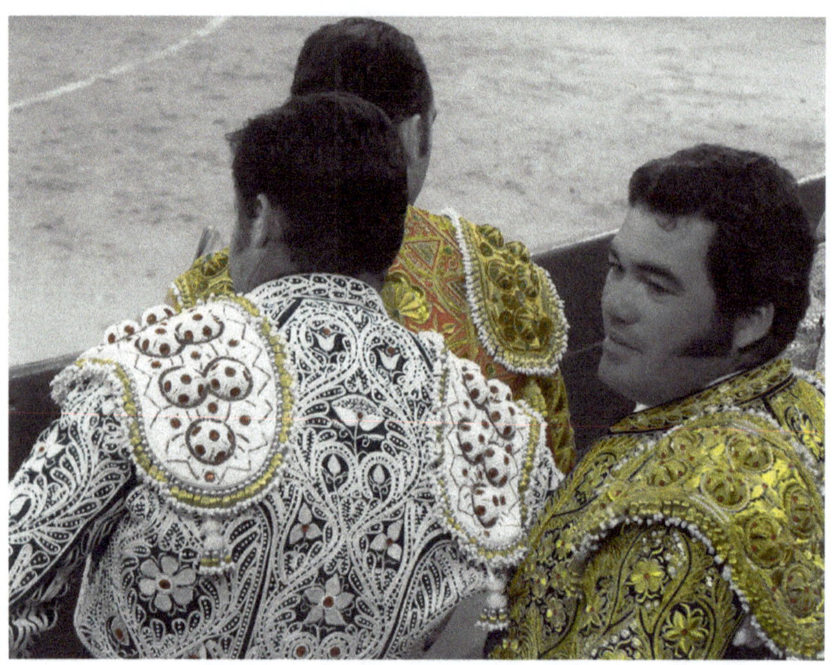

We were entertained by the picadors and banderillos hanging out just below our seats in the 'dug-out'. It sounded like they were wearing tap shoes as they paced back and forth; we noticed that the picador's right pants leg is split so they can wear armor underneath to protect their leg. The click of tap shoes does not fit the seriousness and danger of the bullfight.

The picador, in an elaborately embroidered costume, rides into the ring on a heavily padded, blindfolded horse. His job is to wear the bull down, which he does in two ways. First, he uses his lance to repeatedly stab the mound of muscles on the back of the bull's neck which cuts the muscle and produces blood loss. Then he uses his horse, taunting the bull to get him to charge the horse, to try and lift the horse using his neck and horns which strains the bull's neck muscles. The horse wears a metal blanket under his decorative blanket for protection.

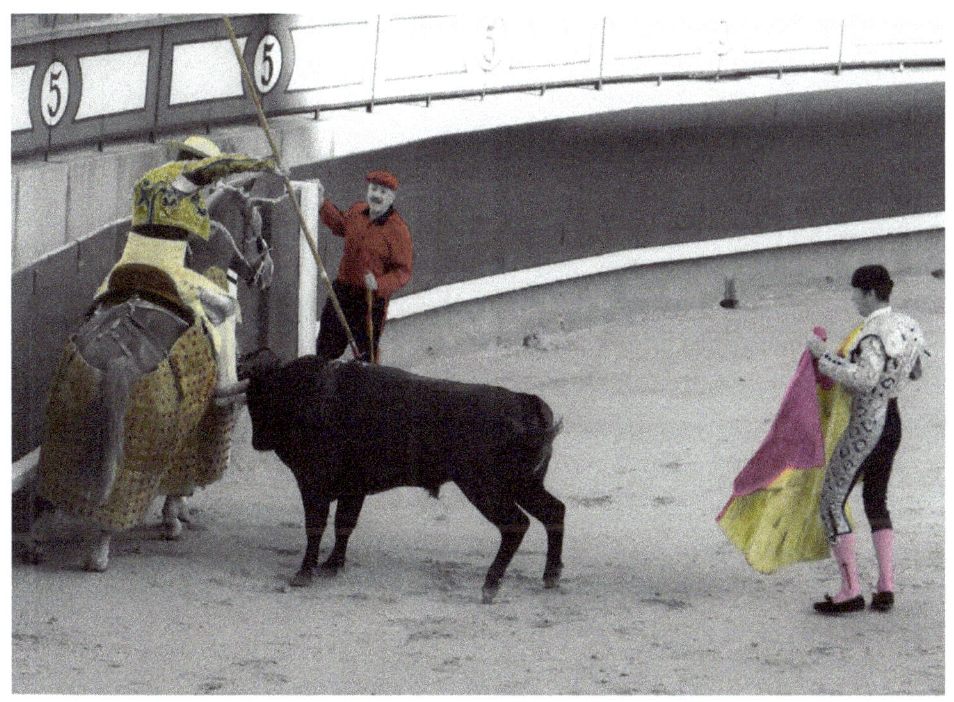

Reporters gather at the exit to interview the matadors just like our sporting events. Only matador number three garnered much attention.

Stage 2: Tercio de Banderilleros (third of flags)

Banderilleros walk into the ring with pink capes and banderillas (sharp darts with flags on them). Each banderillero has three banderillas to plant in the bull's neck. They work together, using the cape to divert the bull so another can get close enough to plant a dart. The darts further weaken the bull as well as anger him.

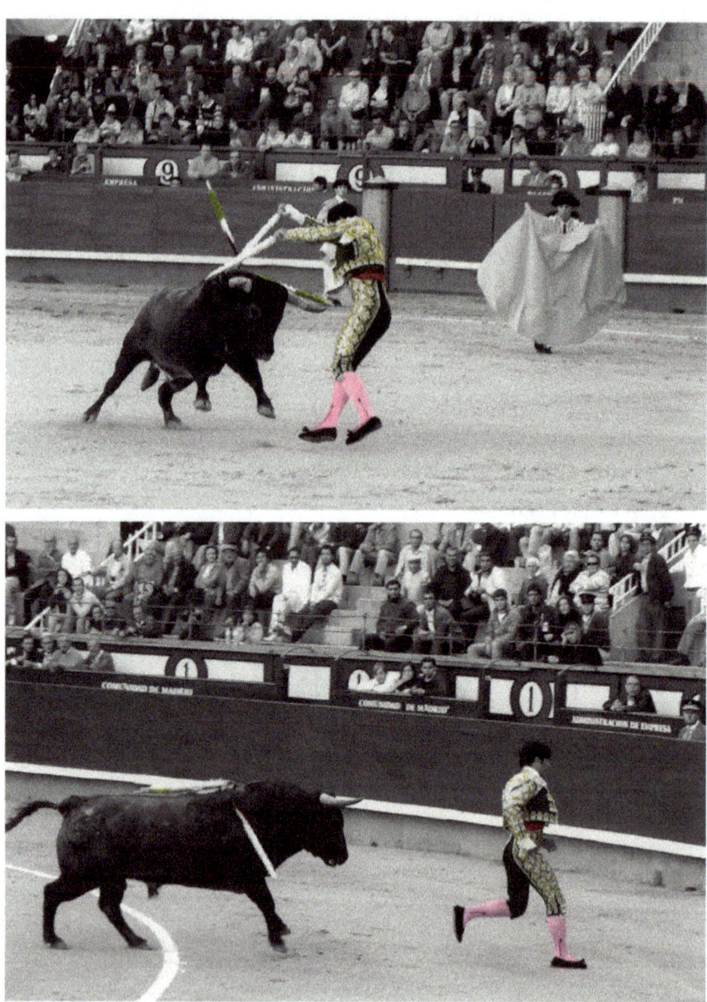

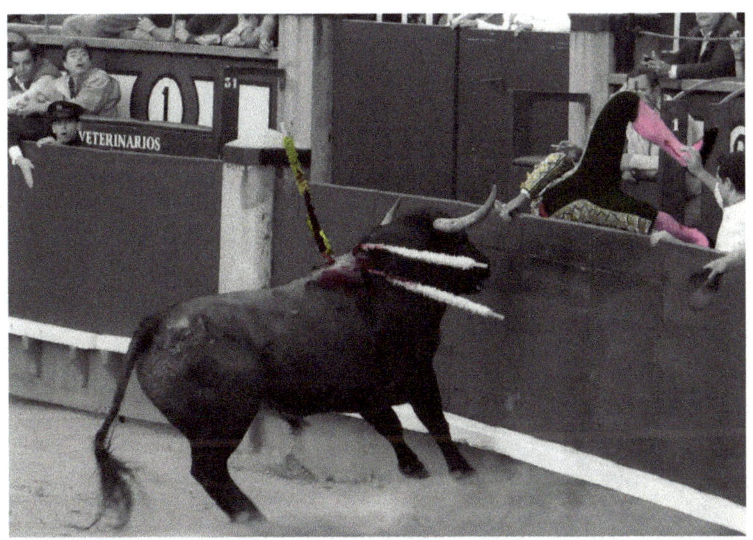

VETERINARIOS

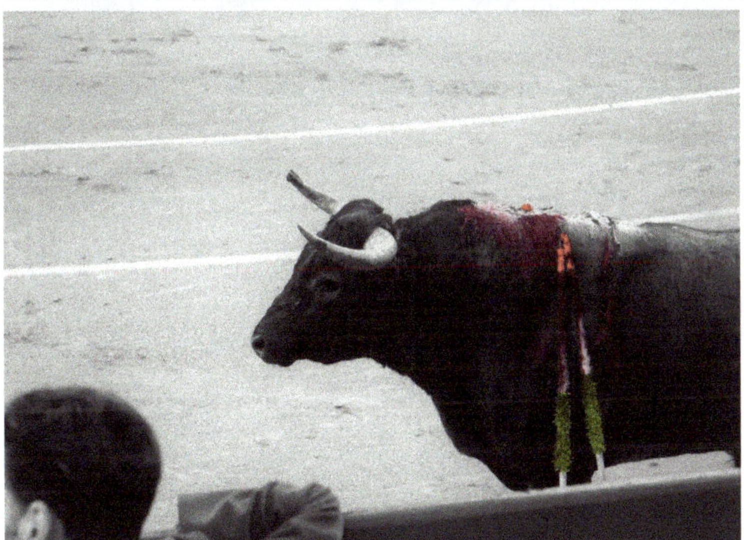

Stage 3: Tercio de Muerte (third of death)

The matador enters the ring with his muleta (a red cape over a wooden dowel) in one hand and a sword in another. Stage 3 is broken into three parts.

•   The matador approaches the presiding official and dedicates the death of the bull to a special person.

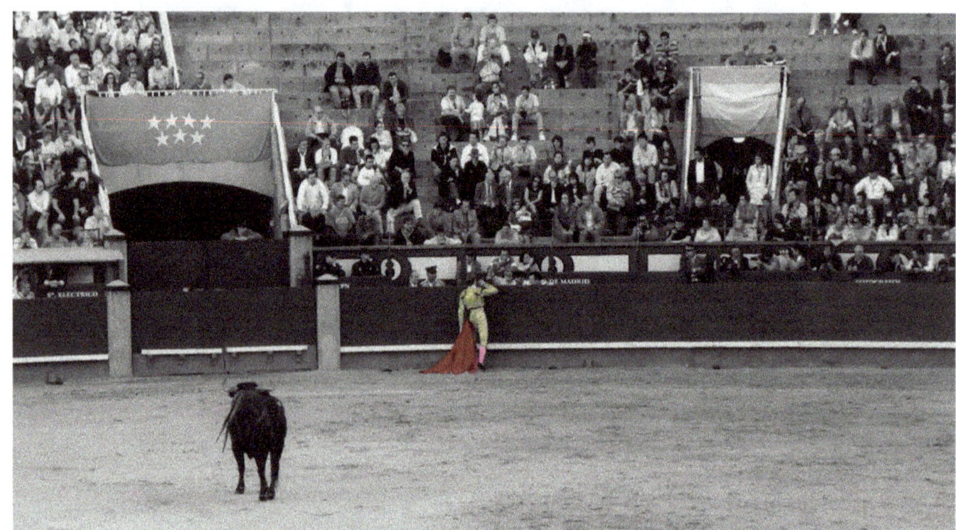

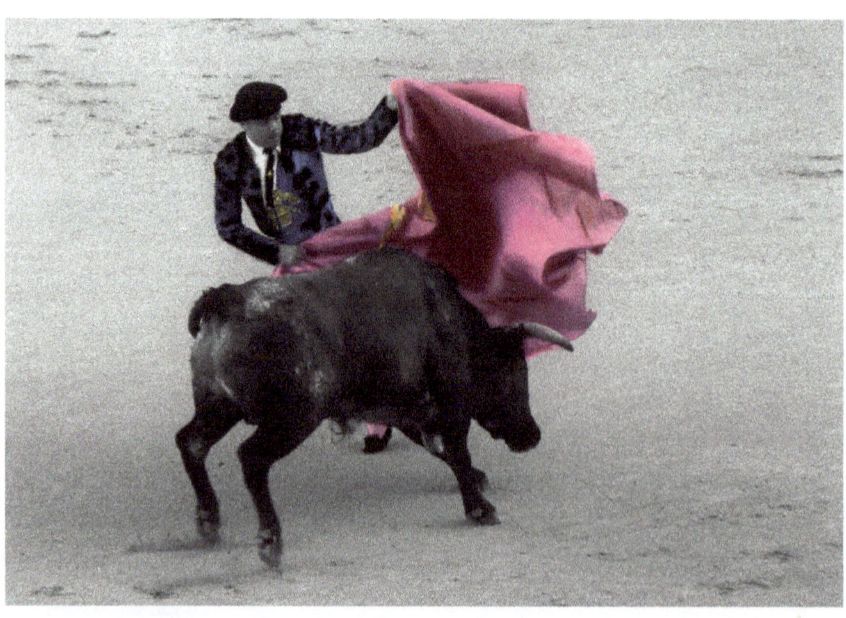

•   He then works the bull with the red cloak to further wear it down. This is his opportunity to show off his skill and bravery. The tandas (passes) each have a specific name.

•   Last is the kill 'estocada'. If all goes well, he will thrust the sword between the bull's shoulder blades and through his heart. If the matador doesn't manage to kill the bull, he will be given a different sword (verdugo) to grab the bull's nose and lower its head so that he can then sever its spinal cord.

When the bull is killed, the presiding official may award the bull the honor of being dragged around the arena for a full lap if he was valiant. Otherwise the mules drag him straight out to make way for the next fight.

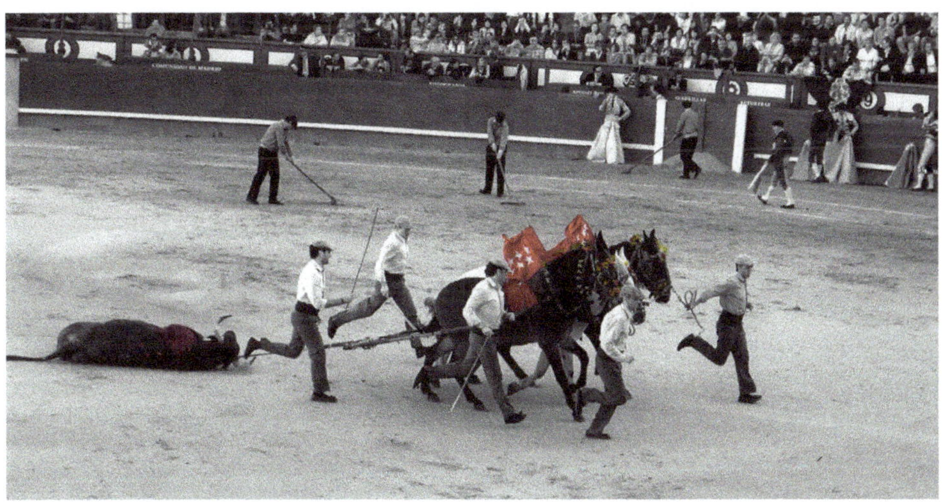

Fight number 2 was an interesting match. I don't think the matador had very much experience. The bull decided that the red cloth was not the target; he went after the matador! The matador's team tried to come to his rescue but he decided he was better off running for it; cleared the wall with room to spare! He managed to escape unharmed.

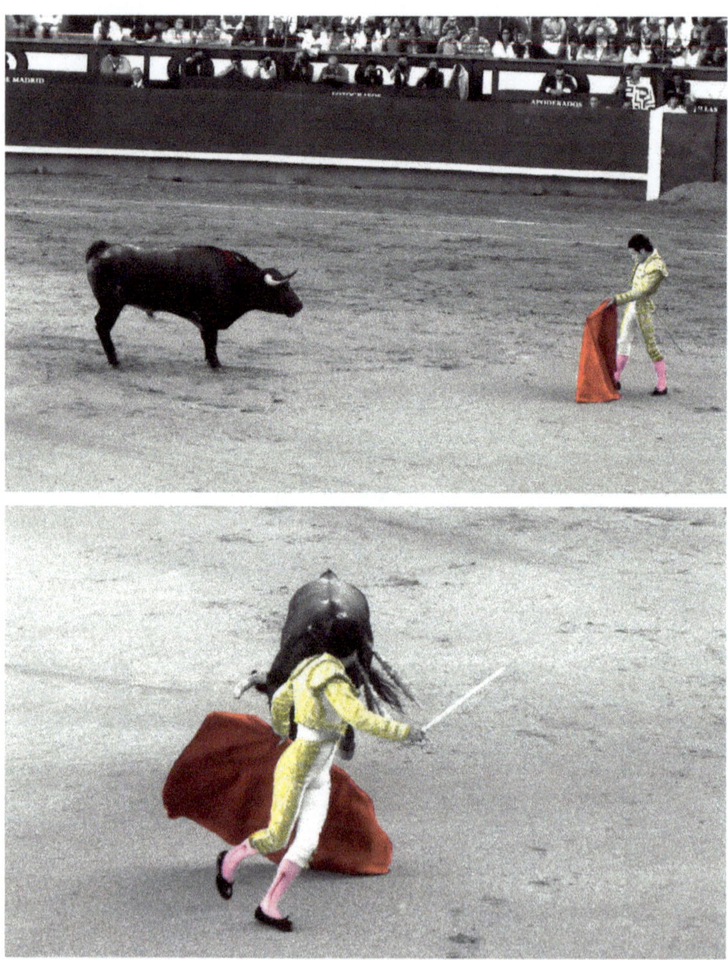

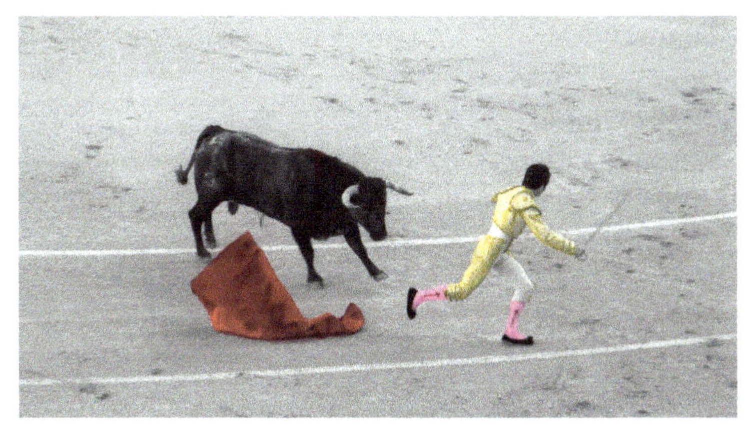

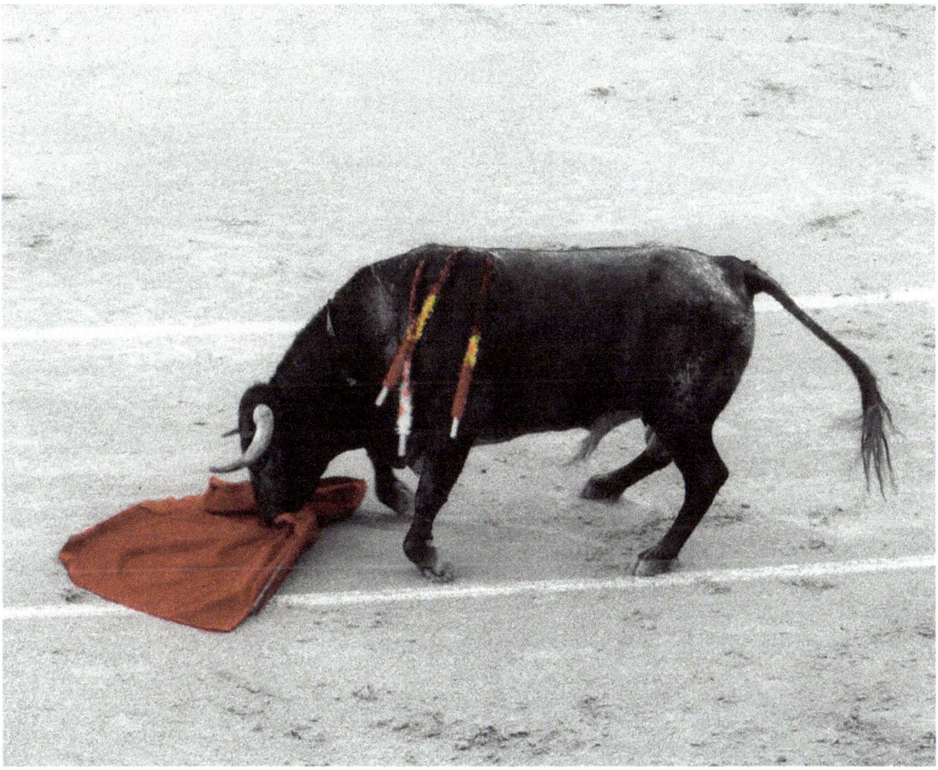

Matador number 3 was the headliner for this corrida. The crowd knew and loved him; he's a very attractive young man with a delightful smile. He entered with grace and a presence that exuded confidence. I knew it was going to be a good experience.

The matador worked the bull in a choreographed manner, with the fluidity of a movie. The red cape held the bull's at-

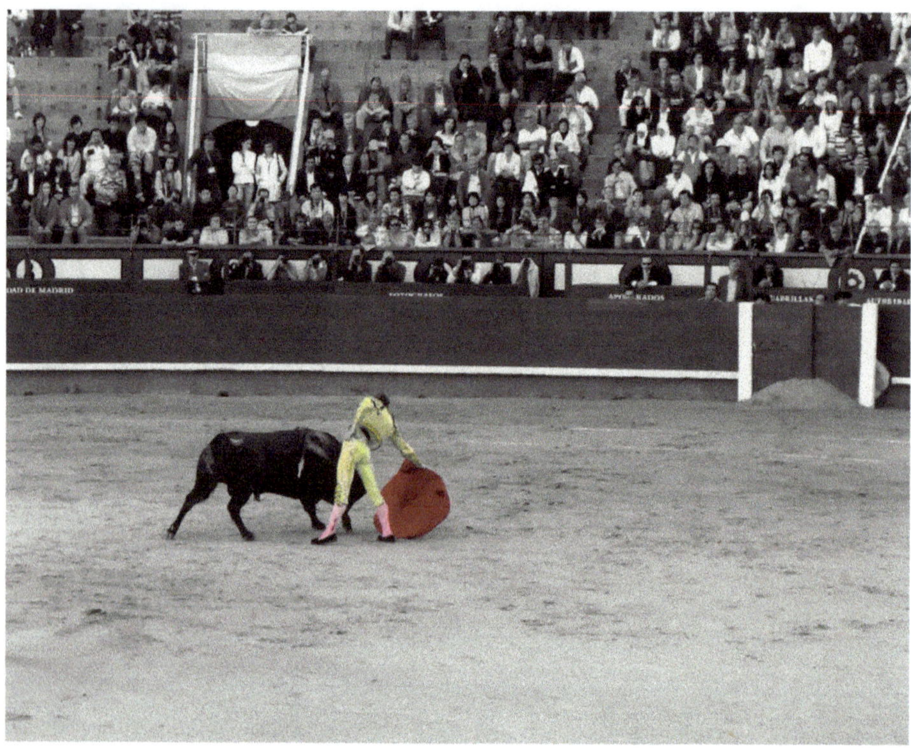

tention and when it was jerked away, the bull quickly did a 180 and prepared to have another go at it.

When the time came, the matador made a clean kill and the crowd went wild! Spectators waved white handkerchiefs or their jackets.

Turns out the crowd has a lot of control over the outcome of a fight; they can boo a matador off the field or they can express their pleasure and ask the presiding official to present the matador with the bull's ear.

For an especially outstanding job, the official may award both ears and even the tail. The matador takes a victory lap, showing his ear to the crowd.

Once the matador cut off the bull's ear, he and his entourage took a lap around the arena to show it off. People threw flowers and jackets to him; his crew carried the flowers and he tossed the jackets back to the crowd. Sitting near us was a group of lovely young women that could have been groupies but I got the impression that one of them had a relationship with the matador; she tossed him a whole bouquet of flowers!

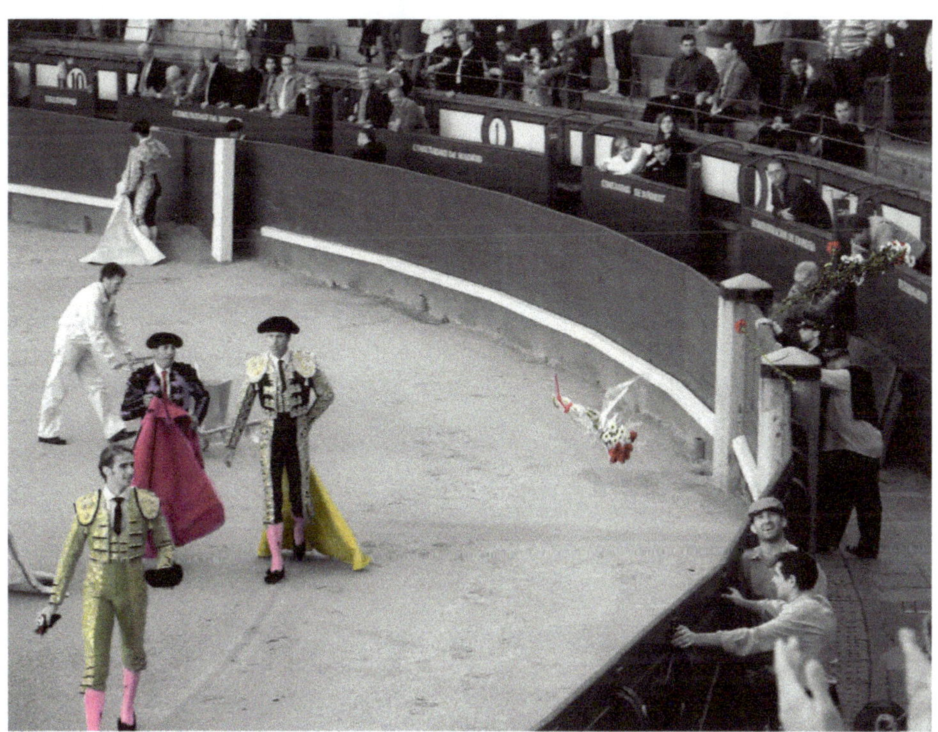

The bull won fight number 4! The matador began the encounter kneeling on the ground with his cape spread out in front of him – a very brave stance. The first few passes were very elegant and professional, then things got interesting.

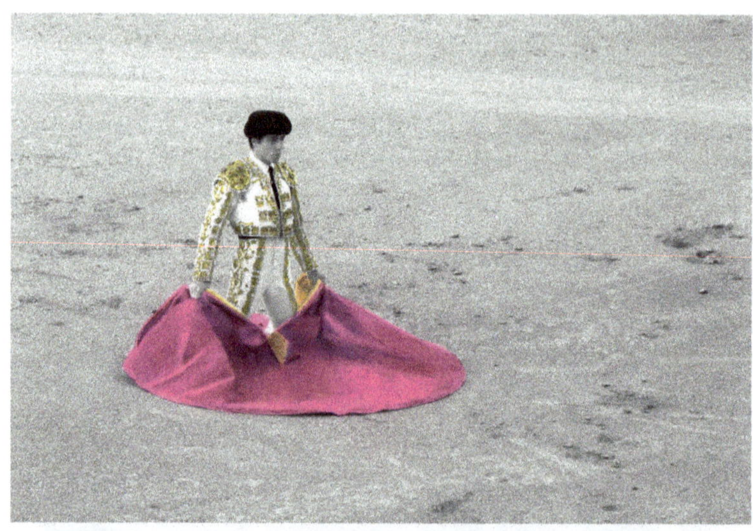

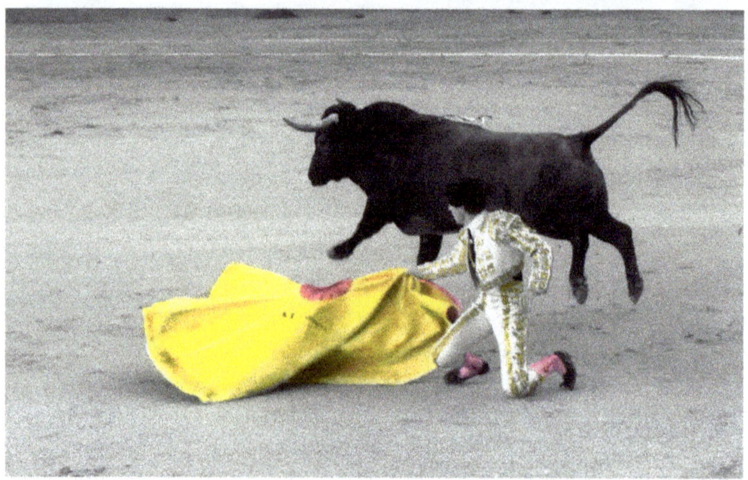

When it came time for the kill, the matador struck him 6 times but the bull continued to rage. The crowd booed the matador from the ring and the bull was granted his freedom.

A herd of brown and white cows, wearing loud bells entered the ring. I thought they were clowns like in a rodeo but they had a serious job to do. Their job is to incorporate the bull into their herd and lead him out of the ring. The bull wins - once a bull has been in the ring, he can never fight again because he is smart and knows what will happen.

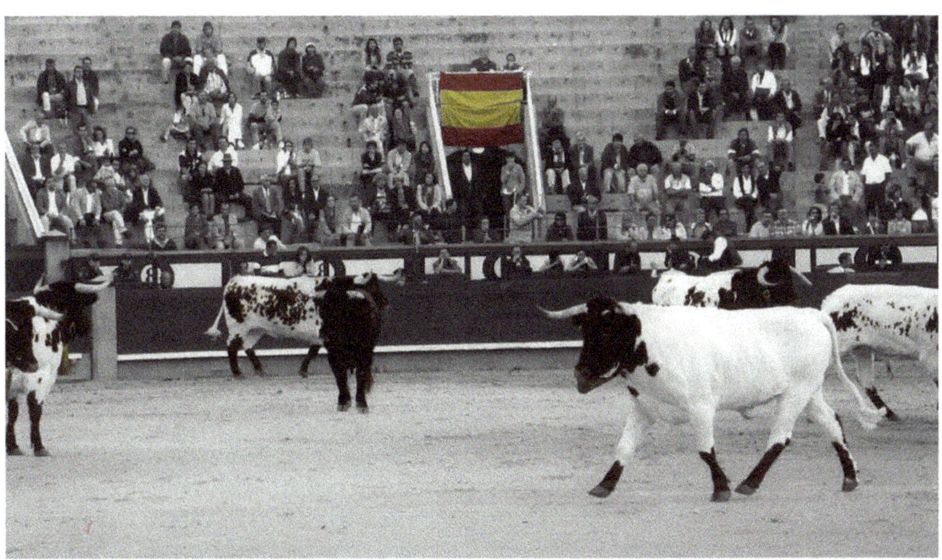

Ferdinand was the star of fight number 5. He sauntered into the ring with his nose in the air, sniffing, and looking at all the people. He was rejected immediately.

The replacement bull was far more energetic and put up a good fight.

The charming matador from fight number 3 didn't do as well in fight number 6. The sparring was split between man and beast. Every time the bull charged the matador, I thought it was over but he got his wind back and charged the bull in return. On the third attempt, he made a clean kill; the crowd went wild, Ole! No ear this round.

The ritual continues once the sixth fight is over. Each matador and his team gather in front of the officials and walk across the ring, exiting just below us. The corridia is officially over.

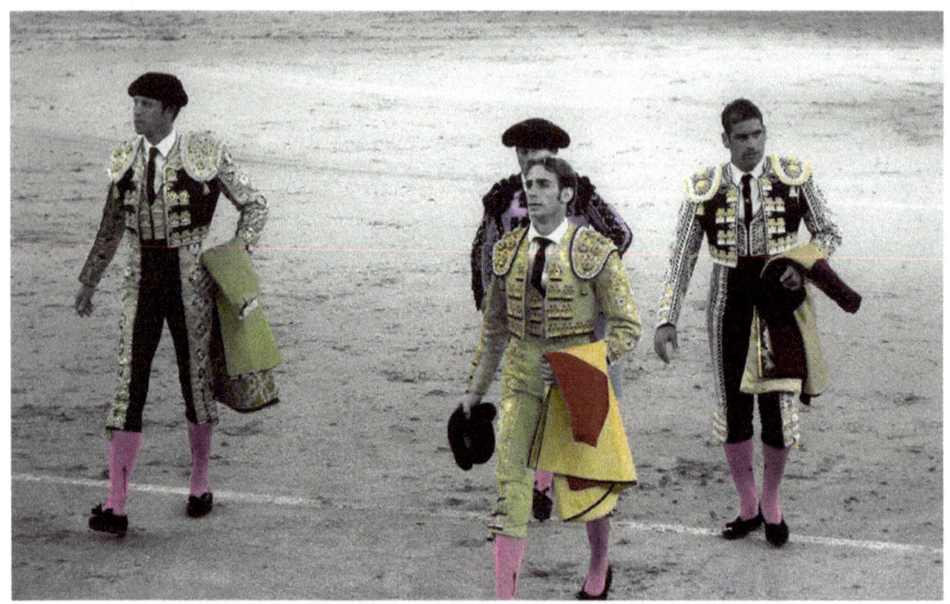

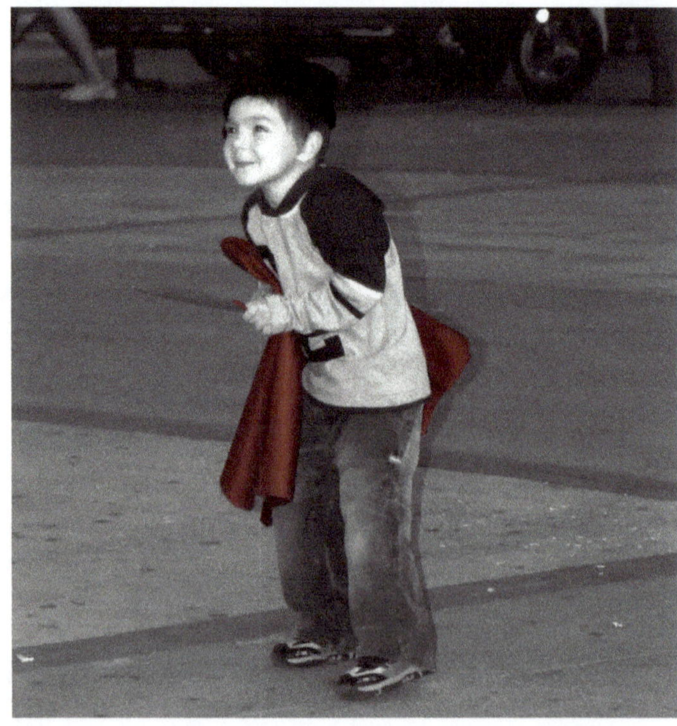

Madrid Day 2

We spent the evening celebrating Liz's birthday. Our intention was to bar hop but one bottle of champagne at the first stop did us in! We couldn't find a bakery open at midnight so we settled for ice cream. Madrid is known as the city that never sleeps. The plaza was densely populated when we set out; we made a wrong turn on our way back and the people disappeared. It got pretty creepy before we realized our error and turned around. The section of Madrid we were staying in sleeps; so did we.

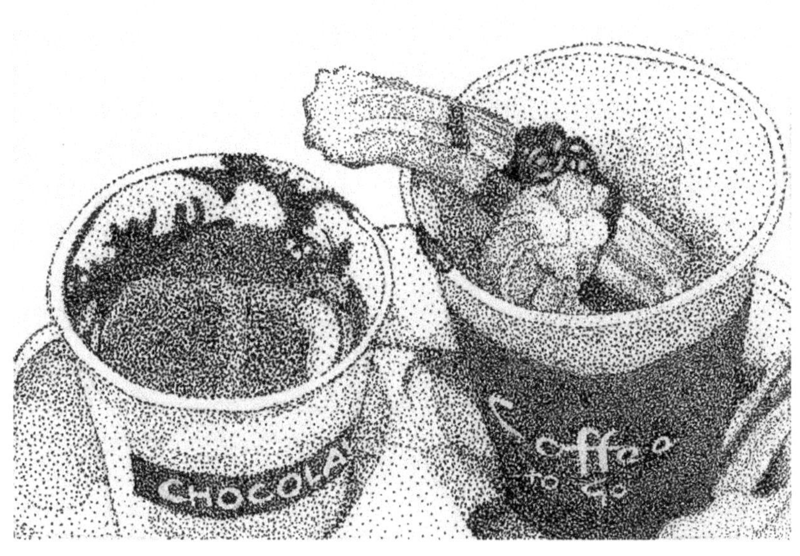

I got great chocolate and churros for breakfast; I'm glad I didn't discover these too early in the trip! Our Madrid objective was 3 museums, a bullfight, and some serious shopping. If Madrid continues to be like NYC and Paris, we should be able to get some good deals.

Madrid is the center of contemporary flamenco so I anticipated numerous flamenco shops but Madrid is more of a fashion mecca. I had a short list of 'the best shops for' from several guidebooks. Our first destination was a shawl shop.

Shopping ended up being a rather hit-or-miss adventure. We tracked down the flamenco shops on our list but their selection was limited. Shoe stores fill every block instead of flamenco shops and they all carry the same inventory. We had a great time wandering through the shops but didn't accomplish much, I still had gifts to buy and Sarah hadn't found a flamenco dress.

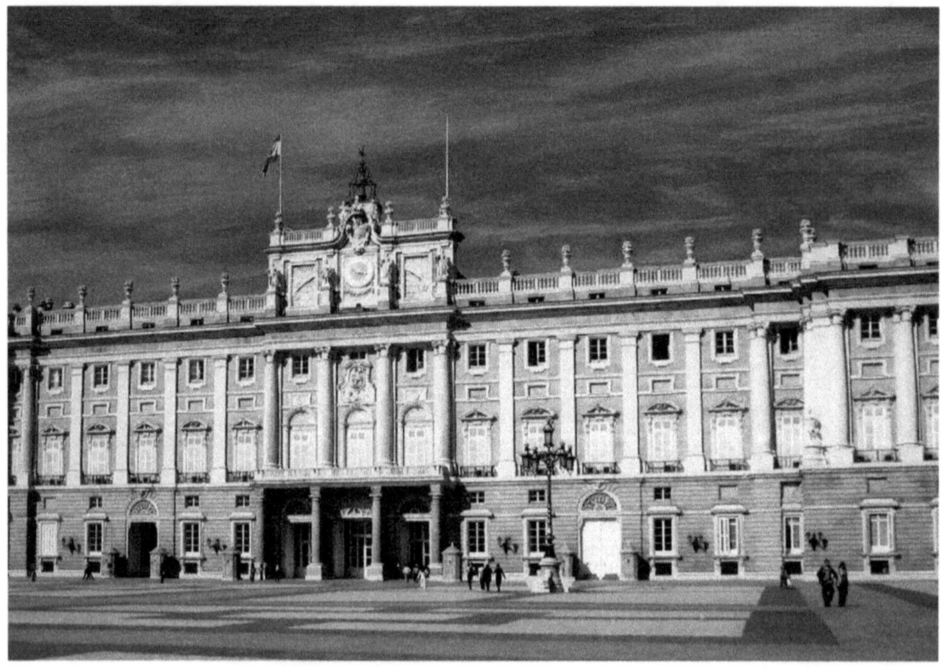

During siesta our destination was the Royal Palace. The Palacio Real De Madrid is a modern palace that is still in use. The palace has 3,418 rooms (1,450,000 sq ft of floor space) that are noted for the many fine materials used in their construction and decoration. The design of the palace was inspired by sketches Bernini made for the Louvre in Paris.

The palace is the largest in Europe and is the official residence of the Spanish Royal family but it is only used for royal functions. The carpets were rolled up away from the tourist trail. Where you could see them, you could appreciate their beauty and how they pull the rooms together.

Several rooms are regularly open to the public. Each of the rooms we visited had a unique style creating a disjointed decorator's show room, tied together by the carpet. All the rooms are heavily ornamented to the point of being gaudy. The porcelain room is covered with beautiful examples of porcelain, floor to ceiling; the oriental room has bright primary tiles. The rooms have fabric covered walls as well as fabric coverings on the wires for the hanging chandeliers. It just screams high maintenance!

After the palace, we were starting to drag so we found an outdoor cafe and ordered our afternoon lattes.

Service in Madrid is no different than the rest of Spain, very frustrating! They waited on us fairly quick then disappeared. We finally decided to go in the bar to pay and speed things up but there was no 'bar' exactly so we hung around the barrier at the kitchen entrance until someone came out and rang up our bill. Hard to believe.

The third and final museum to visit is the Museo Nacional Centro de Arte Reine Sofia, home of the famous Picasso painting, Guernica.

The museum is small (quality over quantity). It houses many famous Dali's, Milo's, and Picasso's along with their contemporaries.

Picasso received a commission from the Spanish Republican government for a large scale painting for the Spanish Pavilion at Paris's World's Fair in 1937. He was having trouble

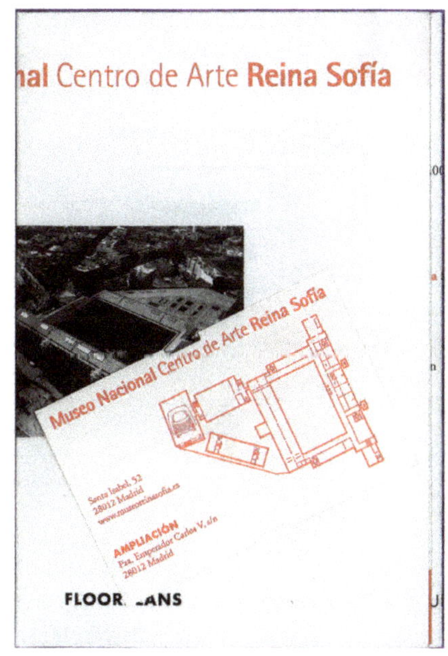

coming up with an idea for the piece until the bombing of the Basque city of Gemika on 4/26/37 by the German and Italian armies during the Spanish Civil War. The bombing inspired him to paint Guernica, a mural-sized painting created with a palette of black, white, and gray, giving it a journalistic quality. The painting has become a timeless, universal symbol, vilifying the implacable and criminal destruction of war. It opened artistic debate on the representation of armed conflict, showing the suffering of innocent civilians.

Guernica was exhibited around the world to raise money for Spanish war relief. It returned to Spain in 1981 and was moved to the Reine in 1992. The museum's exhibit includes the preliminary sketches and photographs of the work in progress, giving some insight into the mind of genius.

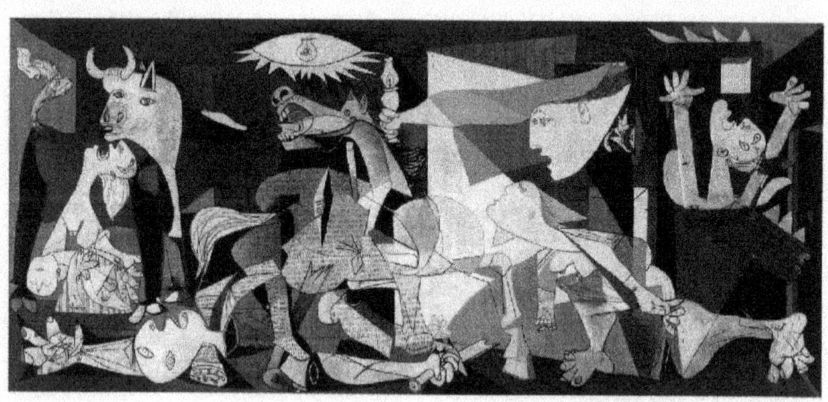

Tonight was pasta - pizza night and beer with lemon. Before we knew it, it was 10:00. Internet time was over so we called it a day on the early side, we were heading to Cordoba on the early train.

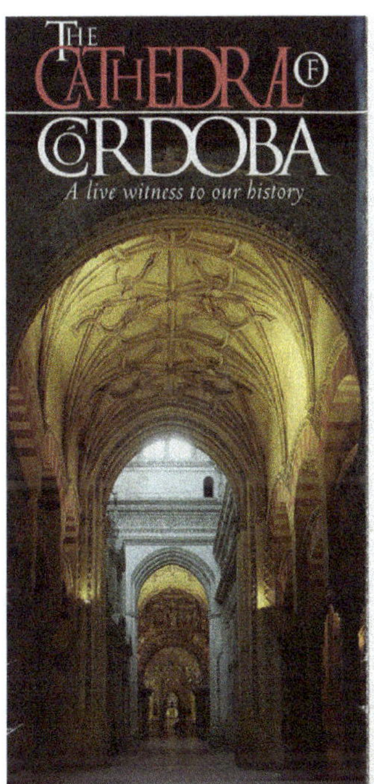

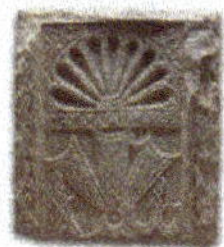

THE MOTHER CHURCH OF THE DIOCESES

The cathedral of Córdoba is not simply a monument or a temple of different cultures; nor is it a mosque, but the Mother Church of the Dioceses. The term "cathedral" derives from "cathedra", or seat of the bishop, from where he acts as the pastor of all his people. That is why a cathedral is the express image of the Church of Christ that preaches, sings, and adores throughout the world. Thus the beauty of the Cathedral of Córdoba does not reside in its architectural grandeur, but in the apostolic succession of the Bishop as a symbol of his pastoral service and the unity of the Church, founded upon the Word of the Lord, the sacraments, and the community of believers.

The Cathedral is alive, it is witness to our history. It acts as a book that conveys the message to those who will read it, the message of the altar, the naves, the alterpieces... teaching us to know and love God, the world, and the human being.

THE ORIGINS

Beneath every cathedral is always a bed of hidden cathedrals. In the case of Córdoba, tradition traces back to its Visigoth origins. This fact is confirmed by archeological excavations, whose remains can be found at the Museum of *San Vicente* (Saint Vincent) and in the pits where the remains of mosaics from the ancient Christian temple can be observed on site.

It is a historical fact that the basilica of San Vicente was expropriated and destroyed in order to build what would later be the Mosque, a reality that questions the theme of tolerance that was supposedly cultivated in the Córdoba of the moment. This was the main church of the city, a martyry basilica from the 6th century, that would be remembered and venerated by Christians, centuries after its destruction.

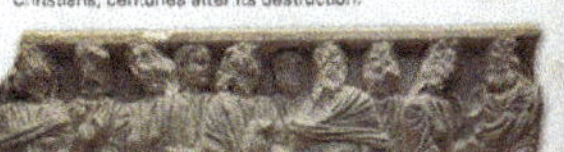

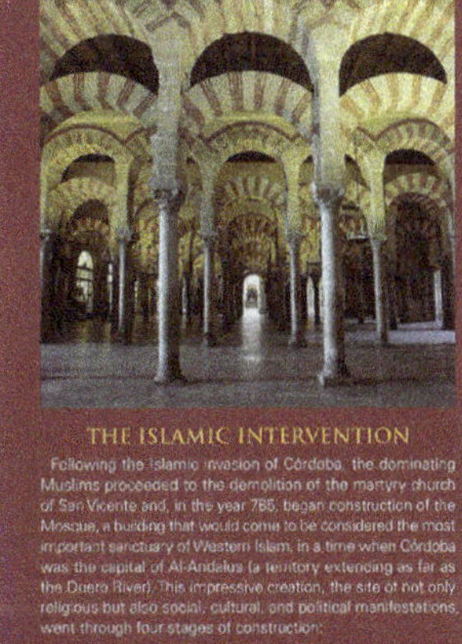

THE ISLAMIC INTERVENTION

Following the Islamic invasion of Córdoba, the dominating Muslims proceeded to the demolition of the martyry church of San Vicente and, in the year 785, began construction of the Mosque, a building that would come to be considered the most important sanctuary of Western Islam, in a time when Córdoba was the capital of Al-Andalus (a territory extending as far as the Duero River). This impressive creation, the site of not only religious but also social, cultural, and political manifestations, went through four stages of construction:

Abd-ar-Rahman I: Inspired by the Mosque of Damascus, with the traditional distribution of *sahn* (ablution courtyard) and *zulla* (hall of prayer). Yet a strong Hispano-Roman influence is perceived, not only from the use of materials that came from the demolished church of San Vicente, but also because the direction of the nave was set towards (and not parallel to) the wall of the *qubla*, as was the case in Visigoth churches. Furthermore, the superposed arches and the alternation of brick and stone (red and beige colors) in the bending of the arches were modeled after the Episcopal palace whose remains are found in the archeological site of *Cercadilla*.

Abd-ar-Rahman II: During this prosperous stage of the Independent Emirate (though also a time of Christian persecution), the first addition to the Mosque was carried out, maintaining the scheme of the preceding ruler and prolonging the courtyard and the aisles of the prayer hall. In this courtyard, the Omeyan caliph Abd-ar-Rahman III ordered the construction of the minaret that is now embedded in the tower of the cathedral.

Our last day in Spain was a busy one! First stop, Cordoba, to visit the Mezquita.

The day began with the 9:39 train. We planned to hail a taxi but one never materialized so we had to hoof it. Luckily the walk was all down hill and only took 15 minutes. The bags continue to get heavier but we are getting stronger! We purchased our tickets and headed for breakfast. Our waitress was surly and slow. We asked for the check when she brought us our food, we didn't want to risk missing the train. Well, she was on Spanish time - no hurry. The train was starting to pull out of the station as we were flying down the steps to hop on board. The train engineer was a saviour! He held the train until we were safely on. Sure gets the adrenalin flowing!

The luggage lockers at the train station in Cordoba were out of service so we headed across the street to the bus station. Thankfully there were a few available. We wasted one token trying to figure out how to work the key. Everything fit, all I took with me were my camera and purse.

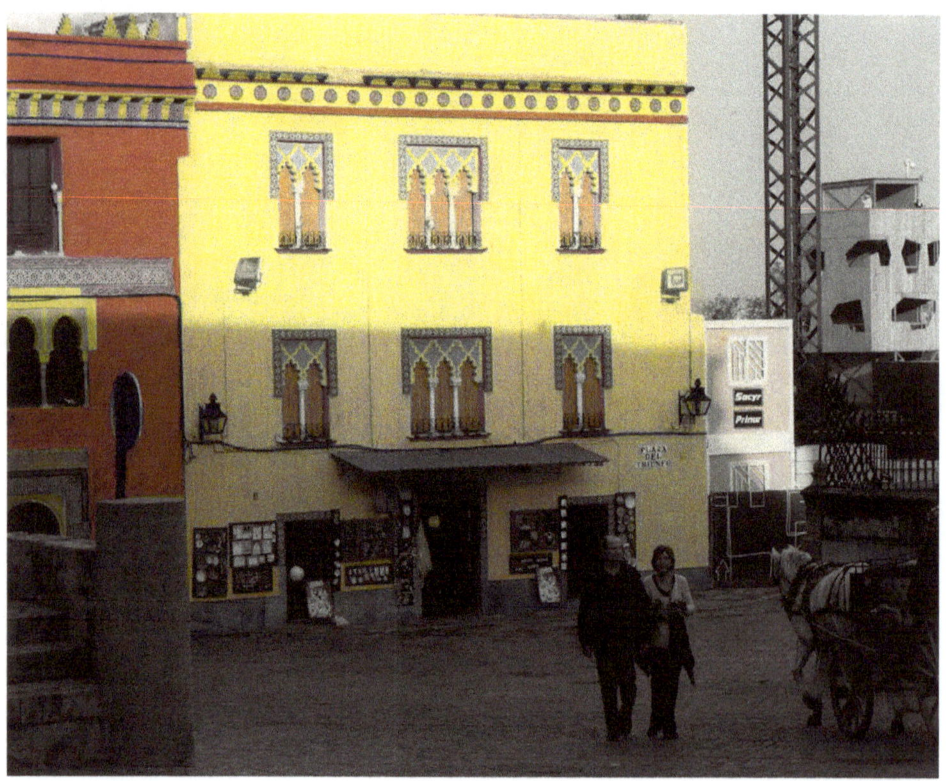

We splurged and took a cab into the city.

Cordoba was considered the intellectual center of Islam. It's relationship with flamenco dates back to the 8th century when Al Zyriab emigrated from Baghdad and founded the first European School of Music in Cordoba. Zyriab is credited with the development of the Spanish guitar from the Arab oud.

In the 16th century, King Charles I held court in Cordoba. The king was fond of entertainment; he hired gypsy families to perform and to organize festivals for the court. Gypsies have remained the keeper of tradition, transforming oral ballads into three or four line coplas (songs). So when in 1956, the Concurso National, a flamenco competition, was established in an effort to revive traditional flamenco, Cordoba was the perfect locale. The competition is held every two years and only recently has been opened to non-gypsy performers.

We came to Cordoba to visit the Mezquita. Construction on the Mezquita began in 785; built on the site of an old Visigoth Christian temple. It's the oldest cathedral in Spain and a UN-

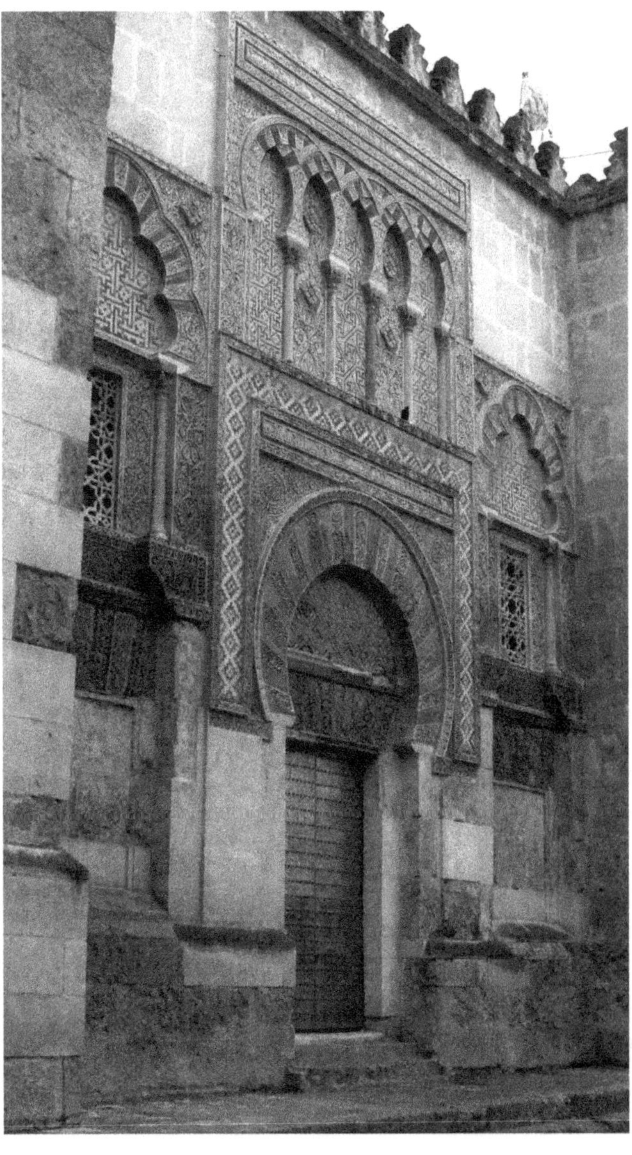

ESCO World Heritage site. The Mezquita is considered one of the most accomplished monuments of Moorish architecture.

For Muslims, the mosque is the center of the community; the site of religious, social, cultural and political events. The hypostyle prayer hall within the Mezquita is huge, containing 856 columns made of jasper, onyx, marble, granite and pieces from the earlier Roman temple. The columns are crowned with double arches of alternating brick and stone like Roman aqueducts. The pillars symbolize rows of palm trees in the oasis of Syria.

In 1236 King Ferdinand III recaptured Cordoba and Christianity took over. The palm tree courtyard was replaced by orange trees which are there today. During the Renaissance, King Charles V approved the addition of a cathedral nave in the center of the mosque. Muslims have petitioned to get their mosque back but it is still in Christian hands.

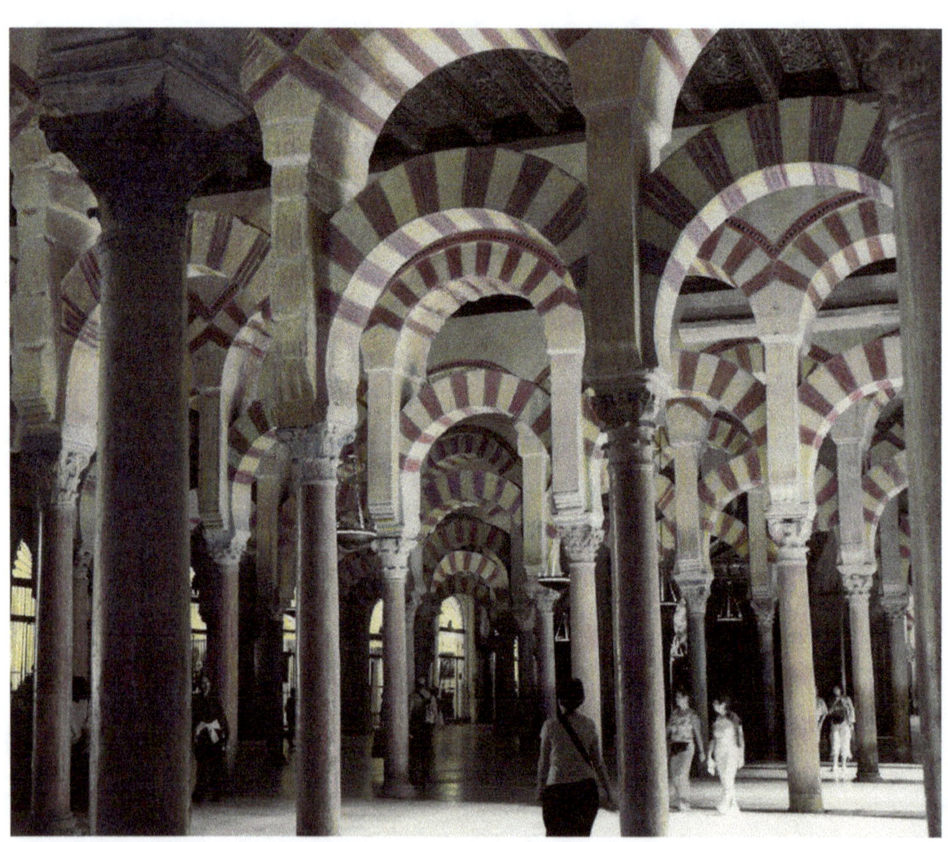

The church has, however, made it a mission to protect the mosque from ruin and to safeguard and inspire its culture and art.

I was expecting the interior to be much smaller and to have more light. I took tons of pictures and even in low light, many appear to have turned out fine.

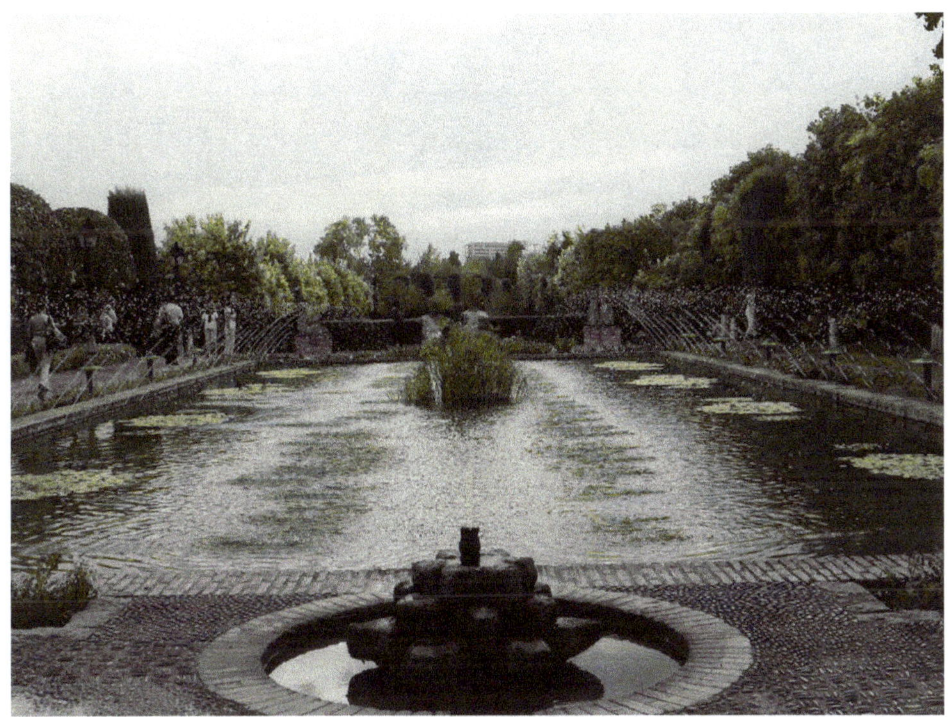

The Muslims that settled in Cordoba in the mid-8th century were mostly desert nomads who arrived without women, so they married local women, integrating with Andalus society. As we had seen in Seville and Granada earlier, they not only introduced architectural styles and improved agricultural methods, they brought their love of gardens.

The garden in Cordoba has hedges that are pruned to look like walls covered with moss; like the Alhambra but on a much more intimate scale. The sound of water is heard throughout the garden and the orange grove is deliciously fragrant. These Muslim gardens are large but designed with many smaller spaces that are perfect places to re-charge.

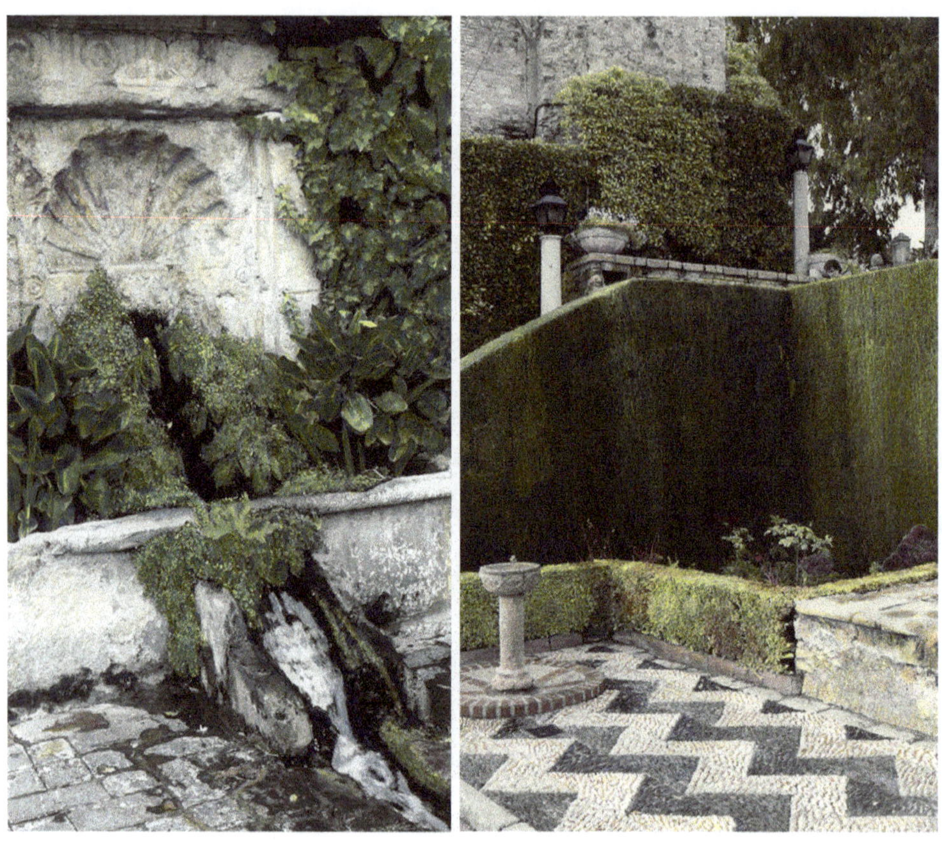

Our afternoon train wasn't until 2:45 so we spent our time
shopping and eating! The shopping area is in the old Jewish
quarter; it's fascinating to observe how the streets were laid
out in narrow alleys that criss-cross to provide shade. Malorca pearls, colorful Caliph pottery (reproductions of pottery
from the Moorish period of the Caliphate), and leather goods
are what Cordoba is known for. We found a bright orange

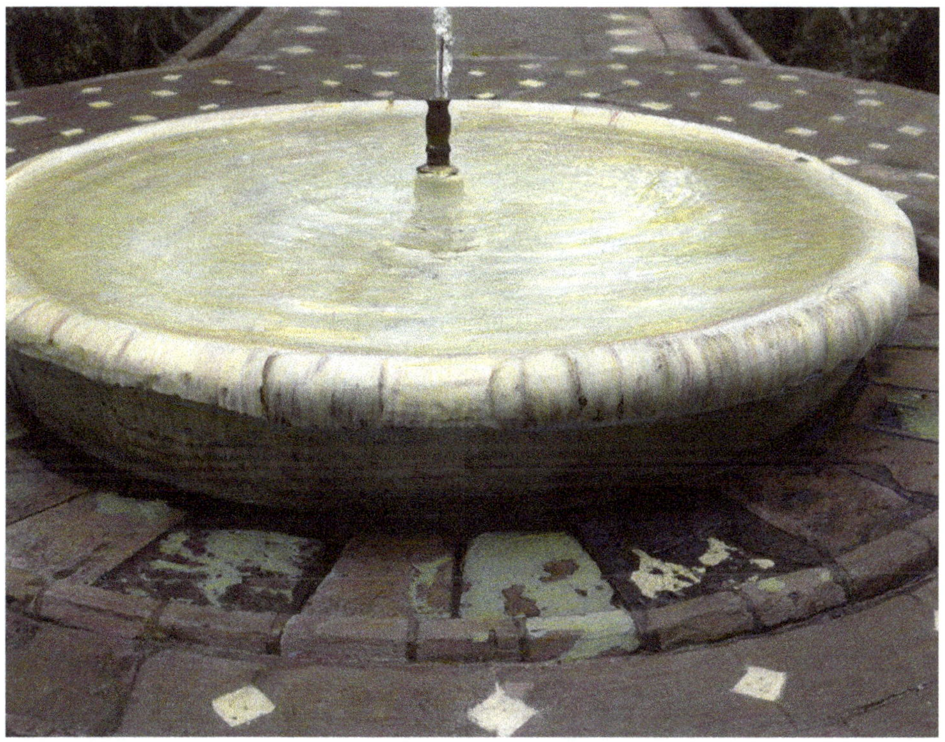

pottery platter, the bride's favorite color, for a wedding gift!
Malorca pearls are large and vivid white. We couldn't resist,
we both got necklaces with nice metal work from a shop
with a very friendly little white dog. He was a very good
salesman!

Then we had ice cream for lunch!

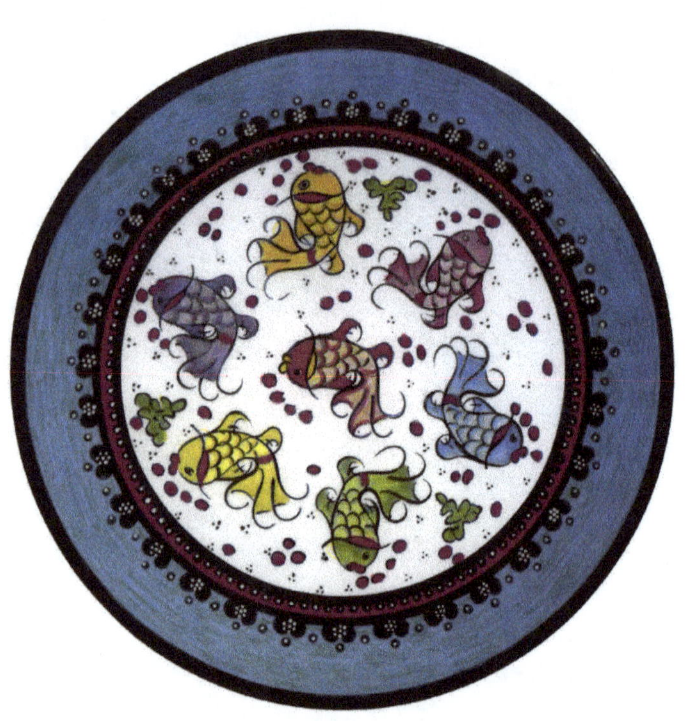

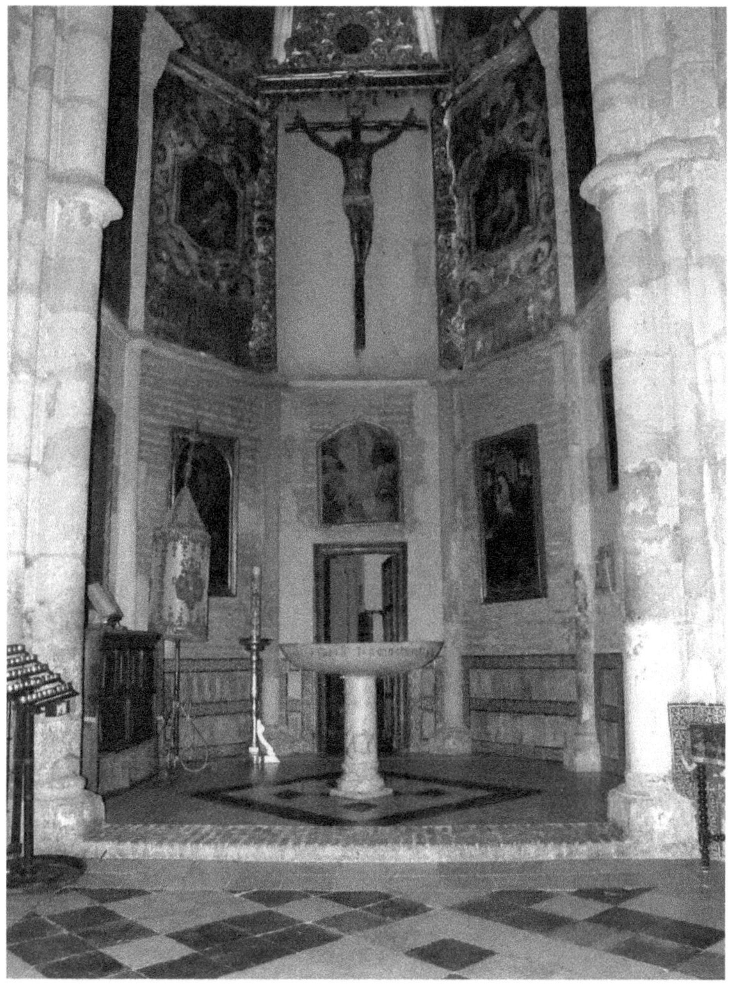

We chose the early afternoon train to Seville in hopes of coordinating our travel with siesta! We still had a little shopping to finish up and a special church in Triana to visit before the flamenco show.

Triana was home to Seville's sailors, bullfighters and flamenco artists because they were not allowed to live within the city walls. So many bullfighters and flamenco artists were born here that Triana is considered the heart of flamenco.

Seville's first church, Santa Ana, is a very small church dating from the 13th century. Local legend says that children baptized in the font here are bestowed with the gifts of flamenco singing and dancing. It's a beautiful church.

Across the street is a community center with flamenco music and singing filtering out the windows!

We had taken the bus when we'd headed out so we felt pretty confident about catching the bus back. The map showed bus stops on the next street. We waited at the bus stop with a group of local women. There was a lively discussion and then, suddenly, we realized they were gone. An elderly man stopped and explained to us that the C3 didn't stop there anymore. Thank goodness he was able to communicate with us, it's a shame he couldn't tell us where it stopped now. We didn't see any buses or taxis until we got to the next major road. We figured out that we could also take the B2 from there, found a bus stop and waited. A taxi got there first which made life so much easier, he was able to drop us real close to our destination and we were only a minute or two late for dinner.

We ate at the little bar where we dined the first night of our trip. We got there early enough to sit outside and enjoy a long and leisurely meal of many different tapas. After dinner we walked to the flamenco café, arriving there in time to get seats much closer to the front.

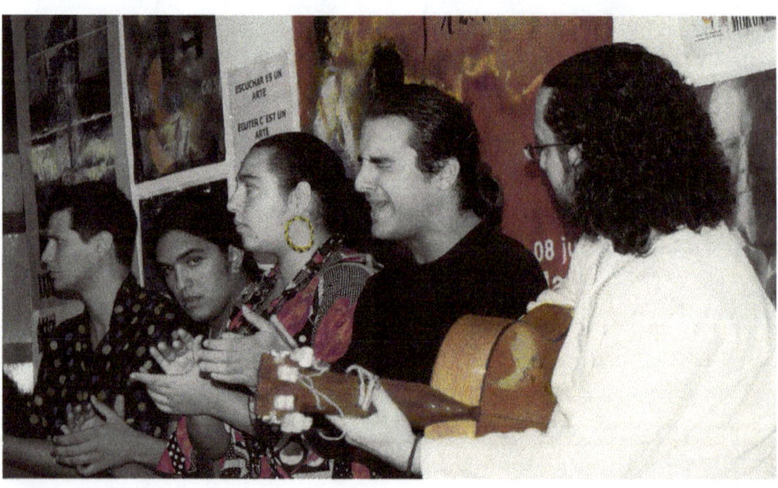

The flamenco group was younger; they really seemed to enjoy performing together, adding to our enjoyment. It was interesting to have a flute as a part of the group since flamenco
centers around the percussion of stomping feet, snapping
fingers, clapping hands, and the tapping of wood.

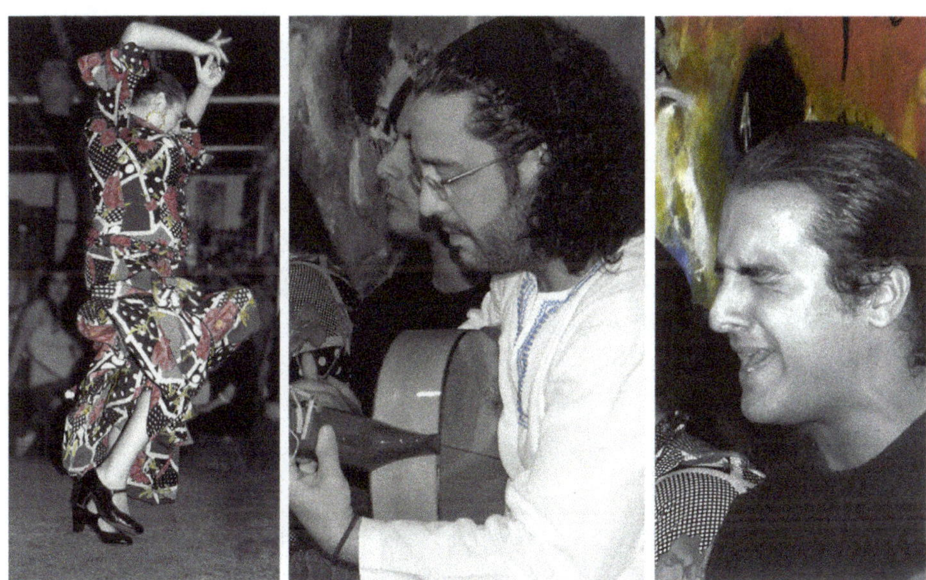

The show was over at 12:15; we walked back, past the bar
where we had called all those cab companies, to the hotel
that had welcomed us the night of the missing keys. We'd
come full circle. We were going to miss Sarah!

We managed to pack up and have the lights out by 1:30 for a
5:00 wakeup call! The young man that had taken care of us
two weeks ago was on duty when we checked out; if he recognized us, he did a good job of hiding it!

The hotel called a cab for us so we had to wait inside for the
cab driver to come in to get us. The older desk clerk went out
front and told us our cab had arrived. Just as we got outside,
a second cab drove up and an argument ensued. The 2nd
driver won and we were on our way to the airport.

Liz was a bit cranky this morning but her demeanor changed once we checked our bags and I went to find coffee. We decided to wait to eat in Madrid since we had a long layover and needed to be a bit more awake first.

Madrid airport is huge. We had to collect our luggage because we flew into terminal #4 and left from terminal #1. We were frustrated but followed the airlines recommendations; we understood once we got there. Terminal #4 is a satellite terminal miles from the other terminals.

The airport is very modern and nice. I got coffee, juice, and pastries in the small café, then we found a small luggage cart that we could load up and push around – we had euros to spend. We got Spanish brandy, shot glasses, Halloween boxers and a sherry sampler for my husband. I ducked into a museum shop and bought a bright bag with bulls on it and a Guadi Lizard for Liz and a few other small things.

Neither of us looked forward to the trip home but we had a 2 seat row on the first flight so we didn't have to share our space. Liz watched movies and TV most of the way while I read and wrote in my journal.

The trip is longer going home by 1.5 hours! Immigration and customs were a piece of cake, which was a good thing since we were running on auto-pilot. I finished reading my book while waiting for our flight to Raleigh, so my entertainment on the last flight was minimal. I was too tired to care. My feet and legs were swollen enough to be uncomfortable; glad it was a short flight.

In Raleigh, we collected our luggage and waited at the curb. I don't remember the last time I was this tired. I was just going in to find a pay phone when Bob came out from baggage claim. We got to carry the luggage one last time – at least we had help this time. I didn't unpack a thing, just hit the sack. By the time Bob got back from taking Liz home, I was asleep. I slept for 12 hours and woke ready to get back to the real world.

Epilogue

It's been thirteen years since I traveled to Spain. I have lived with this project for a long time and I have learned so much as the journey continues. I never achieved duende but I have achieved so much more! My journey was a quest for knowledge and fulfillment. It was a period of growth that some may call a mid-life crisis; I embraced it as the beginning of Chapter 2!

My daughter and I were both at a turning point in our lives, launching new careers and establishing a new and different relationship. Liz finished graduate school and has since traveled the world! I've adjusted to an empty nest and relish the change in my relationships with my children. They've gone from needing me to wanting to have me around!

I would love to report that my art career was lucrative but alas, I continue to make my way as an accountant by day and as an artist by night (and weekends). Art has broadened my horizons and taught me a lot about seeing. It has sparked my desire to learn more about the world around me and to share my observations with others. Through my hand colored images, I hope I shared with you my love for adventure and experiencing new things. While travel is wonderful, it is not necessary for an adventure. Take the time to disconnect, slow down and appreciate the beauty that surrounds you right where you are! Learning to 'see' will change your life.

Writing a book is a major undertaking and a path for growth. As I kept adding illustrations, my colored pencil work took on new nuances and I grew as an artist. Revising and editing meant new research which added to my understanding of flamenco's culture and Spain.

From the technical side, I have learned the technology and skills needed to create an ePub! It sounded so easy when I first started googling how to do it. As I write this, I am trusting that I will figure out publication and if you're reading this, I did!

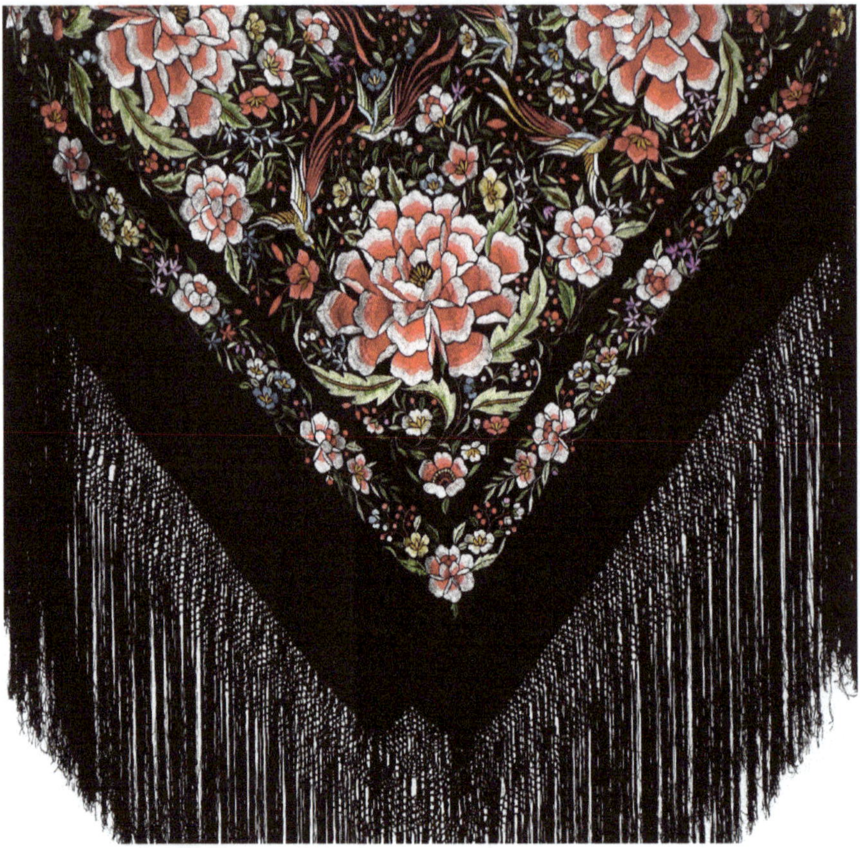

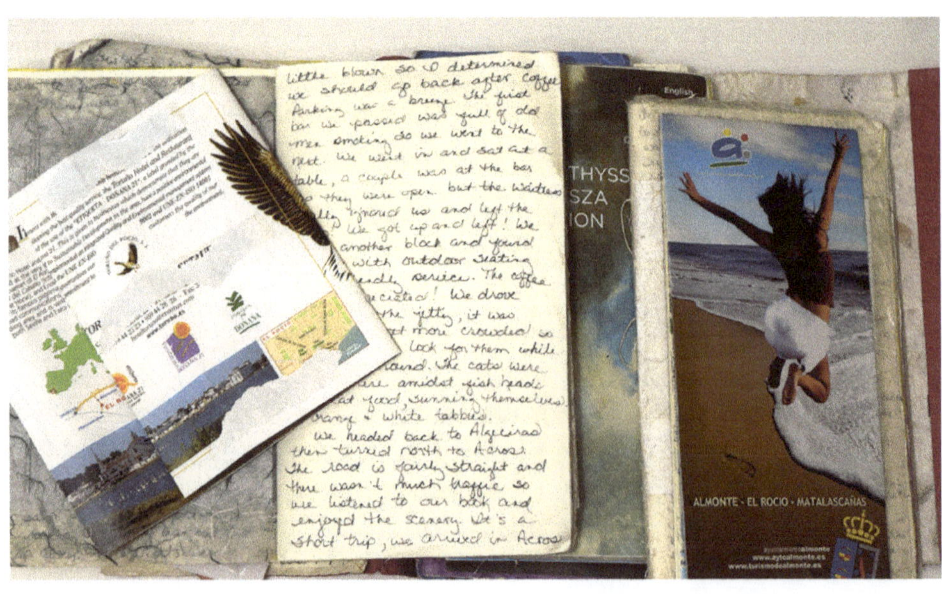

ALMONTE · EL ROCIO · MATALASCAÑAS
www.aytoalmonte.es
www.turismodealmonte.es
English

Glossary

Aficionados – young and dissolute aristocrats that are very knowledgeable and enthusiastic about flamenco

Alegrias – musical form that is lively and vivacious; rhythm consisting of 12 beats

Azulejo – tile that is made up of simple geometric shapes in neutral tones dominated by blues and whites; originated with the Moors

Baile – dance; highly expressive, solo, emotional sweeping or arms and stomping of feet; not choreographed – improvised along palo or rhythm

Baile chico – gaiety, face illuminated, faster, festive palmas and pitos; carefree exuberance; increase footwork, flashing colors

Bailaora grande - female dance; stationary allowing rapid turns to be very effective; uses arms, hands, shoulders and fingers in beautiful circular movements; sex appeal; stomping feet infrequent, may snap fingers; facial expression is very serious

Bata de cola – special dress with a short train

Brazeo – hand and arm movements

Bulerias – rhythmical song, gives one the exhilarating impression of what flamenco was; spontaneity, full of humor yet intrinsically majestic

Café cantantes – public flamenco entertainment began in café cantantes in 1850s; tablas and bar with private rooms upstairs for juerga to continue after the care closed

Campanilleros – traditional cante sung by the members of religious processions

Cantaor – singer; uses his songs to express his sense of hurt as well as his audience's, making them both observer and participant

Cante – song, heart of flamenco; beautiful concise poems; theme of persecution common and pain and suffering; the songs get their meaning from how the singer shapes it through improvisation as there is no set music

Cante grande – ancient roots came out of India; with commercialization, became seen as crude, harsh, and primitive

Cante intermedio – this form of cante lies between jondo and chico; sung with sweet melodious voice; idiomatic gypsy language was overtaken by grammatically correct Spanish

Cante Jondo – (deep song) is an anguished lament that grew from the experiences of marginalized gypsies; condense all the highest emotional moments in life into a 3 or 4 line stanza; most difficult to perform, thus most prized

Cante chico – humor, fast footwork

Castanets – clackers, a percussion instrument; were not a part of original flamenco; used only for baile chico and regional folk dances

Chording – assuming a different chord and single string posture by the left hand

Cofradias – brotherhoods in the Roman Catholic church that were created in 1600s to promote charitable work

Compas – backbone of flamenco; rhythm or beat – like jazz; clapping, hitting table, using cane, feet

Coplas – flamenco song made up of 1 or more short rhyming bursts of 2 to 5 lines

Duende – mischievous poltergeist like spirit; general source of inspiration – drugs, alcohol; must draw close to the earth, acknowledge one's own death and the mortality of all things and the limitation of reason and intelligence

Falsetas – melodic variation inserted by the guitarist in a toque that departs from the basic techniques of rasgueados (right hand playing) and strumming used to give the singer a pause or when his performance is not good

Hypostyle – roof supported by rows of pillars

Gitano – gypsies that entered Andalusia from Egypt fleeing persecution; then had bad reputations due to their vagabond existence, swarthy appearance, rings in ears, strange music and dancing around fires at night which was thought to be a demonic ritual

Juerga – organized gathering for the appreciation of flamenco; aristocracy generally held them in taverns where they could drink and be entertained by gypsies; produced highly charged emotional state; could last days; usually less than 20 people

Jaleo – accompaniment of flamenco, hand-clapping and shouts of encouragement, sometimes finger-snapping and foot stomping

Mantones – fringed shawls

Mantillas – traditional Spanish lace or silk veil or shawl worn over the head and shoulders

Martinets – blacksmiths poured out their souls in song while they hammered away at their work accompanied by the blacksmith's hammer

Palo – music style; sets the mood and tone of the dance

Palmas – hand clapping; it can be either a loud sharp sound made by striking the middle three fingers against the palm or a softer sound made by cupping both hands (palmas sordas)

Parador – luxury hotel usually located in a converted historic building such as a monastery or castle

Peinetas – large combs worn in the hair, usually under a mantilla

Rasgueado – running fingers over the guitar strings in continuous motion

Pitos – a finger snap using the middle and ring fingers against the thumb of the right hand to mark rhythm

Saeta – song of lamentation dedicated to the Virgin Mary and the crucified Christ during Holy Week

Sevillanas – a colorful dance danced by couples and the cante performed by men, women, and children during Sevilla's annual week-long fair; gayest in Spain

Siguiriyas – most desolate cante; release of pent-up hates, persecution, denied liberty and love, tenderness toward a companion-in-misery, and relentless stalking death

Solea – tragic and sad lyrics sung by female

Soleares – central figure, the matriarch, around which all of flamenco revolves

Tablas – flamenco night club; the first one was opened in Madrid in 1954

Tarantas – cante of miners, free from compass, Moorish influence, reflect mining themes

Tertulia – meeting of friends, especially of men; they gather at local bars and clubs to discuss everything under the sun

Tocaor – guitarist; accompaniment, must follow where the singer leads

Tonas – oldest song form, sung unaccompanied except for basic percussion

Toque – all flamenco played on the guitar

Vega – a large plain or valley, typically a fertile and grassy one

Voz affila – rough sounding voice; classic raw, powerful, boozy, baccy soaked jondo voice

Zapateado – footwork, intricate interplay of heel and toe taps, utilizing both feet

Resources

Bakus, Gerald...................Spanish Guitar

Boyd, Alastair...................The Sierras of the South - Travels in the Mountains of Andalusia

Croce, A........................... Writing in the Dark, Dancing in The New Yorker

Dumas, Danielle..............Chants Flamencos

Edwards, Gwynne ....Flamenco!

Harvey, Denis.................. The Gypsies: Wagon Time and After

Havelock, Ellis................. The Soul of Spain

Hecht, Paul..................... The Wind Cried: An American's Discovery of the World of Flamenco

Howson, Gerald...............The Flamencos of Cadiz Bay

Kirkland, Will...................Gypsy Cante: Deep Song of the Caves

Koudelka, Josef................Gypsies: Photo

Lafuente, Rafael...............The Truth About Flamenco

Leblon, Bernard...............Gypsies & Flamenco: The Emerging of the Art of Flamenco in Andalusia

Mitchell, Timothy............Flamenco Deep Song

Morca, Teodoro................Becoming the Dance: Flamenco Spirit

Nartinez, Emma..............Flamenco: All You Wanted to Know

Nevell, Richard............... A Time to Dance

Pohren, Donn.................. Lives and Legends of Flamenco

Pohren, Donn.................. *A Way of Life*

Pohren, Donn.................. *Art of Flamenco*

Schreiner, Claus.............. *Flamenco: Gypsy Dance & Music from Andalucia*

Seymour, Hugh............... *The Bottlebrush Tree*

Totton, Robin.................. *Song of the Outcasts*

Washabaugh.................. *Flamenco: Passion, Policitcs & Popular Culture*

Webb, Godfrey................ *Gypsies, the Secret People*

Webster, Jason................ *Duende*

Yoors, Jan........................ *Gypsies of Spain*

Useful Links

www.spanish-art.org/spanish-dance-sevillanas.html

https://en.wikipedia.org/wiki/
Castle_of_Santa_Catalina_(Ja%C3%A9n)

https://en.wikipedia.org/wiki/Do%C3%B1ana_National_Park

www.andalucia.com/environment/protect/donana.htm

www.barcelona.de/en/barcelona-sagrada-familia-interior.
html

www.sagradafamilia.org/en/home

www.andalucia.com/ronda/history.htm

www.andalucia.com/ronda/bullfightinghistory.htm

www.interlude.hk/front/
new-concepts-in-music-and-art-flamenco-picasso-gaudi-dali

www.timenet.org/detail.html

www.andalucia.com/flamenco/history.htm

https://languagemagazine.com/in-search-of-duende/

www.pablopicasso.org/guernica.jsp

www.museothyssen.org/en/about-us

About the Author

Combining her talents in photography and illustration with a love of travel, Susan K Jones embarked on a project that explores the culture surrounding flamenco and the natural beauty of southern Spain. Each black and white photograph is a work of art, meticulously hand colored with colored pencils. The photographs, combined with pen and ink illustrations, enhance the experience of the journey she took with her daughter to learn not only about flamenco but Modernism arts in Spain that include Gaudi, Dali, and Lorca.

With camera always in hand, Susan captures the world around her and is working on a series of picture books that explore faces in nature, things left behind, old architecture, and travel. Her gallery closed at the onset of the pandemic; her work is now available through her website: skjonesart.com.